Drummer Boy Willie McGee, Civil War Hero and Fraud

Thomas Fox

FOREWORD BY JOSEPH G. BILBY

D1245363

McFarland & Company, Inc., Publishers
Jefferson, North Carolina, and London

LIBRARY OF CONGRESS CATALOGUING-IN-PUBLICATION DATA

Fox, Thomas, 1947–
    Drummer boy Willie McGee, Civil War hero and fraud /
Thomas Fox ; foreword by Joseph G. Bilby.
        p.   cm.
    Includes bibliographical references and index.

    ISBN-13: 978-0-7864-3289-9
    softcover : 50# alkaline paper ∞

    1. McGee, William Henry.   2. Soldiers — United States —
Biography.   3. Drummers (Musicians) — New Jersey — Newark —
Biography.   4. United States — History — Civil War, 1861–1865 —
Biography.   5. New Jersey — History — Civil War, 1861–1865 —
Biography.   6. Medal of Honor — Biography.   7. United States.
Army. Infantry Regiment, 20th. Company K — Biography.
8. Imposters and imposture — United States — Biography.
9. Thieves — United States — Biography.   10. Murderers — United
States — Biography.   I. Title.
E521.M38F695 2008
973.7092 — dc22
[B]
                                                    2007048290

British Library cataloguing data are available

On the cover: The eyes of William J. McGee, New York
bartender who passed himself off as the famous drummer boy;
Confederate drum *(courtesy University of Tennessee, Frank H.
McClung Museum)*

Manufactured in the United States of America

McFarland & Company, Inc., Publishers
  Box 611, Jefferson, North Carolina 28640
    www.mcfarlandpub.com

Drummer Boy Willie McGee,
Civil War Hero and Fraud

For Erin
1974–1997
Lost child of our time —
there are more hurts than cures,
and still no language but a cry.

Contents

Foreword

by Joseph G. Bilby

I was born in Newark, New Jersey, a city I have always loved. Back in the 1950s, I gained a solid education, not only at Saint Rose of Lima Elementary School but also at the wonderful old Newark Library, "downtown" on Washington Street. The library was a quiet world beyond city streets, where a curious kid could roam unsupervised through open book stacks, pulling volumes off the shelves, dipping into worlds and lives well beyond his own.

During that time I was an omnivorous reader of fiction and fact alike, but spent much of my time buried in books on military history, especially the Civil War, then fast approaching its centennial. While perusing the yellowing pages of *New Jersey and the Rebellion*, John Y. Foster's 1868 summation of the state's role in the conflict, I came across the remarkable story of Willie McGee. Willie, a Newark Irish American kid like myself, had gone off to war as a drummer boy with the Thirty-third New Jersey Volunteer Infantry in 1863 at the age of fifteen. He not only came out of it alive but also as a hero; he was awarded the Medal of Honor, and after the war, received a commission as a lieutenant in the United States regular army. Although long gone, young Willie, heroic and ambitious, indeed seemed someone to model a life on.

In the intervening years, I managed to delve deeply into New Jersey's role in the Civil War, but Willie always remained a fascinating footnote. I read elsewhere that his postwar life had not gone well and involved a shooting incident. There was no doubt more to the tale, but I knew that discovering the details would involve much work and probably more than a little luck. Nineteenth century lives, especially those of the common folk, can prove elusive for a number of reasons. And then Tom Fox, in his search for the history of New Jersey's Irish, uncovered the story.

What Fox's assiduous scholarship revealed was not my Willie, the Willie of legend, the Willie that inspired me in the long ago, but the unfortunate real Willie. Willie's tale, like many things in life and history, was not what it seemed. Willie was a scamp, a flimflam man, a manipulator. His string of dupes included not only the three women he married but also an army chaplain, Civil War generals, a governor of New Jersey, a prison warden, the founder of Memorial Day and Lizzie Borden's attorney, among others, in a much traveled life leading to a sad end in New York.

Willie was not the only New Jersey Civil War veteran to fall from grace. One former colonel of the First New Jersey Cavalry ended up dying of a drug overdose in a California brothel, and another spent his final days in an insane asylum. The strange and fascinating career of Willie McGee is, however, perhaps the most bizarre tale to emerge from the state's wartime saga, and Tom Fox has done a superb job of telling it. By digging out obscure sources and doggedly following leads to fill in the many blanks, Fox has brought us Willie, "warts and all." For me, it was well worth the wait.

Wall Township, New Jersey

Joseph G. Bilby is a columnist for the *Civil War News*, the author of six books on the Civil War, and a recipient of the LSU Civil War Center's Award of Excellence.

Preface

On December 7, 1864, just one week after the bloody battle of Franklin, Tennessee, a drummer boy from Newark, New Jersey, William Magee, was credited with leading a Federal force to a sharp and decisive victory over the Confederates in a clash just thirty miles from the carnage at Franklin. This drummer, a fifteen-year-old Irish-American on convalescent duty and acting as an orderly to General Lovell Rousseau, was recognized for the capture of two guns, several hundred prisoners, and the saving of Fortress Rosecrans in Murfreesboro from the famed Nathan Bedford Forrest.

For his actions, young Magee would soon be awarded a Medal of Honor, be written up in both newspapers and books as a glorious New Jersey legend, be commissioned as a lieutenant in the United States Army at age eighteen, and then, inexplicably at the height of his notoriety, would virtually disappear from history for more than 100 years. *Drummer Boy Willie McGee, Civil War Hero and Fraud* is the story of a lost war hero, a man-child with the world at his feet, whose fall from grace is accelerated by fame, lies, alcohol, bigamy, and murder. Given a Medal of Honor through the well-meaning adoration of an adoptive father and a generous congressman, the medal would become an albatross he constantly used for his benefit but never respected. Willie was a boy of many personal gifts, the greatest of which was his lifelong hypnotic ability to befriend and gain allegiances of some of the most powerful men in the country. If a chronicling of McGee's hypnotic gifts were to be fictionalized, they would be deemed unbelievable. The fact that this is a documented work that emanated from the life of a bowery boy forced from school at age eleven to work as a waiter lifts the reader beyond incredulity and into Willie's very real world.

3

In the spring of 2004, I was assisting a student with a history paper at Pope John XXIII High School in Sparta, New Jersey. The sophomore had chosen New Jersey Medal of Honor recipients from the Civil War, and a quick internet search showed that some thirty-three men from the Garden State had been awarded the nation's most esteemed medal. The sixteen-year-old chose one soldier, a William Magee, drummer boy, because of his comparable age and at my urging. I felt certain there had to be an interesting story behind such a young hero, and had no doubt there would be sufficient material for a successful paper.

Such, however, was not the case. The search for Willie Magee turned up nothing, and though the student switched to the better-known Colonel William Joyce Sewell, the assistant librarian kept looking for the lost Magee, and *Drummer Boy Willie McGee* was born. I was intrigued, and disturbed, especially as an Irish-American whose great-grandfather had also fought in a New Jersey regiment, that such a young hero could disappear without a trace.

There was eventually one lead from which all future work proceeded. Joe Bilby and Bob MacAvoy, two intrepid experts and authors on New Jersey in the Civil War, though admitting there was little known about the mysterious Magee, believed he came "to a bad end"; both men pointed to an 1868 history, John Y. Foster's *New Jersey in the Rebellion*. Foster's tale of the hero William Magee, though filled with the hyperbole of the age, nonetheless opened the door that led to the unfolding of this book. I looked forward to uncovering the magical story of a young hero, a story all Americans could embrace, but such would not be the case. William Magee would turn out to be Willie McGee, and the mystery of his enigmatic and troubled life would begin to unfold with the aid of many Civil War buffs, genealogists, historians, and archivists.

Three aspects of McGee's life are embraced in our story. The story begins with the sudden yet seminal decision in Willie's life, his shooting and killing of Doctor Chandler Braman, assistant surgeon of the United States 20th Infantry at Baton Rouge, Louisiana, in 1868. This act, born of Achilles-like pride and anger, begins for Willie a long spiraling descent into a life of prison, poverty, and misplaced priorities, culminating in his conviction for a second murder in 1905 at age 56.

Interspersed throughout this descent are flashbacks unveiling the central theme of the boy's heroic life; the legend of Drummer McGee and his meteoric rise in less than four years from an uneducated Irish waif to a Medal of Honor recipient; friend of governors, generals, and politicians; and then becoming perhaps the youngest commissioned officer in United States peacetime history, at age eighteen. As the story unfolds, we discover some of Willie's origins and the history of the McGees in America.

The third and final act in the life of William H. McGee is his exposure as a Civil War fraud, and his even more inept claim in middle age to be the sole survivor of Custer's Last Stand at the Little Big Horn, a declaration which restored to him temporarily a semblance of the notoriety he had lost as a result of severe alcoholism, before the final end at Sing Sing prison for a second manslaughter.

There are three published works that mention Willie McGee. The first was Foster's *New Jersey in the Rebellion,* a 900 page Victorian history commissioned in 1866 by New Jersey governor Marcus Ward and the New Jersey legislature. Out of print since its publication in 1868, it is still a valuable, though flawed, reference. Foster created the Magee legend, and it would be accepted and never disputed or challenged in any way, until now. In chapter six, where Willie's legend as a hero is contrasted with more accurate historical truths, the Foster revisionist history of 1868 is in italics to simplify for the reader the McGee version of battle with the new account recently uncovered.

The second printed telling of the Willie McGee legend was the 1878 *History of Newark, New Jersey, Being a Narrative of Its Rise and Progress,* by Joseph Atkinson. As rare as Foster's work, *The History of Newark* repeats almost verbatim the Murfreesboro, Tennessee, story as told by Foster, but it does add a brief, though misleading, description of the shooting of the doctor and Willie's "bad end." A three volume *The History of the City of Newark, New Jersey,* edited by Frank Urquhart and published in 1913, is simply a retelling of both the Foster and Atkinson books. It is exceptionally difficult to find, though occasionally it can be found in a New Jersey library, compounding and perpetuating the McGee legend.

The story of Willie McGee not only fills a gap in the history of a missing national Medal of Honor recipient and Civil War boy hero it also tells the tale of a poverty stricken boy soldier in that war. We follow the trail of one young drummer, in his own words, through a near death from disease at Lookout Mountain, Tennessee, to a classic American story of sudden fame and then an ignoble fall from grace. Willie McGee was that Clintonesque character, a street urchin from a broken family, both willing and able to con rich and poor, men, women and children alike. There are compelling life lessons to be learned for all sons like McGee seeking fame and glory on the fast track, only to find the decisions they make are often a huge burden to carry, both in peace and war.

My official introduction to Willie McGee took place in Trenton at the New Jersey State Library, which had a copy of Foster's *New Jersey in the Rebel-*

lion, and the New Jersey State Archives, where Bette Epstein assisted me with the search for the early life of Willie McGee in New Jersey. Several journeys to the National Archives in Washington, D.C., yielded various files on Willie's military career, some of which were misplaced for over one hundred years, including his Medal of Honor file. Jill Abraham, archivist in the Old Army Records Division, provided generous guidance and explanations. The Library of Congress helped build the story behind Senator John Logan's 1880 bill and Congressman Robinson's 1884 proposed bill to aid Willie, which ultimately failed for all the right reasons.

Two days prior to Hurricane Katrina, I requested much information on the Louisiana activities of McGee, including civil transcripts, newspaper microfilm, genealogy of Andrew Herron, and history of Baton Rouge during Reconstruction. Despite being overwhelmed with catastrophe and disaster, the staffs at the Louisiana State University Library, Southeastern Louisiana State University Library, and the Louisiana State Library were exceedingly kind and helpful during a most inopportune time; especially helpful were Judy Bolton of LSU and Charlene Bonnette of the state library in Baton Rouge.

The maladaptive life of Willie McGee led to searches throughout the country. In Minnesota, Debbie Miller and Monica Collins of the Minnesota Historical Society helped me locate records of the Stillwater Prison, as well as newspaper files showing Willie's life in Minnesota. Ted Genoways of the University of Virginia and the author of *Hard Times: Voices from a State Prison, 1849–1914,* shared his knowledge and expertise of the Minnesota prison system.

In Tennessee, Jim Lewis of the National Park Service assisted with detailed information on the Battle of the Cedars, as well as life at Fortress Rosecrans. Mike Schneider of Falls Church, Virginia, whose ancestor fought with the 181st Ohio, helped build the story of the Cedars and is one of the many brilliant unsung Civil War amateur historians in the country. Librarians and historical societies in Jasper, Indiana; Northumberland, Pennsylvania; Springfield, Massachusetts; Marshall and Galveston, Texas, and Syracuse, New York, all provided important documents in tracking down the elusive McGee. John McCabe, of the National Park Service in Springfield, Massachusetts, uncovered the McGee years at the Springfield Armory, a small but important gap long sought.

In Texas, Dianna Baker of the Galveston district clerk's office provided the crucial information in the divorce proceedings of Louise and Willie in 1902, and the Rosenberg Library in Galveston provided further assistance. Dorothy Meadows of the Jarrett Library in Marshall was helpful with the Bonfoey case and the life of Charles B. Clark, as was Hubert Bender of the Harrison County Historical Society.

Internet research enabled me to trace both of the remaining McGee families in Pennsylvania and New York, often, though not exclusively, through census and Civil War database records. When she was discovered, Diane Bretz of the Northumberland Magees was able to provide oral history and photos of Willie's lone surviving daughter with his first wife, Regina. Diane Bretz's early comment when informed that her great grandfather McGee may not have been a classic American father and hero, "Life isn't always what it appears — keep going and find the truth," was just what I needed to hear. The descendants of the New York fraud Magees were initially very receptive, and provided the only known photo we have of the New York Willie McGee.

Numerous civil records were discovered in state agencies in Illinois, Nebraska, Maryland, Louisiana, New York, Massachusetts, Pennsylvania, Texas, and New Jersey, buttressing information discovered either at the National Archives or from family oral history. Much of the research material was found in New Jersey and New York. The New York Public Library, the Newark Public Library, and the Morristown Library in New Jersey all helped build the story, and Sue Kuchinski of the Sussex County Library kindly provided important documents from around the country, but it was the New Jersey Historical Society (NJHS) in Newark which provided firsthand documentation on the life and times of Willie McGee. In the spring of 2005, acting on a hunch, I asked NJHS archivist James Lewis to show me the papers of former Governor Marcus Ward, himself a Newark native. Grasping at straws for the mystery drummer, I thought there might be a mention of McGee, perhaps even a photo, in the papers of Ward, the much proclaimed "soldier's friend."

Astonishingly, James and Brenna King, his assistant at the NJHS, carted out fifty-two boxes of Ward's papers, catalogued by date but unindexed and loose. Over the course of several months almost fifty letters from, to, or about Willie McGee between 1866 and 1882 brought to life our elusive drummer. Letters to and from Louisiana, Minnesota, Pennsylvania, Michigan, Massachusetts, and Washington, D.C., were discovered and provided a unique look at the life of an evasive young man in the nineteenth century. A few more letters were found at the wonderful Alexander Library at Rutgers University, which houses a similar cache of Ward's correspondence between 1860 and 1884, when the governor died. In order to provide a better feel for historical authenticity, the original spelling and grammar is left intact in all letters found in the narrative. The spelling of the McGee surname is also left intact as written. Born McGee, Willie's name was spelled in various ways, and Willie himself used his own surname for whatever benefit he felt he could gain at the time. Likewise, McGee was known as Willie and Will as a youngster, and then Bill or Billy as an adult. I have tried to maintain the consistency and leave it to the reader to understand the differences. All errors, factual and interpretative, are my own.

In the search for Willie McGee on the western front, I was aided by the loyal and generous members of the Little Big Horn Association, especially Billy Markland and Michael Nunnally. Corinne Hallenbeck of Albany was helpful with the Willie of Sing Sing, and Timothy J. Gilfoyle of Chicago and Roberta Arminio of Ossining, New York, are both priceless treasures to all researchers. Debbie Rutkauskas, the town clerk of Meriden, Connecticut, and Jan Franco of the Meriden Library were both gracious on an election day to help with the McGee genealogy, and Hubert Bender of the Harrison County, Texas, Historical Museum, was an aid on the Bonfoey case. Perhaps the greatest reward of writing this book has been meeting and learning from so many people, most of whom can never be acknowledged; to all of them I express sincere gratitude. There are others, however, who went the extra mile to aid a new author.

Most Civil War stories touching on New Jersey, especially this one, have the guiding imprint of Joe Bilby, who has been a mentor of this project from the beginning. Civil War aficionados Bob MacAvoy and Bob Jones, true Jerseymen, have been generous with their time and sources. Pat Foley and Doug Dennis, loyal friends of short and long standing, convinced me I could and should tell the story of McGee, and read each draft with keen insight. Mary Fitzgibbons was a gracious editor, and Carol McBriar and Frank Setlock provided encouragement when most needed. Terry Jones, Louisiana scholar and author, read rough drafts with educated eyes towards the war, while Irish historians Jim Lowney of New Jersey and Anna McHugh of County Galway were my Eire eyes. Special thanks to Rev. Kieran McHugh of Ballybane, Ireland, Dave Johnson and Rich Pompelio, of Sparta, New Jersey, and Mike Kelly of Jersey City, each of whom in their separate ways enabled this dream to become a reality.

Above all, I must express a debt of the heart to Nancy Fox for her utmost patience and understanding during both my presence and absence in the search for Willie McGee and so many other stories, both told and untold. May all writers and husbands be blessed with the loving support I have received from Nancy and the children; Jamie, who served his country with honor for ten years; Bridget, the mother of our wonderful grandson; and Connor, my research running mate since his childhood.

Introduction

In July of 1863, Newark, New Jersey, was then, as now, a city of paradoxes. Once a tiny hamlet founded by Puritan zealots in 1666, whose Revolutionary population was barely 800, Newark had exploded to almost 80,000 during the Civil War. Founded by farmers from Connecticut searching for religious freedom, the majority of its residents in 1863 were now foreign born Irish and German factory workers, and the original wasp settlers were more often found on street names than in homes. Indeed, the factories were so prevalent that the town became known as the Brick City, a moniker it has never lost.[1]

The massive influx of immigrants had begun in the mid–1830s, with the construction of the Morris Canal, which connected the Delaware and Hudson Rivers. Many of the Irish who were recruited to dig the canal eventually settled in Newark, and then thousands more arrived within three years during the building of two railroads, which, along with the canal, positioned Newark to move into the forefront of manufacturing.[2]

As revolutions rocked central Europe in 1848, a large influx of Germans arrived and by 1860 there were more than 20,000 foreign born workers in Newark; added to that were a like number of first generation Irish and German living and working with them.[3] James and Margaret (Doyle) McGee were in the vanguard of the Irish escaping from *An Gorta Mor*, the great Irish Famine of 1845–50. Ireland's population, which had risen to almost nine million in 1845, would count only 4.5 million alive by 1851. At least a million of these Irish immigrated to the East Coast of North America, the McGees among them.[4] Irish America occasionally views its history through rose colored glasses, but immigrants like the McGees often found downtown New York, Newark, and other eastern cities full of desperation, though the shantytowns were still a marked improvement over what they had left in Ireland, where 40 percent of the homes in 1844 were one-room mud cabins; and only at Christmas did many of the inhabitants get a chance to eat meat.[5] Nonetheless, cholera and typhus were always in the lowlands of Newark, and the McGees, like so many of the forgotten ones who ran from Ireland in droves, were often caught in the midst of disease and abject poverty. Crime, despair, insanity, alcoholism, and helpless rage were the lot of thousands.[6] If Willie McGee's people were caught in any of these ills, it should surprise no one.

These immigrants, especially the Irish, were not welcomed, but they were needed. By 1861, when Fort Sumter was fired upon, Newark, the country's eleventh largest city, with its large tannery industry, was producing more than 80 percent of the leather goods in the nation, and, surprisingly, selling 70 percent of that market to southern cities, at a value of more than $21 million a year.[7] Despite being known as "the workshop of the South," Newark provided more men to the Union cause than any city in New Jersey, and many more enlisted in specialized units from New York. For two solid years, regiment after regiment would smartly march out of the Brick City, but as the 87th anniversary of the nation's independence approached, Newark would find itself a city in turmoil.[8]

The joyful news arrived first. On Friday, July 3, the *Newark Daily Advertiser*, the city's largest paper, was already proclaiming in headlines what looked to be a major victory at Gettysburg, "The Glorious Tidings," and "The Rejoicings in Washington" at the top of page one.[9] Finally, after two years of defeat after defeat by rebel forces, the good news from the war brought genuine excitement. Headlines on July 6 and 7 were unrestrained in the feeling that the war had finally turned in the North's favor. "Our Glorious Victory" was the headline on July 6. The story continued: "The proud host which insulted and invaded us, has been driven back in rout and confusion before our victorious arms, and THE NATION IS SAVED!"[10] The next day, four headlines greeted readers: "Vicksburg Captured," "The Fruits of the Glorious Victory," "Rebel Retreat," and "Immense Loss of the Rebel Officers," but also obvious were the long lists of killed and wounded printed each day.[11]

Though this news was long awaited and encouraging to most, the positive mood began to turn slightly after July 10, when, along with the usual long list of printed casualties, a train arrived in Newark loaded with 657 Gettysburg wounded, headed for the town hospital.[12] This was followed in New York on July 13 by five consecutive days of the worst rioting in American history. For weeks the impending draft had inflamed many in the North, particularly the newly arrived immigrants. After two years of volunteer sol-diering, the new federal plan of conscription had many, especially the lower class Irish, in an uproar. They perceived it as a draft, a draft they felt was aimed directly at them. Now, after two weeks of relative joy, pandemonium was unleashed just nine miles away in New York City.[13]

In what amounted to a race riot, the Irish in Manhattan burned hun-dreds of buildings, attacked police, and murdered African Americans. Though the official tally showed a little over one hundred dead, many historians con-cede an accurate total will never be known, and more than a thousand may have perished, most anonymously. If it hadn't been for five Federal regiments of weary soldiers returning home for a rest from Gettysburg, the entire island may have gone up in flames. Though there were demonstrations throughout the city, relative calm prevailed in Newark, despite the fact that smoke was visible across the Hudson.[14]

The July 16 edition of the *Daily Advertiser* was a prime example of the paradoxes facing so many of the residents. One headline proclaimed "Lin-coln Declares a National Day of Thanksgiving" for the recent military tri-umphs, while another story covered the riots in New York. One local item showed just how close Newark was to the troubles in Manhattan: "The body of a young man named Edward MacDavitt, formerly of this city, was brought here today for interment. MacDavitt was one of the rioters in New York, and was killed in an attack by the military on Tuesday. He was 30 years old, and had a wife and four children. The body is at No. 238 Warren Street where his friends reside."[15]

As the pull of emotions ebbed and flowed, July still had one more sur-prise. On July 23, large bounties were publicly posted in all the Newark papers.[16] After two years of paying volunteer soldiers $13 a month, and with the draft (by any name) looming, state and local officials now offered amaz-ing incentives for poor men to fight. Two hundred forty dollars in cash was given for enlisting, another four hundred dollars in six month installments, and additional amounts to unmarried and married men alike. The local Newark bounties, the highest in the state, were offered for residents upon enlisting, as well as city aid and additional money for soldiers with widowed mothers.[17]

The new regiment was to become the 33rd New Jersey Infantry, com-manded by a young and very ambitious Colonel George Washington Mindil.[18] The enlistment offices in Newark opened for business on Monday, July 26, and one of the first in line was a fourteen-year-old who had been out of school for three years. Whether William Henry McGee signed up for the excite-ment, to get away from a dysfunctional Irish home, or for the money will never be known, but his papers were all signed and approved by July 28.[19] For Willie, who was purported to have been eking out a living as a waiter, enlistment was a windfall. McGee received his $240 in cash upon mustering, and with other bounties and incentives, stood to make another $628 by the end of his service. In addition, Willie told authorities he was fatherless, adding to his monthly check, and also avoiding parent permission for a soldier under 18. Suddenly rich beyond his dreams, young Willie was assigned as a drummer to Company C, and he and the other fifteen musicians would learn their craft under the watchful eye of Drum Major Nathaniel "Nat" Morris, a well known Newark band man.[20]

While Willie McGee, whose name changed with his enlistment papers to Magee, was perhaps one of the first to take advantage of the new bounties, he was surely not the last. It was not difficult to understand, as a fortunate full-time factory worker might bring home about $300 a year, more than many citizens living on the periphery of life would ever earn. A married veteran joining the 33rd N.J. Infantry could easily support himself and a family for four years with the $1,286 he would earn as a soldier under the new system. Newark alone paid out more than $75,000 in bonuses to its men, and Jersey City was not far behind.[21]

Hundreds of men, mostly veterans of previous volunteer regiments, reenlisted, were outfitted, paid, and proceeded to walk — or run — away, never to be seen again in their bright blue Zouave uniforms. So many men deserted, sometimes in groups of hundreds, that Mindil was forced to ask for Federal help, and the 14th Vermont Infantry was garrisoned as guard, a necessary but incredibly embarrassing admission to the regiment, Mindil, and New Jersey.[22]

With the sixteen musicians playing at the front of the procession, the regiment left on September 8 with a huge crowd lining the route, as more than 530 of the 950 men were either actually from Newark or claimed to be. One of those drummers, John Mailey of Newark, would never see home or family again, dying in a Southern prison camp. The *Daily Advertiser* remarked that as the band played, "some men looked quiet and sad, while others violently wept; still others laughing and joyous."[23]

Whether Willie's mother was present is unknown, but the *Advertiser* noted that "a great many parting words and a great deal of hand shaking and kissing was done." Unfortunately, many of the well wishers also passed a lot of "wee drop" to the regiment, and soon, under the hot sun and emotion of the day, men were "stupefied and maddened by the fiery liquor and the men became perfectly wild and uncontrollable." Only the presence of the Vermont guards stopped massive insubordination and desertion.[24]

Whatever Willie McGee, now Magee, was thinking while this mayhem continued, there can be no doubt it was an inauspicious entrance to the war. Certainly, no one watching the 33rd Infantry parade out of Newark that Saturday in September would ever dream that four years later the most decorated and famous member of the regiment would be the fourteen-year-old drummer of Company C.

This drunken disturbance would be the last poor grade for the New Jersey 33rd Infantry.[25] They would return home in July of 1865 as heroes, having distinguished themselves consistently.[26] The unit would even produce three Medal of Honor recipients. Colonel George Mindil would be given the medal thirty-one years after the fact, for valor at the Battle of Williamsburg while a captain for the 61st Pennsylvania Infantry.[27] First Lieutenant John James Toffey, a native of Newburgh, New York, was honored in 1897 for his bravery at Chattanooga on November 23, 1863.[28] The third would go to a non-officer, a sixteen-year-old musician named Willie McGee, who would be awarded a Medal of Honor in February 1866, one of the youngest recipients in United States history, but one who soon disappeared from New Jersey and history. This is his story, the lost story of a lost boy who became a bad man.

CHAPTER ONE

The Watch, the Note, the Murder

"The truth of history lies in the pulse of ordinary life."
— Verlyn Klinkenborg

It was August 14, 1868, and Willie McGee was living an American dream. The young man was just out of his teens and already a proud 2nd Lieutenant in the United States Army.[1] True, the former Jersey drummer boy was a long way from home, but there were so many fellow Irish up and down the Mississippi Willie was never short of friends. Friends were never a problem for Willie McGee. Peacetime — Reconstruction — Louisiana — was even better if you were a hero, and McGee was a certified war hero, a Medal of Honor recipient at age sixteen.[2]

William H. McGee was indeed the total military public relations package. Alvin York and Audie Murphy had nothing on the Irish drummer boy from Newark. In the final months of Civil War bloodshed, the Western Theatre was the most vicious. One week in late 1864, following the suicidal Battle of Franklin in Tennessee, where 9,500 men were casualties in five hours, Willie McGee entered the history books a mere thirty miles away. Acting as an orderly for General Horatio Van Cleve, Willie was credited with leading two separate Ohio regiments in an engagement and capturing two rebel cannon, hundreds of prisoners, and saving Murfreesboro, Tennessee, from the outrages of the famed Nathan Bedford Forrest.[3] According to his enlistment papers, McGee was sixteen at the time of the battle, but in truth he was only fifteen years old.[4]

Three years later McGee entered his tent at the Baton Rouge garrison of Company K, the U.S. 20th Infantry, sometime after ten P.M. that sultry August night, confident that life was good and that it was getting better every day. Whatever Willie McGee had in his head that summer night, he could never imagine it would be the last peaceful evening his head would ever rest on a pillow. In less than twenty-four hours, Lieutenant William McGee would face a test of his manhood and maturity — and fail miserably. As the Louisiana night gave way to a red dawn on Saturday, August 15, 1868, the life of Will McGee, a rising young star of America, would disintegrate into murder, alcohol, and lies. It would be an American tragedy, a lost story of a lost boy. As with so many tragedies spawned in the Civil War, it did not have to happen. Lieutenant McGee, whose promising young life was founded on lies, was undone by, of all people, a doctor. But while Willie slept soundly that Friday night, the same could not be said for the regiment's assistant surgeon, Doctor Chandler Braman.

Somebody had stolen Lieutenant Charles Clark's watch. It must have been a nice piece, because the entire 20th U.S. Infantry stationed in Baton Rouge knew it was gone.[5] Clark, like McGee, was a young but much more experienced veteran of the war, a man who chose the army as a career despite the carnage he had seen. Clark enlisted in Syracuse as a twenty-two-year-old first sergeant in 1862, and was promoted three times before mustering out at the end of hostilities in July of 1865 with the rank of captain of the 122nd New York Infantry.[6]

Charles Benton Clark may very well have received his watch as a gift from his grateful unit. From 1862 until the war's end, the 122nd New York fought at a roll call of famous but bloody battlefields. Antietam, Marye's Heights, Gettysburg, Spotsylvania, Cold Harbor, and Petersburg all saw the upstate New Yorkers' heroics and deaths.[7] Clark may also have been given the watch by his father, John Clark, the editor of the Baldwinsville, New York, newspaper, and himself the son of a decorated soldier of the War of 1812.[8] Whatever circumstances enabled Clark to have a fine watch, the theft was the talk of the regiment as dawn broke on Friday, August 14, 1868.

Sometime that morning, Lieutenant Clark paid a visit to the quarters of the regiment's assistant surgeon and fellow Mason, Dr. Chandler Braman.[9] Likely it was a personal, not official, visit. Dr. Braman's first wedding anniversary had been spent alone the previous night, his bride Cecilia at home in Indiana. A second visitor arrived shortly afterward, a shadowy figure named McHenry.[10] Little did the three men realize that Chandler Braman would never see another dawn, much less another anniversary with Cecilia. Within the confines of the comfortable but small second floor quarters, the conversation eventually worked its way to the missing watch.

The only one of the three to leave a record of the meeting was the ubiquitous McHenry, and he is the least reliable source. McHenry was a wily entrepreneur who lived on and operated a steamer on the Mississippi, and laid claims to have been a spy for General Sherman during the war.[11] Braman was out of his league in this company. Chandler Balch and Joseph Balch Braman both left Harvard in May 1864, Joseph enlisting in the 3rd Massachusetts Cavalry, and Chandler following in the footsteps of his father, Dr. Isaac Braman, with the 12 Massachusetts Infantry.[12] Following the war, Joseph returned to school and became a famed lawyer both in Los Angeles and in New York, while brother Chandler returned to Harvard and graduated from its medical school in March of 1866 before reenlisting in the postwar army as a surgeon.[13] The young doctor was eventually sent in March 1867 to his new post at Baton Rouge; he left Louisiana only once, traveling to Terra Haute, Indiana, in August, where he married socialite Cecilia O. Gage.[14] The Braman family had been in Massachusetts since Plymouth Rock, and one gets the impression Chandler was a fish out of water in the turbulent Louisiana of 1868.[15] According to McHenry's later testimony to Mayor James Elam, when he (McHenry) mentioned in passing conversation his previous alleged spying for Sherman, Braman grew "agitated and excited."[16]

There were whispers throughout the regiment that 2nd Lieutenant Willie McGee was the thief, and while there is absolutely no evidence to suspect the young officer of such a crime, the loud whispers may say something about McGee's perceived character.[17] A private in later testimony said, "It was generally thought by the men of the regiment that Lieutenant McGee took the watch," and McGee was later said to be "often on duty under the influence of liquor."[18]

McHenry said that Dr. Braman and Lieutenant Clark were the ones talking about the theft and when McHenry mentioned his supposed detective work under General Sherman, the doctor asked him pointedly to be "his detective." The three men, according to McHenry, agreed to meet on McHenry's boat later that afternoon. On McHenry's steamer, *Irene*, he claimed everything — everything — was Chandler Braman's idea. Braman, he said, offered him $150 to "work up the case against McGee." McHenry added that the doctor, out of friendship for Lieutenant Clark, came up with the idea of a forged note to publicly humiliate McGee. Braman, he said, wrote the note on the boat, hurriedly writing in pencil two sentences, signed McGee's name, and gave it to McHenry.[19] The scribbled note did give the obvious appearance it was written quickly and with little forethought, belying the misery it would cause to so many people:

Steamer *Irene*

En route from Shreveport to Baton Rouge on or about the 10th day of July, Lieut McGee of the 20th Infantry forged a draft at sight upon Lt Chas B Clark, U.S.A. payable at Shreveport.

Witness

Chas B Clark[20]

The rather innocuous sentence never mentioned an amount, though later testimony by various witnesses would throw out numbers like $5 and $10, and the stolen watch was never mentioned. But the note was not about the theft of Clark's watch and missing money. Braman insisted, said McHenry, that the former spy take the note to Mayor James Elam of Baton Rouge. McHenry said it was the doctor's plan to embarrass Willie and perhaps "bring him out in the open" regarding the theft of the watch. McHenry finished his account by saying the doctor insisted that only McHenry himself could take the note to Mayor Elam to better "substantiate the $10 draft and forgery."[21]

Following the afternoon boat meeting, Lieutenant Clark and Chandler Braman returned to the post and their regular duties while McHenry went downtown on a short walk to set the plot in motion with the mayor, arriving a little after 6:00 P.M.[22] In its simplicity, the idea was to assassinate McGee's character and then, who knows, perhaps see what tongues might wag regarding the lieutenant's missing watch. If that was the intent, it backfired completely, and McHenry's role as a detective ended the same day it began.

McHenry delivered the scribbled pencil note to Mr. Elam. The Baton Rouge mayor asked McHenry why he did not go directly to the general, and McHenry replied he had been sent directly to the mayor.[23] Unfortunately for McHenry, and even more unfortunately for Willie McGee and Dr. Braman, the mayor acted quickly and decisively. Mayor Elam may have sensed the fraud in McHenry, or perhaps he was acquainted with one or more of the parties involved. Whatever Elam's reasons, the mayor sent a messenger almost immediately to General George Sykes and asked McHenry to await the reply. Sykes replied within the hour, asking if Mayor Elam himself could bring the note and Mr. McHenry to his office at the Barracks.[24]

In the presence of the commanding officer and the mayor, McHenry caved. The ex-spy and soon to be ex-detective cunningly said he knew nothing "whatsoever" about anything, "except what I heard in Dr. Braman's room."[25]

Can we believe McHenry? Is it possible Dr. Braman, the day following his first wedding anniversary, would concoct such a ludicrous plot to help his friend Lieutenant Clark? Would an assistant surgeon with a salary of less than $300 a year promise a shady character like McHenry $150 dollars just to "work up a case against McGee?" [26] Would the doctor scribble a two-sentence forgery accusing a fellow officer of a $10 theft? It is clear from Mayor Elam's testimony in the first trial that he saw through McHenry when he walked in the door. Maybe he even knew about him before, as perhaps did General Sykes, whose testimony later stated that McHenry lived within a stone's throw of his own quarters. Is it more than possible McHenry, seeing an easy mark in the naïve doctor, convinced him to write the note and trust him (McHenry) to work his spy and imagined detective magic? Dr. Chandler Braman fell for a quick scheme, and, in his excitement, it was over before he recognized his own stupidity. Everyone involved sensed the con man in McHenry but the doctor, and Chandler Braman would pay the dearest price for his naiveté.

General Sykes got to the heart of the matter quickly. Sykes was West Point, Class of 1842, a class that produced no fewer than twelve corps and army commanders during the war. He served the army from 1842 until 1880, when he died of cancer while on duty at age fifty-seven at Fort Brown, Texas.[27] When Mayor Elam and McHenry came to his office that Friday in August 1868, George Sykes had been the commanding officer of the 20th Regiment for six months. Those who knew General Sykes would guarantee one thing about him: he would protect his men, especially his officers. General George McClellan, who had known Sykes during their days at the Point, said of him: "As a gentleman his character was the highest, also the purest, and he endeared himself to all who were so fortunate as to be associated with him."[28] Just to be sure, Sykes brought Lieutenant Clark from his post early Friday after McHenry had left for

General George Sykes, West Point Class of 1842, was the commanding officer of the 20th United States Infantry at Baton Rouge, Louisiana, 1868–69, when Lieut. William McGee shot and killed Dr. Chandler Braman, August 15, 1868 (U.S. Army Military History Institute).

the night and asked him if the note was accurate. "'My God, no!'" was the answer. 'The doctor had no business to say anything of the kind!'"[29]

Because of quick action by Mayor Elam and equally swift leadership by Sykes, Willie McGee would soon be exonerated. Dr. Chandler Balch Braman, the possibly naïve Harvard graduate working in a Reconstruction army post hospital, was about to be exposed, while the mysterious McHenry, the Judas of the story, crawled away to his boat, the *Irene*. It was initially a minor irritation for the 20th Regiment, but one General George Sykes would take care of quickly Saturday morning.

After breakfast on Saturday, the general sent for Dr. Braman. Did the doctor get a warning from his friend Lieutenant Clark? If so, there is no record, but all accounts we do possess — save McHenry, who disappeared into the Mississippi River mist, and McGee, who later found many reasons to discredit the doctor — tend to imply or portray a decent, educated, albeit gullible man eager to please his friends and patients. Sykes, the conservative veteran military man, simply asked Braman two questions. The first question was, "Did you write the note?" to which the doctor replied just as simply, "Yes."[30]

The second question was just as direct. "Did you give the note to McHenry?" (the man who would be referred to in court as "an irresponsible citizen" several times, but never named) and again Dr. Braman replied, "Yes." The commanding officer then informed Braman that during the course of the day he would inform Lieutenant McGee, and the assistant surgeon was dismissed.[31]

Sykes, as was his habit, did not wait long. Sometime later in the morning, he summoned Lieutenant McGee, later testifying, "I felt it was my obligation to inform him of the charges made against him." The general added, "I told Lieutenant McGee there had been trouble of a personal character between [McGee] and Dr. Braman. The doctor had made very serious charges against him affecting McGee's honor and his standing as an officer."[32] General Sykes' testimony at both trials seems to indicate his duty ended after informing both men separately of the charges, perhaps assuming that the two men would work it out. McGee and Braman did, sort of.

Certainly the personalities of both men are revealed in the next few hours. By now it had to be afternoon; later General Sykes testified, "I received a note from Dr. Braman at a later period in the day and he informed me that he had an interview with Lieutenant McGee and he [Braman] 'had made it all right.'"[33] According to Sykes' adjutant, Lt. Carncross, the note said, "I have done injustice to McGee I would try to do away with so long as I remain in Baton Rouge."[34] There is little reason to doubt the sincerity of the doctor. In a letter received by his parents on the very day of his death, Braman spoke of disinterring and sending to their family the remains of two friends who had died in the war and were buried in Baton Rouge. He wrote, "They were both friends of my boyhood, and perhaps someone may be kind enough to thus deal with one of your children, should they be unfortunate as to leave their bones away from home among strangers."[35] Little did Braman know that hours after his parents read this last letter from their oldest son, they would be telegraphed about his death. No other officer or enlisted man ever testified that he was a braggart, bully, or dangerous man, and if there was such a single person, the defense attorneys for Willie McGee, the best in the state, would have called them in a second.

While Chandler Braman was writing and sending his notes to General Sykes and meeting with McGee, what was the lieutenant doing all day? After meeting with Braman no later than one P.M.— his note to Sykes about the meeting was given to the general about 2:00 P.M.— we lose sight of McGee until 5:00 P.M. Again, there is no direct proof, but hints abound.

Willie, at the time, claimed to be twenty years old, but most definitely was only nineteen.[36] His age and size and boyish Irish face made him appear even younger, and he could not have weighed more than 150 pounds, and possibly less.[37] In a later chapter we will discuss McGee's entry into the service as a drummer boy with all its inherent good and bad points. But there was no question Willie McGee had a problem with alcohol, acquired either genetically or as a fourteen-year-old soldier in the war.[38] Did Willie possess some alcohol infused anger in him when he returned to see General Sykes at 5:00 P.M.? Had he spent an hour or two downtown plotting his revenge on the doctor over a few shots of Irish? For sure McGee was not in his tent or anywhere on the barracks, as later witnesses testify. Reconstructed Southerners and his fellow officers in the 20th Infantry would soon test nineteen-year-old McGee's immaturity. Whatever the case, the stage at 5:00 P.M. was set for disaster. Lieutenant William McGee, the man-child hero of New Jersey, would live to regret his lack of patience and maturity in the next two hours of his life.

Shortly before 5:00 P.M. Lieutenant McGee returned to the Baton Rouge Barracks of the 20th Regiment in an undressed uniform and met with General Sykes. The meeting did not last long and Willie ran into Lieutenant Louis Morris and Captain Fletcher, who were sitting and resting on the gallery porch. McGee told his fellow officers he had just come from the general's quarters and had been told by their commanding officer "that Dr. Braman had accused him [McGee] of stealing a watch and some two or three hundred dollars." Willie was "very excited" and told both men, "I'm going to shoot the doctor."[39]

Both men advised McGee to use no violence and urged Willie to take civil action, if he wished, against the doctor "if he had the proof." After McGee explained the scenario involving the note, both Morris and Fletcher said if Willie could get it, he "would have a great case." Without hesitation Lieutenant Willie McGee said, "I'll go and get it" and returned to General Sykes' quarters.[40]

According to General Sykes' later testimony, Willie appeared in his quarters asking for the note. In the first trial, the general said that after giving McGee the note, "He [McGee] said something about wearing a cow-hide out on Dr. Braman." At this point Sykes' testimony is that he told the angry young officer that "it is a personal matter" and as a commanding officer he "could not give any advice on the matter."[41]

In the second trial the general's testimony changed just a bit. As McGee was about to leave the general's quarters, Willie said, "So and so should wear a raw-hide out on Doctor Braman, "but Sykes later stated that while it was a personal matter: "I could give him no advice, but that I know what I would do under the circumstances."[42] Will McGee, stone sober or slightly inebriated, took this last statement as tacit approval to whip and attack Chandler Braman. In this postwar world of rough and tumble Louisiana, that type of beating may have been tolerated and excused, ending the matter. Though General Sykes later amended his testimony in a great example of military political correctness, the bigger mistake was telling his youngest officer, "I can give you no advice."[43]

Why not? Despite General George Sykes' pedigree, this mistake without a doubt contributed to the future actions of our Medal of Honor recipient and what he would do to Doctor Braman. Sykes had been commanding officer of the 20th Infantry for half a year.[44] Is it possible he didn't know McGee and his background? Is it possible this thirty year career officer did not see that his youngest, smallest officer, with an Irish temper and known alcoholic tendencies (testified to in court), needed to be sat down and talked to, or even ordered to calm down? It did not, however, happen, and Willie left the general's quarters for the third time that day.[45]

Returning from the general's quarters, Willie went to his tent, dressed in civilian clothes, and once again passed by and engaged Morris and Fletcher on the way to his destiny. McGee showed both officers the "small, soiled note written in pencil." Both men took notice as well that Willie was also carrying a cow-hide.[46]

McGee stayed with them, conversing "a while" and then crossed the parade grounds towards his own Company K, and still a little later he was seen speaking to a Private McCormack, then Chelsea Walker, the colored

Exterior view of the Pentagon Barracks in Baton Rouge, circa 1960. The well-preserved barracks, constructed in 1824, was the scene of the 1868 shooting of Chandler Braman. The building currently houses several state offices, including that of the Louisiana attorney general (Louisiana Collection, State Library of Louisiana, Baton Rouge).

servant of Lieutenant Thomas Latchford.[47] What was not seen in this period between 5:30 and 6:30 P.M. was McGee's visit to the tent of his sergeant, William Jones. He asked Jones to borrow his pistol, as his own was dirty. Willie told the sergeant, "It's just the thing I want." According to Jones, the lieutenant was "very much excited."[48] Lieutenant William Henry McGee, the New Jersey drummer boy recipient of the Medal of Honor, and one of the youngest officers in the history of the United States Army, a soldier who had spent most of his brief life trying to be a man, now, when it counted the most, behaved like a cowardly boy.[49]

Willie McGee, agitated and excited, had returned from somewhere unknown about 5:00 P.M. and for the next hour and a half had met twice with General Sykes, twice with Lieutenant Morris and Captain Fletcher, with Private McCormack, Sergeant Jones, and, finally, with the colored servant Chelsea Walker. One might say he was a boy looking for someone to stop him, but nobody saw the danger. Doctor Chandler Braman, meanwhile, was working in the hospital, but his mind was clearly not on medicine. Braman had spent the earlier part of the day meeting with McGee and apologizing profusely, and writing notes to General Sykes. While Willie McGee was losing control after 5:00 P.M. Chandler Braman was running scared. Private George Mayhew, a patient at the regiment hospital who was on convalescent duty, spent time talking to him just an hour before the attack. While Mayhew was preparing medicine, the doctor told him that "McGee is not a friend of mine and I anticipate trouble with him." Mayhew also added that Dr. Braman said McGee was innocent of taking Lieut. Clark's watch.[50]

Braman could not possibly have been a tough guy physically, as he asked Private Mayhew to stay close around him should the 5'8" McGee come to his room.[51] Unfortunately for Dr. Braman, when he needed help within the hour, he did not tell Mayhew and went alone to his room for a fatal meeting with McGee.

While Willie McGee was borrowing Sergeant Jones' loaded pistol at approximately six o'clock, Lieutenant Septimus Carncross visited Dr. Braman, at General Sykes' request, on "business." The moment Carncross entered the doctor's room, Chandler quickly handed the lieutenant a letter. "On opening it," he testified later, "I found an application for the annulment of his [Braman's] military contract."[52]

Taken by surprise, Carncross asked Braman what caused him to write such a letter. Braman replied "partly business, but more particularly on account of the displeasure of the General." Lieutenant Carncross was perplexed and asked Chandler what he meant. "The General is very angry with me on account of some statements I have made about Lieutenant McGee.... I had better leave the Post."[53] As Carncross left Braman's room to give the doctor's note to General Sykes, he passed Lieutenant William McGee on the parade grounds.

It was not luck that enabled Carncross to meet Dr. Braman in his room instead of the hospital. Chandler Braman made the mistake — the fatal mistake — of accepting Willie McGee's offer to meet again. It was about 6:30 P.M. when McGee instructed the servant Chelsea Walker to seek out the doctor and tell him to meet McGee in the mess room. The doctor, according to Walker, quickly got up and started toward the mess room as requested, but stopped on the stairs and told Walker to "present Dr. Braman's compliments to Lieutenant McGee and that he [Braman] would be pleased to see Lieut. McGee in his room."[54]

Willie immediately started toward the doctor's room up the stairs and Walker followed a few steps behind. Walker watched Willie enter Dr. Braman's room and he stayed just outside the door and watched through the lone window what was about to unfold. As Willie entered the room Walker said he began whipping the doctor with the cow-hide switch. Braman was seated in his revolving chair and as the whipping continued, he threw up both hands, and yelled, "Look out! McGee, look out!"[55]

To avoid the continued switching, Dr. Braman began to rise and turn from his chair. McGee's pistol rang out with one shot, striking the turning Braman in the back.[56] The doctor, bleeding from the mouth, stumbled away from McGee and out the back door, down the steps to the hospital tent, next to the hospital proper, where he collapsed on a cot face down and died within seconds. Private Mayhew tended to him, but it was useless. The tent filled up with officers and enlisted men, but the doctor died without uttering a sound in the crowded tent.[57]

Willie McGee, on the other hand, ran out the front door of the doctor's room, yelling out, "I will make you howl if you say that about me!" As he passed Chelsea Walker at the window, Lieutenant McGee threw the soiled, two sentence, penciled note on the ground.[58]

Within seconds the barracks were wild. Carncross heard the report of the pistol and ran to the hospital, finding Private Mayhew tending to the dead Doctor Chandler Braman. Officers were running everywhere, but Sykes figured it out silently. He ordered the immediate arrest of Will McGee, and Carncross found him in his tent. After the whipping, shooting, and killing of the doctor, Carncross simply said to Willie, "McGee, you have killed the doctor."[59] Willie McGee, the youngest officer of the 20th U.S. Infantry, blamed the victim: "Oh, my God, Carncross, you do not know how much that man has tried to ruin my character."[60]

Sergeant Jones' borrowed pistol was found fifteen minutes after the shooting on a table in Captain Patterson's tent, through which McGee had been seen fleeing.[61] Saturday night, August 15, 1868, had just begun in earnest in downtown Baton Rouge, but not for Chandler Braman, the Massachusetts doctor who told a lie to help a friend. His widow, barely a bride, would bury her husband in a willowy cemetery in Baton Rouge, the warm and humid Louisiana weather too hot to send his body home to Massachusetts.[62] Drummer Boy Willie McGee was a murderer, and as it would turn out, much more, and less.

The watch was never found.

CHAPTER TWO

The Regiment,
the Drummer, the Medal

> William Magee is one of the mysteries of the 33rd....
> The account of his participation in the battle of Murfreesboro ...
> is almost impossible to believe, but he did get the Medal of Honor,
> so something significant must have happened.
> — John Zinn, *The Mutinous Regiment*

When William McGee, a barely fourteen-year-old Newark waif, enlisted in the U.S. Army in July 1863, his widowed mother surely was concerned for his safety. But if Margaret McGee of Beaver Street knew the kind of regiment her boy Willie was about to join as a drummer, she may have had serious second thoughts about allowing her youngest child to go off to war. The 33rd New Jersey Infantry would be infamous before it was famous, its history ranging from mass desertions at the start to valorous distinction at war's conclusion.[1]

In the summer of 1863, Governor Parker of New Jersey authorized the formation of the Garden State's 33rd regiment under the command of an ambitious young colonel, George Washington Mindil.[2] There would be little problem raising a new regiment that summer, despite a two year losing streak by Union armies. The progress of the Union war effort changed dramatically on July 4, when the news reached Newark about the victory at Gettysburg, which was followed by word of Grant's conquest at Vicksburg.[3] In addition to the wins in the field, Congress had just passed the Conscription Act of 1863, seeming to guarantee an overwhelming supply of Federal man-

Broad Street, the main thoroughfare of Newark, New Jersey, when Willie McGee was five years old in 1854. The beautiful uptown street was a far cry from the swampy, mosquito infested east side where the immigrant Irish resided. The 33rd New Jersey would march down this avenue in triumph on its return home in July 1865, when they were greeted as heroes (from the collections of the New Jersey Historical Society, Newark).

power. Prior to the summer of 1863, all soldiers in the Union army had been volunteers, but the supply of soldiers had declined while the demands of the Northern war effort had increased. The draft seemed an obvious answer.

But not everything was positive that July, especially if you were Irish. Though the Conscription Act was not technically a draft, to the working-class people of the Northeast it was a superficial difference. The infamous draft riots began on July 13 in New York and did not end until 20,000 troops restored order and hundreds of people had been killed, mostly Irish rioters. Though Newark was only ten miles from the flames, lynching, and destruction in lower Manhattan, New Jersey stayed, for the most part, very quiet.[4]

The single biggest reason for the successful recruiting of the 33rd New Jersey however, was not the draft or military success — it was money, and lots of it. Many veterans of earlier New Jersey regiments had returned home after their enlistments were up with little to show, at least monetarily, for their service to the Union except their scant ability to save from their monthly pay, which was about $13.[5] Now, with federal, state, and local bonuses, a man could enlist in the 33rd N.J. Infantry and be paid more than $650 if married, $400 if single.[6] The economics worked, especially as the average salary in Newark for a sixty-hour week seldom exceeded $300 per year.[7] A working-class man could buy a nice home anywhere in the state for what he might receive in bounty money, and it could easily be his first real home, especially for the new immigrants from Ireland and Germany.

These new federal bounties were paid over three years, but the state and local bonuses were given in advance at enlistment. The city of Newark alone paid out over $80,000 in bounties, and the lure of easy money was not lost on veterans or new enlistees.[8] As John Zinn remarks in *The Mutinous Regiment: The Thirty-Third New Jersey in the Civil War*, "Large up-front cash payments created the temptation of bounty jumping: enlistment, receipt of bounty payment, followed by desertion."[9] Drummer boy and Newark native Willie McGee received a $240 federal bonus, and unspecified local Newark and state bounties, as musicians were given on the average about 50 percent of what would be doled out to an enlisted soldier. It was not much by today's standards, but it would have been a fortune for Willie, with a promise for more. Desertions became rampant with the money flowing freely, and on August 30, the day after Willie McGee enlisted and became Willie Magee, fifty-nine men deserted from Company A, and the following morning another 165 left with their cash, for a total of 244 desertions out of the original 902 men.[10]

One week after Magee became the Company C drummer, the 3rd Vermont Infantry, on its way south to fight rebels, was ordered to Newark instead as camp guards of the rapidly notorious 33rd New Jersey, to restore order to the new regiment.[11] As humiliating as it was to have your own regiment under armed guard within the city limits of Newark, it was surely not the proper education for the sixteen musicians, fifteen of whom were under seventeen, and many, like Willie, who were fourteen years or younger. With the regiment's departure for war imminent, another 200 men tried to desert, and by some accounts they were armed.[12] The entire 3rd Vermont was called out, and though fifteen Jerseymen did successfully desert, the rest were restored to order in their units, although two men were killed by the Vermonters, one shot through the heart. The regiment and the state were disgraced, but the 33rd N.J. finally was ushered aboard ships bound for Washington on September 8, 1863, the march to the Newark docks again made under armed Vermont guard, with many — some say most — of the newest New Jersey regiment drunk.[13] After a less than auspicious start, by war's end it would be the only blemish on a regiment that, once pushed into service, was remarkable

The only known photograph or drawing of the 33rd New Jersey Infantry in the field detailing their distinctive Zouave uniforms, chosen by their youthful commander, Colonel George Washington Mindil (author collection).

for all the right reasons.[14] After brief stops in Washington and Northern Virginia, the 33rd Infantry was sent west, where after a tumultuous journey they arrived in Indianapolis by train on September 28; they then went south to Alabama, five miles south of the Tennessee border, on September 30, altogether crossing six states and 1,500 miles in six days.[15]

After a month of living off some of the poorest land in the South, and drilling and performing guard duty while awaiting battle orders, the 33rd New Jersey was moved on November 7 to the brigade camp at Lookout Valley, Tennessee. Immediately there were problems. The sick men, along with the unit's baggage, which was already at a bare minimum, were sent by flatboat on the Tennessee River while the rest of the regiment marched north to the camp. The tragedy that followed has never been adequately explained, but twelve sick men were swept into the water and most of the baggage was lost. Four men, including Oscar Lathrop of Willie Magee's Company C, were drowned. Mourning their comrades, the regiment occupied their new camp in Lookout Valley on November 9, and one soldier wrote home the next day, "The weather had turned very cold with a severe frost the night before."[16] The three previous nights had been difficult, the men "shivering in [their] wretched dog tents" from a severe north wind. Because sudden orders from Washington forced Commander Mindil to leave most of the regiment's supplies and baggage behind when the unit left quickly from the east, and the small remainder was lost on the river, it was simply a matter of time before sickness, especially typhoid and diarrhea, entered the camp.[17] Dozens were already sick and some were dying of the war's biggest killer, disease. Illness killed more than 200,000 men in the war, more than double what weapons accomplished, and easily found the Jersey boys. Union forces soon began the assault to relieve Chattanooga, and for the next three weeks the 33rd N.J. gallantly fought and marched behind Colonel George Washington Mindil's lead through Tennessee before returning to camp at Lookout Valley.[18] The 33rd had forgotten all about their disastrous beginnings in Newark, and had marched to heroically relieve Chattanooga, most without blankets and tents and many without shoes. They performed some of the hardest duty imaginable, admirably surviving frost, rain, and cold. When they arrived back in camp, the 33rd N.J. had begun to establish a proud record of service, a record they would uphold until Lee surrendered, fifteen months hence.[19]

On December 18, 1863, three months after leaving Newark, the 33rd New Jersey Zouaves settled into their first winter's quarters, and within two weeks the worst storm of the year arrived, bringing rain, gale force winds, and bitter cold. Ten inches of snow fell soon afterward and some Union men froze to death overnight. That same night, Colonel Mindil filed a report from Lookout Valley, where he mentioned in part, "As for the officers and men, all performed their duty unflinchingly and where all act well it is impossible to discriminate. For a regiment but of three months creation, without much drill and discipline, the Thirty-third did remarkably well. I feel confident that the regiment can now be relied upon for any emergency, as the men will perform their whole duty.... To Chaplain John Faull my thanks as well as those of the command are due for the fearlessness manifested in relieving the wounded, by personally removing them, with the aid of the drum corps, to the surgeon in the rear. Dr. Stiger remained with the regiment, at all times performing his duty." It was a great testimony for Colonel Mindil to single out the musicians before mentioning most of his officers or field soldiers, so Willie Magee and his fellow drummers had "seen the elephant," and passed their first test with flying colors.[20]

It was the first Christmas the regiment would spend together, and they must have been glad to be back in camp, but John Zinn points out that "almost without exception, Civil War armies suffered the most from disease when they stayed in one place for a long period of time. Remaining stationery contaminated the entire environment which, in turn, became a breeding ground for disease." More than a dozen died of typhoid and related fevers, and hundreds were sick.[21]

Supplies improved after Christmas with the reopening of the railroad from Nashville to Lookout Valley, and it was just in time for the small, four-teen-year-old drummer, Willie Magee. Sick with fever, and, according to Chaplain Holmes Pattison, "close to the jaws of death," Willie and others from the 33rd New Jersey were sent to the hospital at Murfreesboro, 100 miles north, on January 24, 1864.[22] Magee would spend the next fifteen months in Tennessee, not seeing his unit until April 1865, in Virginia.[23] When Willie rejoined his regiment within days of the assassination of President Lincoln on April 14, 1865, the men and boys of the 33rd had much to share with the erstwhile missing musician, as they had spent the past year as part of General Sherman's "March to the Sea." The regiment had fought hard at Resaca and the Battle of Atlanta before the long march north with Sherman, and many had paid a heavy price, including twelve men captured and imprisoned at the infamous Andersonville Prison Camp. Six of the twelve would die there of disease, including Irish drummer John Mailey, or O'Malley, of Company E, like Will McGee the youngest of four children to an immigrant Irish family in Newark.[24]

Who knows what Magee shared with his unit after the long hiatus? Now sixteen, Willie was reunited with soldiers he had known for only four months before becoming ill. Musician Magee had spent the long journey to Alabama with his comrades, as well as the Lookout Valley campaign under General Geary of Pennsylvania, who would become a McGee booster after the war.[25] But for fifteen months the drummer boy of Beaver Street in Newark had been separated from family, friends, and mentors. Had he stayed in touch with his regiment? Mail was the number one priority of all Civil War soldiers, and letters were more important to many soldiers than supplies. Despite the normal disruptions of war, the mail was remarkably efficient, and given Willie's later propensity for writing it would seem likely there had been some contact between Willie and someone in the 33rd New Jersey, in addition to whomever Magee chose to contact back home.

William R. Adams (right) of Company I, who was the youngest musician of the 33rd N.J. at twelve years of age, posed in Newark prior to departure for Tennessee. The unidentified drummer on the left may be the hero of Murfreesboro, Willie McGee. After the war, Adams, unlike McGee, would lead a long and prosperous life back home in Essex County, New Jersey (Donald E. Henningsen collection).

According to the Reverend John Faull, "the only thing on the men's mind was 'Home Sweet Home.'" The regiment arrived in Washington, D.C., on May 19, a long month after Lee surrendered and Lincoln was buried. The entire assembly of the 33rd was present for the Grand Review of the Western armies on May 24, with Willie Magee drumming for his Company C. The crowds in Washington were wild in celebration and looked to the men marching as "a sea of fluttering color." Bands played all day, women cried, many prayed, and people were hoarse with cheering in what was the largest parade in U.S. history.[26]

There was a large New Jersey delegation present for the parade, headed by Marcus Ward, the "soldier's friend." The regiment encamped just north of the city in Bladensburg, Maryland, and remained there for two more months before mustering out on a golden summer day, July 17, 1865. The overwhelming majority of the dispersed Jersey boys hopped the first trains north for home, and stopped at Trenton, where they spent a day being feted by Governor Parker and a huge crowd before finally arriving in Newark on July 21.[27] Willie Magee, soon to once again become McGee, and twelve other musicians were now safely in New Jersey, though none would ever be kids again, and they would be putting away little boys things when they got home.

It was a surreal scene, perhaps, for many of the men and officers. Twenty-two months earlier, a drunken collection of homegrown New Jersey soldiers were marched under armed guard to the Newark docks to begin their military careers with the 33rd Infantry. They returned to joyful celebrations, cheers, flags flying, and banquets, where once again Marcus Ward was the guest of honor and "greeted with vociferous acclaims of the soldiers." Following the wild partying, the regiment was furloughed until July 31, when they were to receive their final pay. Marcus Ward continued proving he was a most generous and considerate man by arranging for each man to be paid through their date of discharge, giving them an extra fifteen days payout. When some of the out of town soldiers from Sussex and Passaic counties had financial difficulties, Ward advanced men $5 to $25 of his own money until their final pay. By August 3, Willie Magee and the rest of the 33rd New Jersey Infantry had ceased to exist. As Zinn remarked in *The Mutinous Regiment*, "The war was over; the men were either at their homes or on their way there. Gradually they would adjust to civilian life, resume their careers or professions, or begin new ones."[28] Willie Magee could now return to civilian life as Willie McGee, a sixteen-year-old–with a man's experience, ready to make his mark on the world.

These were heady days for Willie, who must have been bursting to get home for the first time in two years, and anxious to tell of his first battle at Lookout Mountain, his recovery from typhoid, his adoption, and his fierce escapade at the Battle of the Cedars. Willie remained in Newark working as a waiter for two months or less, when, for reasons unknown, he made the decision to start life over in Michigan with his newly adoptive father, the Reverend Holmes Pattison. Deciding to leave his mother as well as his three siblings for a second time in two years, Willie accepted the $75 for the remainder of his federal bounty, and at least one more paycheck. By October 1865, the drummer boy was living under the roof of Mr. and Mrs. Holmes Pattison in Muskegon, Michigan.[29]

A good assumption can be made that sometime between April when he rejoined his regiment in Virginia, and before leaving Newark for Michigan in the fall to join Holmes Pattison, the Willie Magee story of heroism and bravery at the Battle of the Cedars began to take shape. Perhaps it evolved in campfires prior to mustering out, or over victory celebrations in Washington or on the train home to New Jersey. Surely Marcus Ward heard the Magee tale before Willie left for Michigan, as the story was soon to appear in John Y.

Foster's *New Jersey in the Rebellion*, and it was Ward himself who chose Foster to write the book.[30] Willie's experience in Murfreesboro could not have come from anyone in the 33rd New Jersey, as they were occupied first at the Battle of Atlanta and then were marching and slogging their way through the rivers and swamps of the Carolinas with Sherman. Willie must have told the story to Pattison after he arrived in Michigan late in 1865, and it must have pleased the lawyer and chaplain to no end. The act of heroism and courage could not have sprung from Pattison himself as he was in Michigan at the time of the Murfreesboro battle, and Holmes could not have picked up the story from local soldiers as no Michigan units were anywhere near Fortress Rosecrans at the time.[31] Pattison surprisingly, perhaps even to Willie, spread the marvelous story of bravery, patriotism, youthful passion and leadership to Washington, which resulted in a Medal of Honor, and later, a commission in the Regular Army.[32] The story of McGee's heroism in Tennessee, after Willie almost died in a hospital of typhoid, could never have occurred without the intervention of the Reverend Holmes Pattison.

Pattison, born in Elk County, Pennsylvania, in 1827, is found in the 1860 census living in tiny Colon, Michigan, an hour north of Fort Wayne, Indiana. Holmes was married, with no children, and working full time as a Methodist minister and part time as an attorney.[33] He enlisted in the war early, joining the 11th Michigan Infantry at age thirty-four as their chaplain in August 1861.[34] The 11th may not be one of the storied regiments of the war, but it wasn't for lack of trying, with a casualty rate of 41 percent over a three year period. The Michigan unit was engaged in the midst of vicious fire at Stone River, Chickamauga, and Missionary Ridge before ending their three year enlistment at the bloody Siege of Atlanta in September 1864.[35] In the winter of 1864, the Reverend Pattison found himself in Murfreesboro, doing God's work at one or more of the three hospitals at Fortress Rosecrans. With the 11th Michigan seeing so much action throughout the Tennessee area in 1863, there can be little wonder that Pattison was kept busy at the hospitals throughout the region as post chaplain.[36]

William Magee, as he was officially known in the army upon enlistment, was sent to Murfreesboro with other sick and wounded 33rd New Jersey men — many of whom did not survive the fever or the hospital. At least fourteen Jersey boys of the 33rd N.J. died of typhoid between November 13, 1863, and March 12, 1864.[37] Willie must have presented a very forlorn figure upon arrival at Murfreesboro. Though he listed himself as 5' 2" upon entering the service in Newark, to an observer Magee, sickly, thin, and possessing a boyishly haggard Irish countenance, might easily have passed for eleven or twelve when he was carried into Hospital #2 at Murfreesboro.

Willie Magee, however, was not the only soldier fighting for his life against disease, nor was his age that unusual. The most studied single subject in United States history, the Civil War still offers historians and aficionados some improbable topics, and the ages of its combatants is one. More than one expert has even gone so far as to call this War Between the States "The Boys War." Some historians are convinced that of the approximate 2,700,000 Federal soldiers, a million (40 percent), were under 18, and that "about" 100,000 were under fifteen.[38] Even should this number be significantly exaggerated — and it has not been proven wrong yet — the number of fighting boys is staggering.

Praying men of God thus contended not only with the normal vagaries of inhuman warfare, but in our Civil War, out of necessity, they became temporary foster fathers of thousands upon thousands of young boy-soldiers.[39] At some point in late January or early February 1864, Holmes Pattison, the Michigan chaplain, met Willie Magee, typhoid victim. How long Magee was laid low with fever is unknown, but it may have taken a month, maybe two or more. It is unlikely Holmes Pattison medically saved Willie, but his attention to the young drummer may have gone a long way towards his eventual recovery.

While Willie was fighting for his life, the 33rd N.J. was heading further south, and would spend the remainder of the war a long way from Murfreesboro, Tennessee. The Jersey Zouaves would be involved in the Siege of Atlanta and Sherman's March to the Sea, eventually making the final march from North Carolina to Washington in April 1865.[40] As the spring came and went in Murfreesboro, Willie's health improved. Hospital #2 at Fortress Rosecrans even had a 100-acre vegetable garden, so patients had a much better diet than most field hospitals.[41] The staff at the hospital, and perhaps Chaplain Holmes Pattison, must have decided to keep Willie Magee with them when his unit headed south to Atlanta. It would have been a logical decision. Drummer boys were always trained to assist surgeons during battle, whether as stretcher bearers, nurses, or simply doing convalescent work.[42] Besides, it would be most difficult to do anything else with the little Irishman. The army simply could not put a single musician on a train south to join a combat unit deep in Confederate territory. It made common sense to utilize the Jersey teenager until safe transport could be found. As the summer of '64 came and went, Magee found a home of sorts in Murfreesboro as an orderly to General Horatio Van Cleve.[43]

By all accounts Willie was a most intrinsically gregarious charmer, and as he returned to health, the Reverend Pattison, an attorney by trade, for whatever reasons felt his heart tug and legally adopted our young drummer boy.[44]

Willie must have approved, and it had to have occurred during the summer of 1864, as Holmes Pattison was mustered out in Michigan in late September of that year.[45] The adoption raises doubts, some on Willie's side, and some on Pattison's. For starters, McGee's family was Roman Catholic, while Pattison was a Methodist. Officially, Willie Magee was a fatherless son, but not an orphan. He always — even to Pattison — admitted he had a mother, two older brothers and a sister, and a typically large extended Irish family, though in much correspondence he never, ever wrote their names. It is hard to argue with the adoption evidence. Though no record exists, both Holmes Pattison and Willie admit to such an arrangement in writing several times, as did New Jersey governor Marcus Ward in correspondence.[46]

Maybe Willie was just a scared, sick kid. Perhaps he was worn out or traumatized by war. Possibly he fell for all the attention. Or was he simply a born con man? Could an underage boy be adopted even with his own permission? In a war with the totally parentless numbering well over 20,000 children, why does Pattison have to adopt a boy with at least one parent and three older siblings? One has to wonder about a thirty-eight-year-old man who meets a fifteen-year-old boy in a hospital and adopts him in four months — or less. For certain, from 1864 to late 1872, Holmes Pattison was a very visible protector of Will Magee. After 1872 he disappeared from Magee's life, presumably on bad terms, and in 1880 Pattison and his wife, Fanny, were living and working in Jacksonville, Florida, with another adopted son, a seven-year-old they named Holmes, Jr.[47]

But in December 1865, with whatever family dynamics were involved, our beardless drummer is in Muskegon, and both new father and new son were anxious to please each other. On December 8, Holmes took pen to paper and wrote the following to new Kentucky congressman Lovell Rousseau, former commander of Fortress Rosecrans:

Muskegon, Mich
Decr 8, 1865

Maj. Gen L.H. Rousseau
Washington, DC

General Sir:
I do not know whether you would remember me now, but at any rate I served in the army of the Cumberland for upwards of 3 yrs, in the ole 14th A.C. I was with my Regt (11th Michigan) at Stone River, & subsequently served as Post Chaplain at Fortress Rosecrans at Murfreesboro, Tennessee while you were in command of the Nashville Dist & had called upon you several times on business during that time.
But whether you remember me or not, you will doubtless remember the lad in whose interest I now write. You will doubtless remember Willie Magee of

Co "C" 33rd New Jersey Regt, serving as an orderly to Brig Gen Von Cleve at Murfreesboro a year ago at the time of Hood's move on Murfreesboro and Nashville, & his bravery in the matter of capturing the Rebel Artillery during the fighting in front of Murfreesboro at that time. You will remember that some effort was made, or at least talked of, of procuring him a Lieut's commission as a proper acknowledgment of his bravery & soldierly conduct in leading that charge.

Before I left the service I adopted Willie as my son, & now after serving through the war & honorably discharged he is with me. All he now asks is that you do what you can do so consistently, that you interest yourself in his behalf in procuring for him a Medal, such as has usually been given by the War Dept to soldiers of merit & bravery. If in your judgment his services were of such order as to make him worthy of such mark of National favor &

General Lovell H. Rousseau was the military commander at Fortress Rosecrans in Murfreesboro, Tennessee, on December 7, 1864, when the Willie McGee legend was born. Rousseau would become the catalyst behind the awarding of a Medal of Honor to Will McGee (Dennis Keesee Collection).

would procure it for him, it would greatly oblige him, & so far as I am concerned, if opportunity ever offered I would most heartily reciprocate the favor.

Hoping to hear from you soon I remain

Your obt servt
H.A. Pattison
Pastor of M.E. Church
Muskegon, Mich[48]

Mailing the letter changed forever the life of William H. McGee.

Between 1865 and as late as 1885, veterans, widows, friends and families wrote voluminous notes, letters, and postcards to every possible level of officialdom — governors, congressmen, ex-generals, senators — looking for money, medals, assistance with funerals and burials, and especially jobs. Pattison's letter asked only for a medal and reached Rousseau, a newly elected congressman from Kentucky, in Washington about a week before Christmas. After reading Holmes' letter, Rousseau replied on the back with a ninety-two word response, and sent both the letter and his addendum to the secretary of war. The stars must have been aligned correctly for Willie and Holmes:

Washington, Dec15/65

Respectfully referred to the Honorable, the Secretary of War.

While Genl Hood was between my command in Murfreesborough in December 1864 we had several battles with the rebel Generals, Bates and Forrest on one of which we captured many prisoners and two new 12 pdrs. Napoleon guns, in a charge upon the enemy. The lad was amongst the first who got to the guns & he and one or two others, all mere boys mounted the Artillery horses and took the guns into Fortress Rosecrans. Magee's behavior was very gallant & meritorious and he richly deserves the medal asked for him.

Lovell Rousseau[49]

Following the Christmas and New Year's break, the adjutant general's office sent to Congressman Rousseau the following:

War Department
Adjutant General's Office
Washn Feb 7, 1866

Sir:

Referring to the letter of Rev. H.A. Pattison, Pastor of M.E. Church, Muskegon, Mich. bearing your endorsement of date Dec 15/65 recommending William Magee, late drummer, Co "C" 33rd NJ Vols for a med of honor, I have reply to inform you that the medal has been ordered engraved and will be sent to him in the care of Mr. Pattison at Muskegon, Mich as soon as completed.

(sd) E.D. Townsend[50]
A.A. G.

Less than three weeks later Pattison wrote to Townsend, the assistant adjutant general:

Muskegon, Mich
Febr 26, 1866

Sir:

In behalf of William Magee late drummer of Co "C" 33rd New Jersey Volunteers, I would acknowledge the rect of the Medal of Honor awarded him by the War Dept. It came to hand some ten days since but owing to absence from home I have been unable to acknowledge sooner. With many thanks for your interest in this matter.

I remain very Respectfully

Your obt servt
H.A. Pattison
For Drummer Co "C" 33rd New
Jersey Volunteers[51]

Fifty-three days after Holmes Pattison's plea for his new son was sent by letter to Washington, Willie Magee was the recipient of a United States Medal

F'

War Department,
Adjutant Generals Office,
Washington, February 9, 1866.

Sir:

Herewith I enclose the Medal of Honor which has been awarded you by the Secretary of War under the Resolution of Congress approved July 12, 1862, "To provide for the presentation of 'Medals of Honor' to the enlisted men of the Army and Volunteer Forces who have distinguished or may distinguish themselves in battle during the present rebellion."

Please acknowledge its receipt,

Very respectfully
Your obedient servant,
E. D. Townsend,
Assistant Adjutant General

William Magee, late Drummer, Co. "C"
33d New Jersey Volunteers.

War Department letter to William Magee, Drummer, Co. C, 33rd New Jersey Volunteers, February 9, 1866, awarding him the Medal of Honor. This letter would be used in both the civil trial and the court-martial in Baton Rouge in 1868 as Exhibit F (author collection).

of Honor. Willie received what has become the nation's highest honor three months shy of his seventeenth birthday. The medal was an honor he may have dreamed of but never sought, and while it placed him in the history books it would also turn out to be an albatross around his neck. The paperwork regarding most Medal of Honor awardees is thick, but in Magee's case the above correspondence is the total package in his file. From the initial letter to the acknowledgment of the receipt, four letters were involved, in the incredibly short period of four months.[52]

In the first letter of December 8 from Pattison to Rousseau, Holmes describes the action at Murfreesboro in which Willie was involved.[53] Holmes Pattison, however, was not even in Tennessee, and had not been for four months, having been mustered out in Michigan in September.[54] Holmes' story, as written, could only have come from one source — Willie McGee. The action at Murfreesboro, more properly called Wilkinson's Pike or the Battle of the Cedars, was not reported extensively in Michigan or anywhere else, and was considered a "small action" by most.[55] Indeed, it has not been called Murfreesboro at all except by the people involved in the Willie McGee story. In addition, it occurred one week after and thirty miles away from the carnage at the Battle of Franklin, where 9,500 men were casualties in five hours, and one week prior and thirty miles from the Battle of Nashville, where Hood's Southern army was finally crushed.[56] Both these major battles and the ones back east took up all newspaper coverage in December '64. This is not to suggest that bravery and heroism were not the order of the day for Willie or any other soldier in war, but the only way Pattison could have become aware of the story would be from his adopted son. No Michigan or New Jersey troops were involved in the action.[57] Holmes seems almost to be currying favor for his new son, to get him "something." As he said in the letter, "All he now asks is that you do what you can ... It would greatly oblige him."[58]

Nonetheless, Will McGee was now a proud recipient of the Medal of Honor, and Rousseau, who was the commanding officer in Tennessee, couldn't have been mistaken about such bravery. Willie, now a resident of Muskegon, Michigan, for less than half a year, was not the youngest soldier awarded a Medal of Honor. That honor would go to another drummer, Willie Johnston, a thirteen-year-old from Vermont.[59] Holmes Pattison likely did not care — he had taken care of his boy in grand fashion. Little Willie McGee could grow old and be happy with what he had already accomplished, but such was not to be his fate.

CHAPTER THREE

Baton Rouge, 1868

For the Lord doth hate three things: a proud look,
a lying tongue, and hands that shed innocent blood.
— Proverbs 6:17

The *Baton Rouge Tri-Weekly Advocate* squeezed the story in between stories on the Levee Board and the gold and cotton markets, both of which got small headlines. Buried in the middle of the page of the August 17 edition is the following:

> Saturday evening, a difficulty occurred in the garrison, in which Lieut. W.H. McGee, of the 20th U.S. Infantry, shot Acting Assistant Surgeon C.B. Braman. The latter lived but a few minutes after receiving the fatal wound. Both officers having many warm friends in this city, great regret for the occurrence is expressed and much sympathy felt, for both the living and the dead, who were parties to this unfortunate affair.
> A jury was empanelled by Coroner Patterson and a verdict found in accordance with the above facts.
> Surgeon Braman was interred Sunday evening, his remains being followed to the grave by a concourse of military, St. James' Lodge of Masons and DeSoto Lodge of the I.O.O.E.[1]

In the previous decade, as many as 700,000 American men had been killed or wounded, a president assassinated, a nation torn apart. One more shooting in 1868 Reconstruction Louisiana surely would not garner much news, especially when a Northern soldier shot another Northern soldier. What were important in Baton Rouge were the cotton and banana prices, and the water level of the Mississippi. Still, it is hard to fathom this as a "difficulty" or an "unfortunate affair."[2] But if all politics is local, murder in any form is personal, local, and unforgiving.

Chandler Braman's widow Cecilia and the Braman family were notified of his death by the army, via a telegraph from Lieutenant John Coe, the 20th Infantry post quartermaster.[3] General Sykes wrote to them "It will be some satisfaction for you to know that I had learned to respect his talents, his faithful and conscientious discharge of duty, his skill and accomplishments; and I think he would have attained great eminence in his profession had his life been spared. He was held in high esteem by his associates in the army and by the friends he made in civil life at Baton Rouge."[4] But the family, through spokesman Dr. Isaac Braman, wanted answers.[5]

But the extended Braman family and the United States Army had one question in common: What to do with Lieutenant William H. McGee? The brass decided early on to turn Willie over to the civil authorities and court-martial him as well, a not unexpected or unusual course of action.[6] Within four days, Captain John Patterson of Company K officially turned McGee over to the sheriff of East Baton Rouge Parish, where Willie was charged with fatally shooting Chandler Braman. A grand jury heard eight witnesses, including Chelsea Walker, General Sykes, Lieut. Clark, Private Mayhew, Lieut. Morris, Lieut. Latchford, and Captain Fletcher. The eighth witness was a Doctor Reynaud of East Baton Rouge, who had performed the autopsy.[7]

General Sykes, whose career approach can be best described as totally unemotional and methodical, still had to be perplexed at how such a "difficulty," as the newspaper framed it, had escalated in such a short period of time. George Sykes, who was dealing with all the evils and realities of Reconstruction Louisiana, still found time to write and console the Braman family, constructing a proper investigation to turn over to the civil authorities, yet at the same time trying to be fair in his treatment of McGee.[8] Indeed, Sykes met with Willie several times in jail, and when Willie asked the general to write his family, George Sykes agreed without hesitation. On Saturday, August 21, one week after the shooting, Sykes wrote a letter at McGee's request. The diligence, social grace, and overriding sense of duty in Sykes was evident, but even in this first letter there were questions, the first of many:

> Baton Rouge Brks, La.
> Aug. 21, '68
>
> Mr. H.A. Patterson
>   Muskegon
>   Michigan
>
>   My Dear Sir:
> At the request of Lieut. Wm McGee of my Regiment, I write to make known to you a very distressing matter in which he is involved. A day or two

prior to the 15 inst, some rumors very damaging to the character and honor of Lieut McGee, became in a manner, public, and were brought to my attention by the Mayor of this City. The person instrumental in the charges against Lt McGee was a gentleman named Braman on duty at this Post, as Actg Asst Surgeon.

From conversations with him, I learned that the charges he made against Lt McGee grew out of his suspicions, and his views regarding a note or request made by Lt McGee of a brother officer.

It became my duty to inform Lt McGee of these aspersions, thrown upon him, which I did. An interview took place between Lt McGee & Dr Braman, after which I received a note from Dr B, saying that he had explained every-thing to the Lt, that the latter " seemed to belie his suspicions," that "he felt that he had done him injustice" and that he would do everything in his power to counteract the effect of his acts, so long as he "remained in the garrison." At dusk on the 15 inst Mr McGee visited Dr. B's quarters, and from all the evidence I can gather, some positive, and some circumstantial, a pistol was fired and Dr. Braman was killed — The Verdict of the Coroners inquest was "that he came to his death by a pistol shot fired by Lt. Wm McGee 20 Infy." This is a very dreadful misfortune Sir, & one in which all the officers and friends of Lt McGee are profoundly touched.

Some of his brother officers counseled him to use no violence in resenting the insult put upon him but wither from his youth, need of judgment, and almost frenzied state of mind, he stands charged with an act the nature of which you well understand. Orders from the Dept Commander required me to turn him over to the Civil Authorities, in whose keeping he now is. We will do all that is possible to soften the rigor of his confinement and soothe his mind. Tomorrow his case is to be examined before a Magistrate Court, and if a bill is found against him, he cannot be tried before November when the Courts meet. It is very painful Sir for me to lay before you the circumstances herein detailed but as the Commd Off of Lt McGee it is done both as a duty, and at the re-quest of Mr McGee. He tells me that he is your adopted son. While the officers of his Regt present here, deplore the situation in which he is place, and from appreciation and the kind feeling they have towards him, extend to him every sympathy, yet they cannot in any way extenuate the offence laid at his hands.

We all unite in our expressions of condolence, and trust that a Merciful Providence may temper the mind to your afflicted and unhappy son.

> I am Sir
> Yrs very truly
> Geo Sykes
> Col 20th Inf[9]

Sykes may have wondered how a boy with a widowed mother in New Jersey could ask to have one letter written and that one to his adoptive father in Muskegon, Michigan. In the letter, there is no mention of his mother or family back home in New Jersey. But the Civil War produced many a dis-placed family, so perhaps General Sykes let it go. Despite the gravity of his predicament, Willie was afraid to tell his family, and did not.

The civil authorities in East Baton Rouge Parish must have felt safe and comfortable with their case. A young officer — with no local ties to worry about — loses his temper, and with an eyewitness and almost a dozen military witnesses, including a general and five fellow officers, shoots and kills the assistant surgeon with a bullet to the back. Making the case seem assured for the prosecution, McGee admitted the act and blamed the victim.[10] The authorities downgraded the charge to manslaughter, probably because of the note and the insult to McGee's honor. Willie McGee should have considered himself lucky, as a manslaughter charge could save his life and give him a possible chance at parole by the time he was 40. Certainly, that was a better chance than he gave Chandler Braman. It seemed ordained that Willie McGee — hero or not — would soon be spending serious time in a Louisiana prison. He had been in jail for more than a week and didn't even have an attorney. He made thirty dollars a month and would be court-martialed when the civil trial was over. The drummer boy's prospects, once so bright, seemed extremely bleak when indictment Number 1028 was handed down the last week in August.[11] To the Bramans, it would never, could never, be enough, even though Sykes or a subordinate provided information to the Bramans which found its way to the *Boston Daily Evening Transcript* on August 24, 1868:

Particulars of the Murder of Dr. Braman of Brighton. We have since learned of the particulars of this sad occurrence, from which it appears that a friend of Dr. Braman, Lieut. C.B. Clark of the 20th U.S. Infantry was robbed of his watch and a considerable sum of money. Suspicion fell upon Second Lieut. William McGee, an officer of the same regiment. Lieut. Clark, who is a member of the Masonic Fraternity, as was also Dr. Braman, informed the Doctor of his loss, who, wishing to help a "Brother Mason," took a great interest in the affair, and by his speech and action manifested his doubts of Lieut. McGee.

In some way their suspicions became noised abroad and coming to the knowledge of Gen. Sykes, he ordered an investigation into the affair, but nothing was proved against McGee. Dr. Braman then wrote a letter to Gen. Sykes, regretting his action; said that his zeal as a Mason led him to help a brother Mason (Lieut. Clark); that in an interview with McGee, McGee removed his suspicions; and that he would do everything possible to counteract what had been done.

McGee, however, was not satisfied, and at dusk on the evening of the 15th went to Dr. Braman's room with a revolver, and without any warning shot him while in the act of rising from his chair. Dr. Braman ran to the hospital tent, never spoke, and expired immediately.

As to McGee, his murderer, he is only seventeen or eighteen years of age. He entered the army when quite young, as a drummer boy in the Thirty-third New Jersey Regiment, and a year ago obtained a commission through the influence of friends. Men who have recently been discharged from his regiment and came from Baton Rouge last week represent him to be of dissipated habits and often seen on duty under the influence of liquor. It is to be hoped he will be made to forfeit his own life for the one he took in so cowardly a manner.[12]

General Sykes, however, soon must have understood he had an unusual man on his hands. One week after his first letter to Willie's adoptive father, the general was penning a second, only this one was in response to a letter he received from Holmes A. Pattison, the Muskegon, Michigan, minister and attorney.[13] Pattison, not Patterson, as Sykes was quick to apologize, wrote his letter to Sykes on August 21, the same day as Sykes' letter to him. Willie must have had someone telegraph Holmes after the shooting. Some excerpts from Sykes' second letter raise questions regarding Willie's supposed dire condition: "I [Sykes] learned from him yesterday that he expected to get bail and be released from prison.... He is very well and very cheerful.... I hardly think he realizes the position in which he is placed.... He is daily visited by his friends, and has every comfort necessary to his welfare.... The authorities are very considerate towards him and give him every indulgence possible."[14]

McGee out on bail? One, he had no money; two, he had no lawyer. Yet Willie, even by the account of a dour, unemotional, automaton regular army officer like George Sykes, seemed cheerful, almost happy. Willie was either totally ignorant, the most upbeat optimist in Louisiana, or he knew he had an ace, or aces, up his sleeve. One thing was becoming obvious, even on a local level; despite what McGee had done, he had friends. The newspaper mentioned it; the jailers noticed it; and even a General remarked on it. Willie McGee was turning out to be a very, very engaging young man.

Like clockwork, another letter appeared from Muskegon, Michigan. Holmes A. Pattison wrote a second letter to General Sykes, and the general dutifully responded. But this third letter to Mr. Pattison took on a different tone, both regarding McGee and Sykes himself:

> Baton Rouge, La
> Sept 4, 1868
>
> Mr. H.A. Pattison
> Muskegon
> Mich.
>
> My dear Sir,
> Your
>
> Letter of the 27 I have just read and in answer to your request I will give you such information in regard to Mr McGee as I possess.
>
> The Lt was turned over to the Civil Authorities some two weeks since, and was examined before a magistrate's court a week ago. I was informed that he was committed upon the charge of manslaughter. I have been to see him since his confinement, & he told me that he expected to get "bail" but I hardly think that possible, knowing all the circumstances as I do, and having taken all the

testimony in the case, as became my duty as Comd of the Post. In a matter of this kind dear Sir, it is best to be plain. I will give you my own view of it formed from all that necessarily came under my observation. Although Mr McGee's provocation was sore, yet I do not think he was in the remotest degree justified in shooting Dr. Braman. That he did shoot him, & in my clear judgment, as Dr. B turned to get away from him, I firmly believe. Upon this conviction, and the attendant circumstances, my duty required that I should prefer "charges" of the very gravest and most distressing nature. They await the action of the Civil Court, and cannot be prosecuted until the result of his trial before that Court is known. The fact that McGee was committed upon the charge of manslaughter goes, in my mind, to show a great sympathy for him among the community of B. Rouge. From what I know it is undoubtable, from what I learn it is confirmed — He has the best legal talent here — A.S. Herron formerly Attorney Gen of the State has his case, assisted I believe by other gentlemen. You are the best judge whether your presence would be advisable. The trial will not come off till Nov. In the meantime Mr McGee is very comfortable so far as his surroundings go, & the jailers give him every indulgence possible. His friends are permitted to see him at pleasure and both Ladies and gentlemen do so. I have received letters from the friends of Dr Braman and it is well to say that they seem greatly incensed. Whether they will take any steps to prosecute I do not know. The offrs of my Regt feel very sorry for Mr McGee, but Mr Pattison, they cannot in any way extenuate the deed he has committed. He had sound advice given him, but in his anger he seems to have forgotten it.

As offrs of the Regt to which he belongs, we of course take his act to heart, for it reflects not only upon himself, but upon us, and, while our sympathies cannot be withheld from his friends, the wail of grief comes from those who mourn a son cut off in his youth & usefulness by an act shocking to us all, and shocking to any community in which it takes place. With my respectful Regards Sir,

I remain yrs
Very truly
Geo Sykes[15]

There is no question General George Sykes had not a change of heart but a change in attitude. First, from this letter there was no doubt he believes Willie very guilty. Two, there is no doubt he had heard the cries of the Braman family (those records do not survive). Sykes was unwittingly placed, it seems, between sincere sympathy for the Bramans and honest concern for a young officer defending his honor, a very nineteenth century and West Point mentality, both of which resonated deeply in the psyche of the staid Sykes. As a result, Sykes dutifully communicated with all parties, but after a thorough investigation, became firmly convinced of Willie's guilt. Reading between the lines it also seems possible that he was at odds a bit with Pattison. Sykes may also have been upset with his own officers, some of whom seemed to be vigorously defending McGee, or even with the local community, who also appeared to be "adopting" Willie as a favorite son. The most telling statement in Sykes' last letter to Pattison is the mention of Willie's newly retained attorney, A.S. Herron. Andrew S. Herron was brilliant, connected, wealthy, and beloved in Baton Rouge and throughout Louisiana, and this trial would not be the first time he had fought the United States Army.[16]

Andrew Stewart Herron walked into Will McGee's life during the first days of September 1868. Herron, the "Major" to all in Baton Rouge, did not need the business of representing McGee. In truth, it is not farfetched to suggest that, from 1860 to his death in 1882 at age 60, Major A.S. Herron may have been the most popular, honest, upstanding man in all of Louisiana. "One of Louisiana's noblest sons," said the *Capitolian Advocate*. Herron, the paper reported at another time, possessed "Kindness and generosity of heart, amenity of manners, geniality of soul, and zealous devotion to his state, his party, and his friends."[17]

Though Herron, a resident of Baton Rouge since 1833, was probably a stranger to Willie McGee, the forty-five-year old attorney and the youthful second lieutenant did share some interesting similarities. Andrew Herron, like McGee, was the product of Irish immigration; the Herrons' beginning in Pennsylvania and going west to Tennessee, where Andrew was born in Nashville in 1823. As with so many wayward Irish, the Herrons ended up in Louisiana, settling near Baton Rouge about 1830.[18]

Like McGee, who told army authorities when enlisting that he was fatherless, Herron's father died in a duel of honor when the boy was ten. McGee, as Sykes found out, had an adoptive attorney father, and Herron, after his father's death, had been raised by an older relative named Burke, an eccentric but learned lawyer in Baton Rouge. Both men could charm people of all ages and all classes. Throughout his life, phrases such as "his characteristic heartiness" and "there was no more attractive and delightful man" were used about Andrew Herron,[19] while McGee had a mesmerizing personality which captured many people's hearts, when he was not shooting doctors.

The service record in the recent war also seemed to portray both in a memorable light. McGee's Medal of Honor career has been briefly discussed, one which resulted in his recent commission in the regular army. Herron's defense of the Confederacy was renowned throughout Louisiana. Taking the early lead in Baton Rouge, the Irishman enlisted in the 7th Louisiana Infantry, where he was elected (a common practice) captain of Company B, the Baton Rouge Fencibles.[20]

From 1861 through 1863, Louisiana units in the Army of Northern Virginia, among them the 7th Louisiana Infantry, were known as the "Louisiana Tigers" for their ferocity in and out of battle; they fought at Bull Run, Cold

Harbor, Cedar Mountain, Second Manassas, and Antietam, among others. The 7th Louisiana was typical of all the legendary Tiger regiments — tough, willing and unpredictable. As author Terry Jones has said in his standard work, *Lee's Tigers: The Louisiana Infantry in the Army of Northern Virginia,* "The Tigers were the Dr. Jekyll and Mr. Hyde of the Confederacy. They were drunken, lawless, renegades ... yet when it came to fighting, the Tigers were rated among [Robert E.] Lee's most dependable soldiers."[21]

Even their own Confederate comrades feared Louisiana men. Comprised mostly of Cajun, Irish, and tough renegade stock, they were a strange, volatile mix: "The same men who pillaged towns and delighted in drinking and fighting also knelt in knee-deep snow at Fredericksburg to celebrate Easter, held frequent revivals and prayer meetings, and astonished everyone on the dreary Petersburg line by building an elaborate chapel for religious services."[22]

Andrew Herron ably led these "ferocious rascals," who suffered massive casualties, and was in turn, loved by them, but there all similarities with Willie McGee ended.[23] Captain (later Major) Andrew Herron led his Baton Rouge Fencibles through almost every battle in Virginia for two years, being wounded twice, the second time at Chancellorsville severely, after which he was assigned by Robert E. Lee himself to Mobile, Alabama, and promoted to colonel for judicial duty. At the conclusion of the war, Herron returned home to Baton Rouge a revered man. His illustrious career as a wartime leader led to an even greater and more famous one in peacetime. Herron entered the political arena and was elected to numerous posts, including that of Louisiana attorney general, and Congress. His law firm was considered the best in the city of Baton Rouge.[24]

Perhaps the best way to judge the respect citizens of East Baton Rouge Parish had for Andrew Herron would be that, when the only Confederate monument ever erected was built in Louisiana in 1886, "raising no sectional feelings, sinking all political differences," the people chose to place on the top the statue of one man — Andrew S. Herron, "the beau ideal of a patriotic citizen."[25]

Willie McGee must have been surprised when Major Herron and his esteemed partner, Colonel E.W. Robertson, walked into his jail cell, but no more so than the United States Army and the populace of Baton Rouge. By September 20, Herron petitioned the court for a bail hearing, and reminded the court that bail was allowed for manslaughter charges. He also informed the court that McGee's "pecuniary means are small and he will be unable to furnish bond in a very large amount." Herron then provided a statement McGee had given to the sheriff when arrested, perhaps as a preliminary defense.[26]

Though no known photograph of the Louisiana soldier and attorney Andrew Herron exists, this edifice, the only Confederate statue erected in Louisiana, placed the Irish-American Herron on the top "as the beau ideal of a patriotic citizen." The statue, located at Third Street and North Boulevard, was photographed in the early 1950s (Louisiana Collection, State Library of Louisiana, Baton Rouge).

The Fifth District Court judge heard the appeal, and agreed on September 26 to the bail request, setting bail at $2,000 cash bond, roughly equiva-
lent today to about $220,000. McGee, who had been in the regular army for
about sixteen months, hardly could be expected to have such money on hand,
even though an officer. To the surprise of many, Will McGee walked out of
the East Baton Rouge Parish jail the same day as the bail hearing.[27] Temporarily a free man, the only stipulation Willie McGee had to heed was that he
appear at 9:00 A.M. on November 2, 1868, on a charge of manslaughter in
the shooting of Dr. Chandler Braman. Reading Willie's preliminary statement
it was no surprise what defense tactic Andrew Herron would be taking in
November:

> On Saturday, the 15th of August, 1868 late in the evening Gen Sykes command-
> ing post at Baton Rouge who had sent for me showed to me a note which I was
> told was in the handwriting of Dr. C.B. Bramin in which note I was accused of
> a crime of forgery and stating also that Dr. Bramin had set a detective to cook
> up a stolen watch, and he has had reason to believe I had stolen it, also under-
> standing that those accusations were known in the town of Baton Rouge and
> were or soon would be a matter of public town talk. I of course became indig-
> nant and exasperated, and immediately started to inflict chastisement upon him,
> who had falsely attacked my good name and reputation, on my way to him I
> armed myself for self defense and sent word to Dr. Bramin that I wanted to see
> him. He not coming and sending me word that he would see me in his room I
> went to his room. I showed him the note accusing me of forgery [and] asked
> him if he written it. He replied he had. I then struck him with a small cowhide
> I had procured for that purpose. He then rose and moved as I thought he went
> for his weapons. I knew that he kept loaded pistols in his room. I then drew the
> revolver I had with me for purposes of self defense. It went off while I was in
> the act of cocking and holding it with both hands. It was not intentionally dis-
> charged at him. I had no idea or intention of shooting him and had drawn my
> weapon to defend myself from his weapons that I thought from his movement
> he was about to use against me.
>   Wm McGee[28]

The stage was set for November in Baton Rouge. Second Lieutenant
William McGee, Medal of Honor recipient, hero of Murfreesboro, and
Andrew Herron, most popular man in Baton Rouge, a veteran of Antietam,
lined up against the State of Louisiana and the memory of Doctor Chandler
Braman, who had been shot in the back and was dead.

CHAPTER FOUR

The Legend
of Willie McGee

The first casualty of war is the truth.
—Hiram Johnson,
California Senator, 1917

After less than two months at home in New Jersey in late 1865, Willie McGee hurried to Muskegon, Michigan, and Holmes Pattison. A later published work in New Jersey stated that McGee returned to Newark "upon the close of the war [July] and resumed his old vocation, that of an eating-house waiter"; but he was not there long, for in several letters, Pattison said that his drummer boy had been in Michigan with him since October 1865.[1] The young Irishman was awarded the Medal of Honor six months after mustering out on February 9, 1866, and both the medal and the official written notification were sent to Willie at his new hometown and his adoptive father.[2]

Flush with pride of his medal, new hometown and family, and emerging status into adulthood, Will McGee spent seven months in Michigan with the Pattisons before Governor Marcus Ward of New Jersey tracked him down, possibly through Margaret McGee, Willie's widowed mother, who was a domestic servant in Newark and an acquaintance of Ward. Governor Ward, known throughout the East as the "soldier's friend," was determined at war's end to portray his brave citizen soldiers of the Garden State in history's best light. Towards war's end, Ward, a great aficionado of the arts — indeed one of the founders of the New Jersey Historical Society — pushed through the

New Jersey Legislature an act authorizing the governor himself to appoint "a competent man to prepare for publication a history of the record made by New Jersey in the recent war."[3]

Coincidentally on Willie's sixteenth birthday, the governor, according to the *Newark Advertiser* in a May 13, 1865, article said, "[H]e has very satisfactorily performed his duty by selecting John Y. Foster, Esq., who possesses in an eminent degree the ability and industry required for the faithful performance of this important task." The paper added the hope that "Mr. Foster may produce something that 'the world will not willingly let die' and that the future historian may implicitly rely on as a true and faithful record not only of the services of our soldiers in the field but of everything done by our people at home for the salvation of the Union."[4]

Foster certainly took the job to heart, producing within two years an 872-page comprehensive volume titled *New Jersey In the Rebellion: A History of the Services of the Troops and People of New Jersey in Aid of*

The Medal of Honor awarded to Willie Magee in February 1866. Entirely gold-leafed, with the exception of the red, white, and blue cloth, this was the first design of the Army Medal of Honor, issued from 1862 to 1896, after which time the design changed slightly.

the Union Cause.[5] Full of detail and local color, Foster also collected with commendable diligence a large amount of miscellaneous information in regard to the part played by New Jersey during the war. In the forty-sixth, and last, chapter, Foster chose two young soldiers who epitomized the "spirit, courage, and daring" of New Jersey soldiers who fought so gallantly. John Foster picked one officer of the patrician class, Major Peter Vredenburgh of the 14th New Jersey Volunteers. The Vredenburghs were of Dutch descent, venerable lawyers from Monmouth County in Central New Jersey, whose ancestors fought in the Revolution and had been in America already for centuries.[6]

The second soldier singled out among the more than 80,000 New Jersey combatants was musician William H. McGee, soon to be famous as Willie Magee.[7] Where and when Foster heard the story of Willie McGee, drummer boy, during a siege in Tennessee is unknown, but when the book was published in February 1867 Willie McGee was an official war hero. Though Foster's hyperbole was typical of nineteenth-century authors, his four-page story of the exploits of Willie was generous even for the time. *New Jersey in the Rebellion* was the first record of the state in the war, and is still referred to by many historians. The following excerpt recounts the history of Willie Magee, a story that, until this publishing, was known only to a handful of people, a legend that has become part of New Jersey history and, along with the Medal of Honor, shaped and changed Willie's McGee's life forever:

INSTANCES OF GALLANTRY

The careful reader of these pages cannot have been struck with the numerous instances in which high gallantry and soldierly ability were exhibited by very young men. Indeed, the war and its objects seem to have appealed with peculiar force to this class, and of those who attained marked distinction and came out of the strife as Generals and officers of exalted grade, at least one-half were men below thirty years of age. This was, perhaps, but natural — the soldier's life and excitements having peculiar charms for the adventurous spirit of youth; and possibly the same fact was true of other States; at least we remember that among the earliest martyrs of the conflict were young men like Ellsworth and Winthrop, and others no less noble, representing alike the East and the West; but certainly in no State was the proportion of young men who entered the service greater than in our own, many of our regiments being almost exclusively composed of volunteers who had barely attained their majority. Mindil, Bayard, Hall, Sewell, Price, Zabriskie, Janeway, Tay, Ramsey, Yorke — these, with scores of others whose deeds were equally illustrious — were all young men, some of them scarcely come to man's estate, and all rose by sheer and resistless merit. So among the rank and file, many of them deserving soldiers, many whose heroism embellished the grandest fields, and whose lofty, patient self-sacrifice gave an almost royal splendor to the saddest scenes of suffering and peril, were, as the world counts the years of life, mere boys — beardless striplings — whose lives, up to the day they went afield, had coursed only in the calmest currents. Hundreds of such — nay thousands, bravely defending the flag under whose stars their grandfathers nobly fought, fell in the carnival of battle; hundreds still, maimed and scarred, meet us on our daily paths, living epitomes of that sublime instinct of nationality which lifted the nation from the misty lowlands of barbarous self-seeking, to the broad relationship with all the highest aspirations of humanity — the serene heights of justice — where it stands today. The records of these epistles are written in blood, which we may well send down to coming generations as embodying the very loftiest and purest teachings of the crucial period of our life as a nation.

Obviously, it is altogether impossible to record, in these pages, all the instances of dauntless heroism, of wonderful achievement, and of almost precocious skill which, in sifting the narratives of our various regiments, have come to the author's knowledge. We can only select one or two types of the whole body of similar cases, and as such give them in evidence that New Jersey still has sons who are worthy to rank with the noblest and best of her younger Revolutionary patriots.

Among the many instances of youthful intrepidity and daring, none, perhaps, exceeded in all the points of real sublimity those which are furnished in the career of drummer William Magee, of the Thirty-Third Regiment. This lad, for he was only a lad, entered the service at fifteen years of age — leaving a widowed mother in the city of Newark — to aid in maintaining the unity of the Nation. From the first he displayed qualities of the highest order. Intelligent, fearless, vigilant, he was at all times an example alike to superiors and inferiors. Though entering the service as a drummer, he by no means confined himself to the duties of his specific sphere. He had a knack of fighting as well as drumming, and withal exhibited an appreciation of the methods of warfare, which qualified him for the most surprising exploits. One of these, at least, was equal in splendor of execution and grandeur of result to any which the history of the war records. It will be remembered that in the Fall of 1864, after Sherman had swung loose from his base and started on his stately "March to the Sea," Hood with an army of forty thousand men laid siege to Nashville, defended by General Thomas. Here, for a period of two or three weeks, our troops were penned up with little prospect of relief.

At Murfreesboro, thirty miles away, General Thomas, reluctant to relax his hold on the railroad to Chattanooga, had stationed a small garrison under General Milroy. This garrison, as the rebels gathered in greater force, beleaguering the post, soon became comparatively isolated, all avenues of escape being practically closed. But the men did not lose heart. At length, on the 2nd of December, it was determined to strike a blow for deliverance. At this time, young Magee had become acting orderly to General Van Cleve, and to him, youth as he was, the order was given to charge the enemy. It may be that a smile accompanied the order — a smile at the mere thought of committing such a work to a mere stripling; but it is certain that the confidence of the commander was not misplaced. Taking the One Hundred and Eighty-First Ohio Infantry, Magee sallied out of the works, and rushed upon a battery posted on an eminence hard by. The charge was made most gallantly, but the fire of the enemy was resistless, and slowly the column fell back. But the intrepid orderly did not for a moment falter in his purpose. One repulse only stimulated his appetite for his work, and accordingly, selecting the One Hundred and Seventy-fourth Ohio, he again moved out, again charged the foe, again met their withering fire, still, however, pressing on until at last the victory was his. And it was no ordinary victory. Two heavy guns and eight hundred of the enemy killed, wounded, and captured, were the trophies that he brought out of the contest. Nor was this all. This signal success at once dispiriting the enemy and reviving the hopes of our own men, proved the first of a series of victories which resulted, finally, in driving Hood from Tennessee and restoring that whole section to Federal control. The readiness and gallantry displayed by young Magee in this affair very naturally attracted the attention of those around him, and he received the hearty commendation of Generals Rousseau, Milroy, and other officers in the command. Subsequently he received a medal of honor from the War Department, inscribed, "The Congress to drummer William Magee, Company C, Thirty-Third Regiment, New Jersey Volunteers."

Upon the close of the war, the young hero was appointed by the President Second Lieutenant in the Twentieth Regiment of Infantry, being strongly recommended by Governors Ward and Geary. The latter, in his letter to the War Department, spoke of him from personal knowledge: "He served in my command, and from personal observation I can speak unreservedly in his behalf." Upon appearing before the Examining Board for examination, Magee found that he was deficient in several studies — having never enjoyed educational advantages — and much to his disappointment he returned home, expecting to be obliged to abandon his cherished design of entering the regular service. Governor Ward, however, learning the facts of the case, succeeded in securing an extension of the time for the final examination, and then, with characteristic generosity, at once placed Magee in the care of capable instructors, by whom he was soon fitted for a second appearance before the Board — his progress, owing to his intense application to study, being most rapid in all the branches in which it was necessary he should acquire proficiency. To-day, the drummer boy of the Thirty-third, the hero of Murfreesboro, now only nineteen years of age, wears the uniform of the regular service, and should our flag ever again be assailed, we may be sure that among its brave defenders he will not be the last to write his name high on the scroll of fame.[8]

Ten years later, in 1878, Joseph Atkinson wrote *The History of Newark, New Jersey: Being a Narrative of Its Rise and Progress,* and repeated the legend created by Foster for a new decade of New Jersey readers. Once again, the author chooses two "conspicuous hero-figures furnished to the military service and history of the nation by this locality, one representing the higher and the other the humbler walks of life." The first outstanding leader Atkinson picked is the still famous Philip Kearny, born in New York in 1815. The millionaire Irish American's family originally settled in Shrewsbury, Monmouth County, before spreading throughout the state, and the Kearnys can safely be said to rank with the Kean clan as competitors for rank as the First Family of New Jersey. General Phil Kearny was just one of many truly exceptional Kearnys to grace the state's history, and author Atkinson is not alone among Civil War historians who believe Kearny's early death at Chantilly in 1862 was the only roadblock to his being named commander in chief of all Federal forces. But the "One-armed Devil" from Newark, where he made his home, is a story of another time. As Atkinson said, "From the hero given to us by wealth, education, culture and refinement, we turn to another hero, furnished by poverty and illiteracy. We turn from 'Fighting Phil' Kearny to little Willie Magee, the drummer boy of the Thirty-third New Jersey Regiment."[9]

Much of Atkinson's history is a rehash of Foster's, and though some new "facts" are included and others are embellished, it is nonetheless remarkable that in two significant histories, one of the state and the other of its largest city, William Magee's story is told in both. Atkinson begins:

Governor Marcus Ward of Newark, circa 1865. Historians have long neglected Ward, one of the finest one-term governors in New Jersey history. He created with his own money the first veteran's hospital in the state, helped found the New Jersey Historical Society, was the chairman of the Republican National Committee, and served a term as a congressman. He was the savior and enabler of Willie McGee, until his death in 1884 (from the collections of the New Jersey Historical Society, Newark, New Jersey).

William Magee was probably born in Newark. His parents were of Irish birth, and of the humblest class. When the war broke out William was about eleven years of age. When, in the summer of 1863, the Thirty-third New Jersey was organized, he joined the regiment as one of the drum corps. He was then not quite fourteen years of age — a bright, sharp-eyed, intelligent, full-grown and very handsome lad. After leaving Newark, it was not long before Magee gave evidence that he could handle the rifle skillfully as well as the drum-sticks. He was the hero of many surprising exploits. "One of these, at least," as another writer [Foster] remarks, "was equal in splendor of execution and grandeur of result, to any which the history of war records."[10]

Atkinson proceeds to retell the Foster version almost word for word with just a few sprinkles of change. In describing the condition before the battle, he writes: "Gradually the Confederates encircled the garrison, until every avenue of escape was practically closed." Atkinson does add, "owing to illness, Magee had been left behind in the hospital by the Thirty-third."[11]

When retelling the final portions of the battle, Atkinson added to the Foster version: "But this time fortunately the brave youth had with him hearts as gallant as his own. On through the surging smoke dashed the little band — on! On! On! Until success, a most glorious success, crowned with the valor of Magee and his brave spirits. The battery, with its entire force, was captured! The victory was a brilliant one in itself and the virtual salvation of Milroy's garrison." Atkinson finishes the military version of the Magee legend thusly: "The army and the nation rang with the praises of Newark's boy-hero and his magnificent exploit!"[12]

With the publication of *New Jersey in the Rebellion* in early 1867, William McGee was famous in Michigan as a Medal of Honor recipient, and in New Jersey as a published war hero. Governor Marcus Ward, one of the great New Jersey philanthropists of the nineteenth century, was thrilled to have a fellow native of Newark portrayed so eloquently, and in May of 1867 he decided to reward Willie, for the great honor the drummer boy had bestowed upon the Garden State, with even more accolades. As it turned out, the meteoric ascent of the Irish waif from the slums of Newark to war hero was still on the rise, but even a setback, which only the president of the United States could overcome, was not enough to stop the quixotic Willie McGee. Andrew Johnson, like so many others, would fall under the spell of the drummer boy from Newark.

CHAPTER FIVE

The Trial

The best stories are the ones
we are most thoroughly ashamed of.
— William Faulkner

In November 1868, Baton Rouge was struggling. The war had been over for three years, yet the United States Army was still stationed in the river city as an occupied force of government, and would stay another nine years, longer than any other state in the country. Officially, there was a civil government, but it was puppet reconstruction. The native populace, more precisely the white populace, was not buying in to the scalawags and Northern carpetbaggers who flooded the state following the war. The future of Louisiana would be a peaceful, sometimes not so peaceful, battle where some residents championed conciliation and cooperation, while others strongly resisted any show of reconciliation and sought vengeance for Southern deaths and honor. They instead advocated white supremacy and the need for social control within a changed racial order.[1]

The soldiers of the 20th U.S. Infantry, now career men in the regular army, were caught between two forces, the government backed Republican reconstruction party of President Andrew Johnson, and the Democratic Party of the Louisiana people, in particular, the Louisiana white people, Americans all. The 20th U.S. Infantry was individually accepted, but the army as a unit was seen as an occupying force. The *Baton Rouge Tri-Weekly Advocate* in the summer of '68 said, "Doubtless, with few exceptions, the soldiers stationed in the South are opposed, heart and soul, to the entire programme of persecution and outrage. They did not wage war upon us to obtain a prize for a wandering handful of adventurers to fatten and grow rich upon."[2]

A similar situation was found in 1972 in Northern Ireland, where the British Army was called in to be a buffer between the local native population of Catholics and the official British-backed government, all Irish. Just as that Irish problem was not supposed to be about religion but was; Louisiana of 1868 was not supposed to be about race, but was nothing else. The new Louisiana constitution of mid–1868 allowed "Negroes" to vote, but prevented many whites, all ex-Confederates, from voting.[3] In real terms, this new constitution did little beyond look good on paper. When blacks tested antidiscrimination in courts and won, the law was seldom enforced. The color line was rarely challenged and even when it was, most blacks could not afford to pay the costs of bringing offending people and institutions to court. In addition to the ever-present racial "situation," taxes were crushing, yet the state remained atrociously maintained. As Willie McGee was about to be tried for manslaughter that fall of 1868, Louisiana did not have a single hard surfaced road, and New Orleans, the largest city, contained only two hospitals.[4]

As the November trial approached, much was going on in Baton Rouge other than the shooting of one Northern soldier by another. The July 20, 1868, *Tri-Weekly Advocate* contained a front page story which said in part, "We are not on the eve, but in the midst of a contest upon the result of which everything possessed by the white race in the South depends.... We must exert ourselves to rouse the people as they were never roused before."[5]

On August 19, two weeks after Dr. Chandler Braman's death, the *Advocate* ran another front page article, which challenged the populace: "The Radicals are aiming at inaugurating a new government under the rule of a military Dictator (President Grant).... Grant proposes to perpetuate military authority throughout the land.... The bayonet that was found all powerful to maintain the Union has proved powerless to protect the organic law."[6]

Sixty days before the shooting, the *Advocate* again attacked what it considered to be an uncivil government with its three times a week verbal challenge:

All ye Northerners, who were awaiting Grant's election to come down South and purchase farms, plantations, etc., now is your time! It was "Grant in Peace," "Grant and Capital," before the election. Come on with peace and capital, the more white men, the more Democrats, whether they come here Radicals or not, a few months of negro rule soon changes them! Come on then with your men and money. There is plenty of land for sale, plenty of cheap laborers to hire, plenty of bargains to obtain. Come on and invest with us, live with us, and struggle with us to re-establish a free government once more in Louisiana.... No more thieves, no more carpetbaggers, no more professional office hunters, but solid, working men, with money, COME ON![7]

In such a polarized political and racial atmosphere, where 6,500 white people and 11,300 black people uneasily existed separately together, it comes as no surprise that the trial of Willie McGee caused no sensation whatsoever. But fate goes as fate must, and on the first Wednesday of November, Judge R.T. Posey began the work of jury selection and opening arguments in the manslaughter trial of 2nd Lieutenant William McGee of the United States 20th Infantry.

Reuben Thornton Posey was no stranger to Southern justice. Born in Kentucky in 1830, R.T. Posey turned early to the law, working first in his native Kentucky before settling in Sabine County, Texas, just over the Louisiana border, where he was an attorney and judge. He moved to Baton Rouge after the war, and was now at age thirty-eight, the head of the Fifth District Court.[8] The jury, which was seated the first day, was, despite the new Louisiana constitution, all white, a surprise to absolutely no one.

The prosecution was either overconfident, inept, or, more likely, just did not wish to convict McGee, a Northerner who shot another Yankee. Nonetheless it was an easy case. The lieutenant had, after all, shot the doctor in front of an eyewitness; had told another man, "I'm going to shoot the doctor"; was observed by a general and several other officers planning the deed; and had admitted shooting the man.[9]

Five witnesses were scheduled for the prosecution, but only four were called. The first man on the witness stand was 1st Lieutenant Thomas Latchford. Latchford's testimony is damning to Willie McGee. "While standing in front of my quarters in the garrison, I heard the report of a firearm, and immediately afterward a shout which went in the direction the report came from. I met the accused, William McGee, descending the stairs with a pistol in his right hand." Lieut. Latchford added, "I passed the accused and went to the room occupied by Dr. Braman. I found smoke in the room, and blood on the door sill, on the opposite door from where I entered." Latchford continued, saying he then went to the hospital tent, found the deceased doctor, "lying on a cot, blood flowing from his mouth, and unable to speak."[10]

Under cross-examination by Andrew Herron, Lieut. Tom Latchford said he went back to Dr. Braman's room ten to fifteen minutes after finding him dead in the hospital tent, where he found two pistols, one a six-barrel loaded, and one a five-barrel pistol with one barrel loaded. Latchford added, "Both pistols were in a drawer of a table which was closed."[11]

Second up for the State of Louisiana was Private George Mayhew. Private Mayhew testifies that he was at the barracks hospital and saw Doctor Braman going down the stairs immediately after hearing a shot fired. Mayhew said the doctor then "went into the hospital tent, where he looked back behind him, as if he were expecting someone to follow him." Braman, he added, then fell unto a cot face down and died without speaking a word.[12]

When cross-examined, Mayhew said he was a patient at the time of the shooting, doing convalescent work at the hospital. He admitted McGee was not a friend, and added, "Dr. Braman anticipated trouble with McGee," while also stating the doctor felt McGee was innocent of taking Lieut. Clark's watch. Mayhew, under questioning by Herron, said that Dr. Braman asked him (Mayhew) for help should trouble with McGee materialize. The private also said "it was assumed among the enlisted men that Lieut. McGee was guilty of taking Lieut. Clark's watch."[13]

The third witness for the prosecution was a local man, Baton Rouge physician Louis Favrot Reynaud, who performed the autopsy on Chandler Braman. Reynaud was typical of the great diversity of the native population of Louisiana. Born in Baton Rouge in 1842, Dr. Reynaud studied medicine in New York City and New Orleans, and was the same age, twenty-six, as his assistant, Chandler Braman. Reynaud's ancestors were truly Louisianan. His grandfather, William Reynaud, was born in France before coming to New Orleans and then Baton Rouge as a merchant. Dr. Louis Reynaud's father, also William, was a famed doctor in Baton Rouge and his maternal grandfather, Judge Louis Favrot, was born in Louisiana and was known throughout the South. Dr. Louis Favrot Reynaud served in the war with the 4th Louisiana Delta Rifle Brigade, and, after the war, had a magnificent forty-year career as a physician, lecturer, and teacher at Tulane and L.S.U.[14] But at the time of the trial, Louis Reynaud was under contract as the surgeon in charge of caring for soldiers at the Baton Rouge barracks. His assistant was the late Dr. Chandler Braman.[15]

After being sworn, Dr. Reynaud testified "the ball entered the back of Dr. Braman, near the spine, and passed through the lungs." Reynaud added that the death ensued from internal hemorrhage to the chest, with the ball piercing near the sixth rib and ranging upwards to the third and fourth ribs.[16] There was no cross-examination of Doctor Reynaud, who of course was a member of several social clubs with both defense attorneys Herron and Edward Robertson.[17]

The fourth and last witness for the State vs. William H. McGee was the servant Chelsea Walker. It was noted in the trial transcript that Walker was "colored." Though it was not mentioned that the other witnesses are white, this was still standard operating procedure in 1868 Louisiana. Walker told the court "I found Lt. McGee in the kitchen and he told me to go to Dr. Braman and tell him that he [McGee] wished to see him in the mess room." Walker said he did as ordered and as Dr. Braman got up and started towards the mess room he stopped on the stairs and "told me to present his compliments to Lt. McGee and that he [Braman] would be pleased to see him in his room."[18]

Walker said he went back, told McGee what the doctor had said, and the lieutenant started toward the doctor's room as he (Walker) followed behind. Chelsea then saw McGee enter the room while he stood outside in front of Dr. Braman's window "so I could see in." Walker said Willie "commenced switching Dr. Braman with something." Dr. Braman, said the servant, "threw up both hands, exclaiming 'Look out! McGee, look out!'" Walker continued, saying Dr. Braman started to get up from where he was sitting and did get up when Lieut. McGee shot him, "just as he was getting up." The doctor, Walker added, ran out the back door hollering. Lieutenant McGee came out the front door and, as he passed Walker, he was yelling at Braman, "I'll make you howl if you say that about me." Chelsea Walker concluded his testimony for the prosecution by adding that Willie went down the stairs with his pistol in his hand.[19]

The only true eyewitness was then cross-examined by Andrew Herron. The only change or verbal confusion Herron was able to elicit was when Willie was switching Dr. Braman they were standing by the side of each other, "That is, Lt. McGee was standing on the side of Dr. Braman who as I said before was sitting down."[20] The fifth prosecution witness was supposed to be Captain Louis Morris, but for whatever reason, he was not called, and the prosecution rested its case.

The following week court resumed. The trial, which began on November 4 and reached a verdict on November 25, was conducted each Wednesday of the month. Andrew Herron introduced two statements before he called any witnesses. The first, Exhibit A, was the voluntary statement Willie gave the sheriff two days after the shooting. In the written admission, while admitting to most of the State's prosecution, Willie claimed he followed only "in self defense when he felt Doctor Braman was going to shoot him." He also added that the shooting was "accidental and he had no intention of shooting the doctor."[21]

The second exhibit entered by Herron was the infamous penciled note that caused so much pain and heartache. The one-sentence scribbled and soiled message was labeled Exhibit B, and entered into evidence.[22] Despite the anger and death that it produced, it is still hard to fathom how such a nebulous note led to such mayhem. Because of this single sentence, Braman was killed, and his young bride became a widow. Braman's mentor, Dr. Louis Favrot Reynaud, would go on to have forty years of an eminent life, and raise a family of ten children, with ancestors still in Louisiana to this day, but his assistant, Chandler Braman, would be buried in a cemetery unvisited by even his own family, more than 1,000 miles from home. If convicted, Will McGee, one of the youngest American heroes to be awarded a Medal of Honor, would be branded for life, a promising career lost to a single pistol shot. It would be up to Andrew Herron to pull off a miracle.

Herron and his law partner, Edward White Robertson, centered their defense not on whether Willie McGee shot Chandler Braman, but on why he shot the doctor. Herron and Robertson, along with the judge, coroner, sheriff, and likely the entire jury, were either veterans or civilian victims of the war. The issue for the South — for generations to come — centered on pride. Conquered people the world over have always grasped at words like pride and honor in order to survive defeat, but for ex-Confederates it was even more difficult as it was a civil war. Honor and pride are difficult words for history books, but not for those living the history. Andrew Herron knew his people, but could even he help save Willie McGee?

Herron would begin his defense by throwing out the "note" as Willie McGee's badge of honor. Herron's first witness was the commanding officer himself, General George Sykes. Herron would use the army against itself. General Sykes, sworn for the defense, was no doubt a formidable witness, and not unhappy to testify. The general may have been surprised at not being called as a prosecution witness, but, as is obvious in his third letter to Holmes Pattison, Sykes was convinced of Willie's guilt and believed the manslaughter charge was generous.[23] Sykes repeated the version of August 14 and 15 so eloquently expressed to Pattison in his August letters. He said, of course, that "Lieutenant McGee was accused of theft and forgery," and that in front of the mayor, the man McHenry swore, "Dr. Braman wrote the forged note."[24] Herron never gave the general a chance to expound on his army investigation, instead making him stick to the conferences with Mayor Elam, McHenry, Braman, Clark, and McGee.

General Sykes gave a lengthy testimony, telling judge and jury he had interviewed both Lt. Clark and Dr. Braman. Clark, said Sykes, replied, "My God, general. Lt. McGee never committed a forgery on me, and I never said so." According to the general, Dr. Braman, when asked by Sykes if he indeed wrote the note and gave it to McHenry, said "Yes," to both questions. Sykes continued to testify that he also met with Willie McGee and gave McGee the infamous note, and that Willie was agitated. "I will wear a cow-hide out on him," the general said McGee told him. George Sykes responded to McGee's oath by saying it "was a personal matter," and as the commanding officer, he "could not give any advice on the subject." The remainder of the general's testimony was in direct agreement with the prosecution witnesses.[25]

The East Baton Rouge Courthouse, as seen in 1901. Built in 1857, it was only eleven years old when Willie McGee was tried for the murder of Chandler Braman. The courthouse was razed in 1921. (Louisiana Collection, State Library of Louisiana, Baton Rouge).

Andrew Herron, however, had accomplished just what he wished. A distinguished, respectable and well spoken general (who believed the defendant guilty) spent most of his time in the witness box discussing the "injustice" to McGee; and "accusations" against McGee," as well as the "personal matter," to which he could "not give any advice."[26]

General George Sykes was not cross-examined by the prosecution, and was therefore not provided any opportunity to explain what happened in his other two meetings with Willie on Saturday, August 15. Sykes does not have the chance to explain Braman's attempts at reconciliation. In short, Sykes is given no window to tell the jury why he knows Willie McGee is guilty of killing his assistant surgeon. In retrospect, General Sykes may have felt he could do all this and more once he took the stand, but instead he fell victim to the snares of a wily Louisiana Tiger. The general would not be the last.

The second witness for the defense would involve another attempt by Herron to play the honor theory. Mayor J.E. Elam was sworn in, and, though he played a minor part in the affair, testified longer than any prosecution witness, including the only true eyewitness, Chelsea Walker. Mayor Elam recounted in great detail the origins of the note, how McHenry appeared at his office, and how the mysterious McHenry blamed Dr. Braman for the entire affair. As his testimony closes, Elam uses — what else — the words "honor" and "matter of justice." Though Herron kept the mayor on the stand a long time, Elam used the word "McGee" only once — in the phrase, "McHenry told me Dr. Braman could not furnish proof against McGee when called upon."[27]

Again, the witness was not cross-examined, and had he been pressed the mayor would have had to admit he really had no idea what Lt. McGee or Dr. Braman said or did to each other on August 14 or 15. Mayor Elam had never seen or talked to either one at any time. But the jury had just heard from the two most influential people in Baton Rouge; the commanding officer of the U.S. Army and the mayor of their own city — and both had testified that Willie McGee's honor was greatly besmirched by a forger, and thus less than an honorable man.[28]

The third witness for the defense was Lieutenant Septimus Carncross. Carncross was General Sykes' adjutant, and had been a professional soldier since 1849. Born in England in 1829, Carncross became a career soldier as soon as he reached legal age. In 1868, at the time of the McGee trail, Septimus was almost forty and perhaps the most respected soldier in Baton Rouge. Carncross had begun military life as a private in Saint Louis and had risen through the ranks from lieutenant to captain to major. Septimus Carncross had served in the artillery, the infantry, and as an aide-de-camp for some of the most prestigious leaders of the Civil War.[29] He was a soldier's soldier, and it seemed his testimony was sure to be somber, direct, and truthful. He, like Sykes, may have wondered why he was a defense witness and not speaking for the prosecution, but would, as he had done for twenty years, perform his duty admirably.

The defense attorney led Carncross through the story Herron wished to tell, just as he did with Elam and Sykes. The lieutenant admitted to the "excitability" of Dr. Braman when he met him just prior to the shooting. He told the jury how the Doctor was planning on resigning from the service for his poor behavior. Herron elicited from Carncross the statement by Dr. Braman, "I was very wrong." Later, when Lt. Carncross found McGee and said to him, "McGee, you have killed the doctor," a statement seeming to damn McGee, Willie responded, "Oh my God, Carncross, you do not know how that man has tried to ruin my character." The jury and audience, who had been beaten at war and also in peace by the federal government and were still fearful for their way of life, understood well the phrase "tried to ruin my character." [30]

Carncross told the jury that after the shooting he arrested McGee on the orders of the general; and then he said, "McGee appeared terribly excited." Herron then asked Carncross if he had seen Willie at any time earlier in the day — presumably before his "honor" was attacked — and Septimus replied, "Yes, he was in the best of health and spirits."[31] Lt. Carncross, like Sykes, stumbled headlong into the Herron web, and, like his commanding officer, was never cross-examined and thus could not tell the jury that not only were the doctor's pistols in a closed drawer, they were in a locked drawer at the opposite end of the room, which Carncross had discovered in the military investigation.[32]

Andrew Herron, however, was not finished, and he continued his assault against the prosecution with another officer from the 20th Infantry, Captain William Fletcher. The choice of Fletcher was somewhat surprising, as the Sykes investigation showed him in a minor role, but he would not be a surprise to Herron or McGee.

According to the army in-house investigation, Fletcher and Lt. Louis Morris met Willie on the barracks gallery as they rested about six P.M. on the fateful Saturday. Both men tried to dissuade Willie from any violence, urging him to seek civil redress. They even convinced Willie to see the general again and retrieve the note, which McGee did, and returned to show his fellow officers, who were still resting on the porch.[33]

On the stand, we meet a different Captain Fletcher, or a witness close to perjury. The captain's initial statements followed the Herron plan of upset hubris. "McGee was in a great state of excitement near sunset on the fifteenth of August," said Fletcher, as he recounted the meetings on the gallery porch.[34] But then Fletcher went in an unexpected route, at least to the prosecution, and many officers of the U.S. 20th Infantry.

Fletcher told the jurors that on Saturday morning he visited the room of Dr. Chandler Braman, and Braman told Fletcher he (Braman) had found out who had stolen Lt. Clark's money, and that he had employed a detective on his own responsibility to work the case up, and Lt. McGee and "someone else [not naming the person] [were] was concerned in it." Dr. Braman allegedly added that Lt. Clark "found a great deal of fault with him." Braman, according to Fletcher's new testimony, said the doctor admitted he had done everything out of friendship for Lt. Clark. Braman also told Fletcher, "Lt. McGee had forged an order on Lt. Clark, for ten dollars." After hearing all this from Braman, Fletcher left in disgust, saying, "I became indignant at such an accusation against Lt. McGee, whom I have known a long time."[35]

Fletcher had more. He claimed he immediately sought out Lt. Clark, telling him what Braman had allegedly told him. Clark, according to Fletcher, replied, "My God, no! The doctor had no business to say anything of the kind!" Fletcher claimed Clark added, "I would not have made such an accusation for fifty times that amount lost." Topping off his testimony, Captain Fletcher said that upon visiting his friend McGee in jail eight days after the shooting, he noticed a wound to McGee's hand. Willie told him, "I must have had hold of the cylinder of the pistol when it went off."[36]

The prosecution may have been intimidated by the presence of General Sykes and Mayor Elam, and perhaps by the extremely officious Lieutenant Carncross, but not to challenge William Fletcher was criminal. His story of visiting Braman was patently bogus. For starters, Braman had been with General Sykes twice and also met with McGee. Though neither meeting was long, the doctor had admitted writing the note to both men, and was in a somber, dejected tone the rest of the day. He had written letters — after those meetings — both to Sykes and McGee.[37] Additionally, he was working in the hospital with Mayhew. Doctor Braman spent all of Saturday remorseful and scared of his own shadow.[38]

Why would Braman, in that frame of mind, knowing Fletcher was McGee's friend, brag about the entire affair? There is no record that Fletcher visited Clark on Saturday. Clark had already been summoned the night before by General Sykes and thus knew the situation. Why would Clark respond so emotionally, and, most interestingly, using the exact same words to Fletcher he had when responding to General Sykes the previous night?

Fletcher ended his testimony with the "wound" he noticed on Willie's hand eight days after the shooting, a wound never mentioned by any sheriff, soldier, doctor, or even McGee himself. It was not mentioned in three separate letters by Sykes, who visited Willie twice, to Holmes Pattison, or by Herron at the bail hearing. Why even bring up such a strange statement? It goes to the self-defense nature of Willie's statement. No veteran soldier like Willie would have "grabbed the cylinder" unless it was spontaneous and accidental. Incredibly, Fletcher walked off the witness stand with nothing but the thanks of Andrew Herron and Judge R.T. Posey, shocking many officers in the audience, and, perhaps, himself.

While the prosecution may have wasted three months preparing the case, Andrew Herron certainly did not. The "best lawyer in the state," according to General Sykes, next called to the stand a local druggist named Jardot.[39] Mr. Jardot told the jury Dr. Chandler Braman was at his store the morning of his death — Braman surely had a busy morning!— looking to buy "pistol cartridges." Jardot told the doctor he had none in his store and gave him directions to the establishment of a Mr. Lefebvre.[40] Lefebvre then took the stand and said Dr. Braman "positively" was in his store the day of the shooting and bought fifty cents worth of No. 36 Remington cartridges.[41] Needless to say, the cries of the dead were not in the ears of the prosecution, and no questions were asked — again.

The last witness for the defense was Doctor Thomas Buffington, a Baton Rouge physician. Buffington said he examined Willie McGee's hand eight days after the shooting and found marks of powder sticking in the skin, and marks of inflammation.[42] As Dr. Buffington left the stand, there were no questions from the people responsible for speaking for Chandler B. Braman.

The defense rested, as Andrew Herron chose not to let Lieutenant William H. McGee testify about the grave injustice done to his honor and pride. There is, however, no transcript of the closing arguments, for either the prosecution or the defense. But before the Honorable R.T. Posey charged the jury, we have been given a virtual replay of what Major Herron must have pleaded before the jury. As will be seen during the court-martial that followed the criminal case, Andrew Herron was allowed to represent Willie McGee. At the conclusion of the court-martial, Herron provided a twenty page written argument in defense of Willie. Though of course aimed at the military justices conducting the military trial, the arguments Herron used cannot have been much different than what he first used to the Baton Rouge citizens jury. If anything, the civil closing may have been more "down home," perhaps even with a tinge of humor.

Herron spent most of the civil trial playing the honor card, following up with what must have been perjured testimony by Captain Fletcher. In the following, aimed at a jury he knew well, Andrew Herron played the ultimate cards, heroism and race, both words the jury — all Baton Rouge white men — understood well. What follows, in Major Andrew Herron's words are some of what he was likely to have explained to the jury in late November 1868:

> This charge embraces a most grave accusation, and if fully sustained, show the accused to be guilty of one of the most heinous crimes known to the laws, deliberate, willful murder.... You would take the life of the moral, social, penitent man, although the mere physical animal man might still live, an object of scorn and contempt to his fellow beings. This I am satisfied you will not do, unless you are satisfied beyond all doubt that he is guilty.[43]
>
>   That Dr. Braman came to his death by a shot from a pistol in the hands of the accused is not denied, but it is denied that the circumstances, which led to this unfortunate result — are of a nature to fix criminality — on the accused.... The facts are developed by the evidence are substantially as follows. On the 15th of August, 1868, in the evening, General Sykes commanding post at Baton Rouge, sent for William McGee, an officer in his command, and informed him, that Dr. Braman, an acting assistant surgeon in the same command had charged

him (McGee) with committing a forgery on Lt Clark, and had also put an irresponsible citizen (McHenry) to look up the evidence against the accused on a charge of stealing a watch and some money.[44]

The General also exhibited to the accused, a note, admitted by Dr. Braman to be in his handwriting, in which the accused was charged with the commission of the crime of forgery. The accused was also informed that the accusations had been made known to the Mayor of Baton Rouge, and perhaps to others, and were thus likely soon to be a matter of public town talk.[45]

The accused immediately afterward held conversations with officers in the command relative to the matter, and as to what he would, and ought to do. He returned to the General, and procured from him the note accusing him of forgery, written by Dr. Braman.... He sought the General's advice, or made remarks, which elicited from the General the reply, that he could not advise him what to do, that it was a personal matter between the accused and Dr. Braman, that he knew what he would do.[46]

The accused sent a message to Dr. Braman saying he desired to see him, the Doctor answered by the same messenger that he would be in his room, whither the accused immediately proceeded, he entered the Doctor's room, struck him with a whip or a cow-hide, a pistol shot was fired, immediately the accused came out the front door of the room and down the stairs with a pistol in his hand. Dr, Braman simultaneously passing out of the back door, and down the back stairs to the hospital tent about fifty yards from his room, where he died from the effects of a pistol shot wound.[47]

Major Herron remained consistent with the defense strategy; keep focusing on the note, the forgery, the crime committed by Dr. Braman. Minimize the shooting, the murder of Dr. Braman. Eventually, the ex-attorney general and future congressman gets to the heart of the matter:

But here arises a very important question upon the solution of which depends to a very great degree the guilt or innocence of the accused. Was the shot fired intentionally or was it to a very great degree the guilt or innocence of the accused. Was the shot fired intentionally or was it fired accidentally...? The theory of the prosecution is that it was fired deliberately and intentionally, while the accused maintains that it was unintentional. The question must be solved almost entirely by circumstantial evidence.[48]

Then, with one small sentence Andrew Herron cut to the quick: "For outside the testimony of Chelsea Walker, colored, there is no other direct testimony upon the subject."[49] The "Major" made no further mention of Walker or his race — he did not have to — Herron knew well his people, and each member of the jury was from East Baton Rouge Parish. Herron finished up by referring to the shooting:

The accused [Mr. Herron used the names "McGee," "Lieutenant McGee," or "Mr. McGee" almost not at all] maintains that after striking the deceased, he [Braman] made a movement which the accused thought was to procure his weapons, and the accused drew his pistol and accidentally discharged it in the act of cocking it. This position is sustained ... by the high and distinguished character of the accused as a brave courageous and gallant soldier. The act of shooting a fleeing antagonist in the back would not only exhibit the characteristics of a vengeful, cruel and brutal disposition, but it would also indicate the perpetration of a base coward destitute of courage and gallantry. Can you believe that the boy, who by his valor upon the field of battle fought his way to distinction and honor, could so soon degenerate into the base and cowardly assassin?[50]

But Herron was just getting started:

Can it be possible that this boyish form, that four years ago rode at the head of gallant men, amidst the whistling bullets and bursting shell, confronting danger in its most threatening shape, in the very midst of the enemy, driving them from their guard and bringing them off in triumph, has already even before attaining man's estate, fallen so far as to be the cold-blooded cowardly murderer...? I feel that your knowledge of human nature will apply the answer. NO! NEVER![51]

Although the accused may not be justified in strict law for the means of redress he resorted to, for the grievous wrong done to him by the deceased, are there not, taking all the circumstances into consideration, weighty reasons for excuse, extenuating and palliation, just about entering the threshold of manhood, by his good conduct, and services rendered his country, the architect of his own magnificent fortune, consisting as yet only of his good name, and fair unblemished and spotless reputation as an officer and a gentleman; just emerging from boyhood his whole life is his future and it before him, his foot just placed on the first rung of the ladder that leads to renown." [Herron completed his impressive closing with a statement each juror would certainly understand.] There may be a variety of opinions on the subject. It is certain, however, that many honorable high minded men would have acted just as this youth did.[52]

Herron's plan was brilliant and complete. Dazzle the jurors with honor, won and lost, injustice to McGee, forgery against McGee. Attack the victim. Throw in a friend's favorable if not perjured testimony, finish it off with a wonderful closing of youthful heroism, and sneak in race just to be sure the jury didn't notice Chelsea Walker's skin color. Herron was paid to win. Had he judged the jury correctly? One indication of the white male attitude in East Baton Rouge Parish might be understood better by reading the front page article of *The Tri-Weekly Advocate* on Friday, December 4, one week after the trial ended for Willie McGee:

THE NEGRO

They want him to remain, because His ballot at the South is needed to chain the lately rebellious States to the Union. This fact may not be pleasant to our chivalric neighbors, but it is nevertheless a fact. Other facts will, ere while be demonstrated if this outrage of negro suffrage be persisted in. The negro is not apt to control the general current of popular opinion here. He is more apt to float with and follow it and before many years if the cruel, ungenerous and unjust scheme of the extremists in the North is insisted on, we of the South will give you cause for unlimited howling and gnashing of teeth, in the use that will be made of this same negro suffrage. That we do not love nor even like the Radical North is true, we have cause for enmity. For many cogent reasons we protest against the last insult to the white race, and when the cry of "repudiation" rings through the land there will be no friendly feeling here to save you, Messrs. Radical.[53]

It is probable that Judge Posey proceeded to charge the jury on Wednesday, August 25, as that is also the date the verdict was given. Posey gave the jurors seven options. The first four charges are standard legal definitions of the differences between murder and manslaughter, and the differences between voluntary and involuntary manslaughter should the jury find McGee guilty. The charges are the same as would be expounded upon today, with a fair amount of necessary legalese. Charge numbers six and seven were also the standard rules regarding innocence and reasonable doubt, ending of course with the well known phrase, "Should there be any doubts resting upon reasonable grounds as to whether he is guilty of either of those crimes, you should acquit him."[54]

But Posey had one charge, number five, which was spelled out a bit differently than the rest. It reads as follows: "If 'A' from previous angry feelings, on meeting with 'B' strikes him with a whip with the view of inducing 'B' to draw a pistol, or believing he will do so in resentment of the insult, and determines, if he does so, to shoot 'B' as soon as he draws, and 'B' does draw — and 'A' immediately shoots and kills 'B,' this is murder."[55]

Judge R.T. Posey, unlike the prosecution, was up to the task, and, like Andrew Herron, knew his people. Charge number five, perhaps, was not necessary. But Posey eschews legal terms a bit and spells out to the jury in one paragraph the entire case. Substituting "A" for McGee and "B" for Braman, it could not be any plainer, at least from the judge's standpoint: "If Lieut. Willie McGee from previous angry feelings, on meeting with Dr. Braman, strikes him with a whip with the view of inducing Dr. Braman to draw a pistol, or believing Braman will do so in resentment of the insult, and determines, if he do so, to shoot Dr. Braman as soon as he draws, and Dr. Braman does draw — and McGee immediately shoots and kills Dr. Braman, this is murder." Not only does Judge Posey cut to the quick, he even takes away McGee's self defense: "Even if Dr Braman does draw," this is murder.[56]

With all seven charges explained, the jury retired to judge the innocence or guilt of Willie McGee. There is no record of how long the jury was out, but sometime on that Wednesday, November 25, foreman George W. Roberts led his fellow citizens back with a verdict. There are two distinct newspaper records of the decision, one from the *Tri-Weekly Advocate* and the other from the *Boston* (Massachusetts) *Globe Evening Transcript.*

In the Friday, November 27, 1868, *Tri-Weekly Advocate*, and under local items, below a local baseball box score between the Southern Jr ball club and the Pattersons, won by the Southerns 46–18, and just above a mention of seed tomatoes taking root between two bricks on the Levee, is the following two sentence article: "The trial of Lieut. McGee on a charge of manslaughter terminated in his acquittal Wednesday evening. The trial was by jury and the accused was ably defended by Col's Robertson and Herron."[57]

From the Boston paper comes a different approach:

The Murder of Dr. Braman — Law and Justice in Louisiana — The following letter from Baton Rouge, La., has been received by an officer at the Watertown Arsenal:

Baton Rouge, La., Nov. 26, 1868.

Yesterday Lieut. McGee was acquitted of the crime of murdering Dr. Braman, though the testimony was POSITIVE and the whole community was knowing to the circumstances, yet a jury of white men set him free.

The trial was a farce, and was conducted in such a manner as to disgust all the officers of the regiment. I told some that killing a human being was a less offence in their eyes than stealing a horse, which is a fact. McGee will still be tried by a military court for the same offence; but of course his life is no longer in jeopardy. I have done all that was in my power to have justice meted in this case. The witnesses were present who saw the transaction, and gave their evidence, but it had no weight with people whose interest or sympathy was not much given to either party, and who, I think, cared nothing about it. This is one of the many results growing out of the war, and the wisdom of commissioning men who have no business in the service.[58]

This letter was sent to Chandler's father, Dr. Isaac Braman, who ironically enough was the acting assistant surgeon for the U.S. Army Arsenal at Watertown, Massachusetts, just outside Boston. The author of the letter was 1st Lieutenant John Coe, a fellow officer, but not a friend, of William McGee.[59]

Nonetheless, Willie walked out of the Baton Rouge courthouse that Wednesday in November a free man — sort of. Did the New Jersey Irishman celebrate with Andrew Herron, "Colonel" Robertson and friend Captain William Fletcher? Holmes Pattison, Willie's adoptive father and a Michigan lawyer, was not present, and there is no record Willie's family back East were even aware of the trial. Pro or con, the barracks at Baton Rouge must have been in an uproar. While McGee and his entourage must have enjoyed the verdict, the specter of the court-martial could not be ignored. Willie McGee, the irrepressible Medal of Honor recipient, may have believed he was invincible, but Andrew Herron knew better. Both Herron and McGee knew that Willie faced two trials, civil and military.[60] The more serious, the one holding Willie's life in the balance, went in McGee's favor, and Andrew Herron, who must have been well paid — by someone close to McGee with money — may have felt his job was done. But if the major or Willie knew the letter to Dr. Isaac Braman was testimony to the feelings of his fellow officers, Lieutenant William McGee should not have felt very safe or comfortable.

CHAPTER SIX

The Battle of the Cedars

For every one of us, living in this world means waiting for our end.
Let whoever can, win glory before death.
When a warrior is gone, that will be his best and only bulwark.
— Beowulf

Drummer Willie McGee was about to enter month eleven in Murfrees-boro, Tennessee, in December 1864.[1] His unit, the 33rd New Jersey Infantry, was outside Atlanta, about to embark on Sherman's March to the Sea campaign.[2] That was real action, and since Willie had enlisted in August of 1863 in Newark, the only military action the drummer boy had seen was at Lookout Mountain, and that two day affair was over a year before; a year to a fifteen-year-old boy is a lifetime, war or not. For Willie, the past twelve months had held no adventure, no gallantry, no valor, and no excitement. So many thousands of boys just like McGee entered the army just for such adventure, as did other young men who left loving wives and children.

Though only a young drummer, Willie was still a soldier. He had as yet little to show for his time, and now that he was healthy, McGee would be anxious to prove his manliness. In *For Cause & Comrades: Why Men Fought in the Civil War,* James McPherson says, "The sheer boredom of inactivity caused some men to crave the alternative of action." McPherson could easily have had Willie's name on his mind when he quoted two army psychiatrists from World War II: "They become very restless for combat and impatient of delay.... The men seldom have any real, concrete notions of what combat is like. Their minds are full of romanticized, Hollywood versions of their future activity in combat, colored with vague ideas of being a hero."[3]

Was Willie McGee, the drummer boy from Newark, New Jersey, going to end the war sweeping floors in a hospital, growing vegetables in the hospital gardens, emptying bedpans, and carrying messages for others who had seen "real action"? Would he go home with hospital stories while his fellow boy musicians in the 33rd N.J. had real tales of war? Was the fifteen-year-old waiter sharing letters from his friends as they fought and marched throughout the South, or writing letters home to his mother, brothers and sister describing his improved health and distaste of war, that he was sick and tired of war and wished he could go home?

McPherson quoted a sergeant in the 70th Indiana who had spent the first twenty months of his service guarding railroad bridges at the rear — much like Willie in the hospital — and who wrote in disgust, "We are not gaining much honor here.... The boys are very anxious to see a little of the elephant, and would jump for a chance to have the name of at least one battle inscribed on the flag."[4]

As Willie McGee enjoyed an Indian summer day on November 30, 1864, he had no idea the thirty-mile triangle between Franklin, Murfreesboro, and Nashville would provide all the action any soldier would ever need to experience. Tens of thousands on both sides would regret it, but not Willie McGee. At four P.M. in Franklin, thirty miles west of Murfreesboro, blood began to flow in earnest, and there would be heroes aplenty, both Blue and Gray.[5] Confederate general John Bell Hood was both personally and professionally desperate, but so was the whole Southern mind. In the east, the Army of Northern Virginia was being squeezed, and in the south, Sherman would become an evil household name.[6]

Indeed, the entire Confederacy was desperate, but, even more, they were committed. John Hood, in command of some of the finest leaders in the Rebel army (among them Hiram Granbury, A.P. Stewart, Patrick Cleburne, Daniel Govan, and Nathan Bedford Forrest), made a decision to leave Atlanta and strike north, hoping to lure Sherman away from the sea.[7] It was a gamble for sure, but the Confederacy in November 1864 was faced with nothing but desperate decisions. At what point do a people so truly committed, a people who had spent three years fighting on their own soil for a cause that now seemed lost, at what point do they say "enough"? The thought, though often not expressed aloud, was certainly on the minds of all Southerners, especially the men on the march into Tennessee.

But Sherman didn't take the bait, and Hood with his almost 40,000 men crept closer and closer to Tennessee, looking to regain the Western Theatre. As his army moved west, and then north into the Volunteer state, the Federals in the area barely retreated ahead of them, racing ahead to safety in

Nashville, where General George Thomas waited with almost 50,000 soldiers. In a scene reminiscent of Napoleon in Russia, Hood's larger numbers and minor successes pushed him further and further north, giving him a false sense of bravado. In truth, no Southern army had been this far north for three years, and this is where John Bell Hood lost the West and hastened the fall of the Confederacy. Hood, ambitious, egocentric, and as desperate as any private, dove headlong into tiny Franklin, Tennessee, and in late afternoon on the thirtieth committed himself to career suicide and his army to mass murder. Without even waiting for morning, J.B. Hood sent almost 24,000 infantrymen into a worse debacle than Pickett's Charge at the Wheatfield at Gettysburg in July of '63. Within five hours, 9,500 men on both sides would be killed, wounded or captured in a frenzied attempt to save the South. In these five hours, almost 5,000 Rebel soldiers died or lay wounded in piles near the fortified Union lines, and one division lost almost 600 men in minutes as they charged the earthworks in front of the town.[8]

By midnight, the cause of the Confederacy had taken a most mortal hit. Hood had sacrificed almost 7,000 men, one third of his army, "to make himself famous," in the words of one of his own officers. The brutality of the assault was not confined to the infantry alone. Sixty-five Confederate commanders of divisions, brigades, or regiments were causalities, and thirteen of the twenty-eight Rebel generals were wounded or captured, and six generals, including the brilliant Irish-born Patrick Cleburne, lay dead in open fields. The courage shown on both sides has still not been ingrained in the American mind, but it is not an accident that one third of all Medals of Honor awarded during the entire war in Tennessee were bestowed at Franklin, a fact which speaks not only of the valor of the Federals, but also of the ferocity of the Rebel soldier's will, determination, and bravery.[9]

The Battle of Franklin was grotesque madness, and though it marked the end of the Confederacy in the West, Hood incredibly pushed the remnants of his mentally and physically spent army north twenty miles to the outskirts of Nashville, all the while declaring, pathetically, victory at Franklin. "We attacked the enemy at Franklin and drove them from their center lines ... leaving their dead and wounded in our possession," read his first dispatch sent to Richmond.[10]

The enormous carnage was exceeded only by the loss of morale among the survivors, as officers and soldiers alike knew their cause, if not over, was close to extinction. Hood had risked all and lost, but he camped outside Nashville with the remainder of his forces, approximately 20,000 men, and dared Union general George Thomas, with his now combined 60,000, to fight. Thomas, one of the most underestimated generals in the entire war, would make Hood wait two weeks, until he was good and ready to finish Hood's career. On December 15, the Virginia born Thomas obliged John Bell Hood and routed the Confederates not only out of Nashville but also out of Tennessee, effectively ending the war west of the Appalachians. At the end of the day, the Confederate Army of Tennessee panicked and fled south back through Franklin, a tiny town still in shock, where thousands were still in makeshift hospitals, mass graves greeted those retreating, and the smell of death from two weeks prior was omnipresent. By the time Hood and what was left of his forces were safely in Alabama, he had suffered over 23,000 causalities out of an army of 38,000 men. No American army had, up to that moment, ever suffered so, and yet the Union losses were less than 6,000. In the midst of these two weeks of carnage, courage and, finally, capitulation, 8,000 Union forces at Fortress Rosecrans in Murfreesboro, thirty miles east of both Franklin and Nashville, protected the small town of 4,000 and the vital railroad links that ran through it. None of the Union forces at Murfreesboro saw action at Franklin or Nashville, but on December 7, the garrison would find itself involved in a firefight historians would call "a minor irritation."[11]

The forty-five minute action would be variously referred to as the Battle of Wilkinson's Pike, Murfreesboro II, or the Battle of the Cedars. It would feature the famous, the brilliant Confederate general Nathan Bedford Forrest; the forgotten, Union major general Robert Milroy; and a boy, William H. Magee, a fifteen-year-old convalescent at Hospital #2. Surprisingly, the celebrity Bedford Forrest would lose and in anger shoot and kill a retreating Florida color-bearer in the head at point blank range; the forgotten Milroy would have his tarnished reputation somewhat restored; and though it made few history books, the Cedars would propel drummer boy Magee into a regional legend, and in the process enable him to receive a Medal of Honor. But it all started at Fortress Rosecrans, in Murfreesboro, Tennessee, which had become a home for the Jersey drummer for almost a full year.[12]

Following the Battle of Stones River in December 1862, the Union Army controlled the heavily Confederate Middle Tennessee area, and decided to maintain its hold by constructing the largest fort built during the Civil War just outside the town limits of Murfreesboro. Planned as a massive Union supply depot, the construction of the more than 220 acre bastioned fort was begun in January 1863 and not completed until June 1864 under the direction of Brigadier General James St. Clair Morton, the chief engineer of the Army of the Cumberland.[13]

More than 40,000 men, led by the Pioneer Brigade, an elite Michigan building unit, were involved in its construction, with four thousand soldiers working eight hour shifts each, clearing land, excavating moats, positioning the abatis, building walls, lunettes, and redoubts. The geographical placement planned by St. Clair Morton was brilliant, with the fort of eight strategic lunettes and four redoubts linked by walls and abatis, all placed astride the junction of the Stones River and the Nashville and Chattanooga Railroad and adjacent to the intersection of four major roads. The fortress, which was never successfully assaulted by Confederate forces, supplied the Union armies west of the Appalachians for the last two and a half years of the war.[14] Within Rosecrans were sawmills, warehouses, depots, magazines, quarters for thousands, and, luckily for drummer Willie Magee, several hospitals. When Willie entered Hospital # 2, he was one of approximately 1,800 Union soldiers within the earthen-post grounds all under the command of Brigadier General Horatio Van Cleve.[15] Van Cleve had been seriously wounded at Stones River, but upon recovery had been placed in command of the forces of the post at Murfreesboro in June 1863, though it was largely an administrative position. An engineer and surveyor by profession, the West Point graduate was perfectly suited for the job, which he held until the end of the war.[16]

During Willie McGee's first ten months at Rosecrans the population of the fort was a relatively stable 1,500 to 1,800, with convalescents being a large minority, the hospitals having beds for more than 500 patients. Though a small force of generally raw troops, it was enough to control the fortress, enforce martial law over the 4,000 residents of Murfreesboro and surrounding area, and staff and supply the depots and hospitals.[17] At some point in his recovery from typhoid, Willie would have been assigned to convalescent work. As a resident of the post for almost a full year, McGee, with his effervescent personality, was probably known to most if not all the full time personnel, and by October 1864 he was assigned as an orderly to the commanding officer, General Van Cleve.[18] Being commander's orderly, which had to be the prime convalescent position in any camp, perhaps best suited the amiability of our young Irishman. The noncombative, almost bucolic lifestyle for Willie and the other convalescents at Fortress Rosecrans changed dramatically, however, when Hood began his suicidal push north in November of '64 towards Franklin, a short thirty miles from Murfreesboro.[19]

General George Thomas, the sometimes misunderstood but incredibly efficient commander of the Army of the Cumberland, had anticipated John Bell Hood's every move and decided to fortify Murfreesboro with some veteran troops in his well-planned defense of Nashville. Thomas first sent 3,000 infantry north from Alabama on November 24, and one week later another 3,000 who had been guarding the railroad near Tullahoma, Tennessee, under the command of Major General Robert Milroy. General Thomas, not taking any chances, and aware that Van Cleve had been primarily an administrator at the fort the past year and a half, assigned Major General Lovell Rousseau from Nashville to take personal command on November 28. It was clear the duty for Rousseau was a temporary assignment until Hood and his struggling army were emptied out of Tennessee, and there is no record showing that General Van Cleve, at fifty-five years of age, was angry at the move. Rousseau would be in charge of all military action, and Van Cleve still post commander and chief administrative officer.[20]

Rousseau had been given but one order by General Thomas — "hold Murfreesboro secure" — just days before the telegraph lines were cut to Nashville and Rousseau was on his own.[21] Altogether, by December 5, Rousseau commanded about 8,000 men, approximately 6,000 of whom were soldiers fit for combat, an even mixture of veterans and newly formed raw units.[22] The 1,800 convalescents, doctors, warehouse soldiers, and clerks saw their world turned upside down overnight by the influx of Rousseau and his new troops. When news of Franklin reached the post at Murfreesboro, excitement had to be at fever pitch, and when communication was broken on December 2, officers, soldiers, and drummer boys alike were alive with anticipation of impending action.[23]

The Confederate leadership response after the massacre at Franklin was continued stupidity. Of the 40,000 he led into Tennessee just a fortnight before, Hood camped outside Nashville with barely 23,000 men, one third of whom may have been barefoot.[24] Hood compounded his mistakes by dividing his forces even more, sending General William Bate with 1,600 men southeast thirty miles to harass Murfreesboro and any Federals he could find. Bate and his depleted division arrived outside the fortress only to discover the newly arrived Union reinforcements; and Bate realized at once his small force was at a serious disadvantage. He reported the news to Hood in Nashville via courier and the Confederate commander further depleted his Nashville numbers, sending the legendary cavalry leader Nathan Bedford Forrest to join with Bate and his infantry. Forrest took over command based on seniority and with his 2,500 men brought the Rebel troop strength to more than 4,000, which by December 6 would swell close to 6,000.[25]

While Hood and barely 20,000 men waited at Nashville for Thomas and his 60,000 to attack him, Bate and Forrest were given orders to force the issue at Murfreesboro. On December 6, Forrest ordered Bate to employ skirmishers against the fortress, but to little avail. After Forrest himself made a reconnaissance with one of his Mississippi cavalry regiments, he agreed with Bate that a frontal assault against Fortress Rosecrans would be impossible, especially with the fifty-seven artillery pieces Rousseau had at the ready.[26] Forrest hoped his presence would force the Federals to come out after him, and indeed Rousseau took the bait, deciding that the Rebels "were very impudent."[27]

"At Murfreesboro thirty miles away, General Thomas, reluctant to relax his hold on the railroad, had stationed a small garrison under General Milroy. This garrison, as the rebels gathered in greater force, beleaguering the post, soon became comparatively isolated, all avenues of escape being practically closed. At length, it was determined to strike a blow for deliverance."[28]

Early the next morning, December 7, the day of glory for Willie McGee, General Rousseau ordered a heavy reconnaissance force of just over 3,300 men under Major General Robert Milroy to find out "where the main body of the enemy was."[29] At 10:00 A.M. Milroy took seven regiments of infantry, one cavalry unit, and a small battery of artillery south out of Fortress Rosecrans and headed down the Salem Pike.[30] Where was Willie, the orderly for General Van Cleve? Would he have been sent with Milroy's unit to report back to Van Cleve? Milroy would have had his own orderlies, and though it is possible Willie may have been reassigned to Milroy temporarily, never in his postwar life did McGee ever mention "The Gray Eagle," Robert Milroy, even once, and Willie McGee was a name dropper without peer. It is also possible Van Cleve loaned his orderly to Rousseau during the general's short three-week assignment at Murfreesboro. Possible, but not likely, as neither McGee nor Rousseau made mention of such an arrangement — ever — even when Rousseau was asked by Holmes Pattison to recommend Willie for a Medal of Honor.

"At this point young Magee had become acting orderly to General Van Cleve, and to him, youth as he was, the order was given to charge the enemy. It may be that a smile accompanied the order — a smile at the thought of committing such a work to a mere stripling; but it is certain that the confidence of the commander was not misplaced."[31]

Milroy and his troops marched almost four miles southeast along the Salem Pike, meeting sporadic but ineffectual resistance, mostly skirmishers and scouts, before stopping at the Spence farmhouse, where Mrs. Spence, a native of Ireland and the mother of four, informed the Union general for reasons unknown that "General's Forrest and Bate, with a large force of infantry, artillery, and cavalry," were posted north along the Wilkinson Pike, two miles north of the Spence house, and three miles directly west of Fortress Rosecrans.[32]

The decision for Milroy to look for a fight was easy, as the major-general had been waiting for a vindication of his own tarnished reputation for two years, when he had been embarrassed and almost court-martialed for his leadership at Winchester, Virginia.[33] Before continuing the search for Bate and Forrest, Milroy thanked the Spence family by taking their "60 fine fat hogs" and ordering a company of Ohio boys to bring them immediately to the fort.[34] We have no record if the talkative Mrs. Spence regretted her conversation with Milroy, or if she was ever invited to the post banquet.

It was now early afternoon, and if Milroy knew where the butternuts were lying in wait, Nathan Bedford Forrest's scouts were just as aware of the bluecoat's presence.[35] Forrest had planned to trap Milroy just south of the Wilkinson Pike with Bate's infantry, then swing his own veteran cavalry south behind the Union forces and cut off Milroy's line of retreat to the fortress. At first, Milroy appeared to walk right into Forrest's trap. The Union troops approached the Rebels, who were barricaded at the end of an open cotton field south of the Wilkinson Pike.[36]

Milroy had deployed his forces into two brigades, and the first took the front line of attack with four of the seven regiments. Milroy sent the 61st Illinois out as skirmishers and brought up his six gun battery, as both sides began an artillery duel of equal guns, hoping to draw each other out into the open field. After half an hour, "The Gray Eagle" realized the Confederate lines were not advancing, and his own artillery, which had begun the reconnaissance patrol with limited ammunition, had run out and had to go back to Rosecrans for resupplying.[37]

Had the Union artillery been better equipped, Milroy and his 3,300 men may have indeed taken the bait and walked into Forrest's trap, but Robert Milroy then made a move Nathan Bedford Forrest never anticipated, one of the few times Forrest would be bested in the war.[38] Milroy ordered his men to fall back through the thick cedar woods and then reform northeast back on the Wilkinson Pike with Fortress Rosecrans at their back. The idea was to get a better look at the Confederate strength, and perhaps avoid the open cotton field. In addition to the timber cover, the Federals were also hidden behind a small ridge shielding their movement, and none of the Confederate forces were aware of the circle back to Wilkinson Pike, since Forrest had kept the entire cavalry with him poised for the trap. Both rebel commanders, Bate and Forrest, thought Milroy believed his position was untenable and had simply retreated back to the safety of the fort.[39]

Whether by luck or design, Milroy was astride the pike at right angles to Bate's infantry, and still partially obscured by the thick cedar woods. It was now the Confederates who were surprised to see the newly constituted bluecoats, and Forrest hastily attempted to shift his lines, but gaps and overlaps of 100 yards were evident to all. Milroy needed to strike quickly, and his men did not disappoint him. It was now after three P.M. and Milroy acted with alacrity, sending the 61st Illinois out as skirmishers again, and the veteran unit quickly unleashed a volley which put the Rebel outposts on their heels.[40]

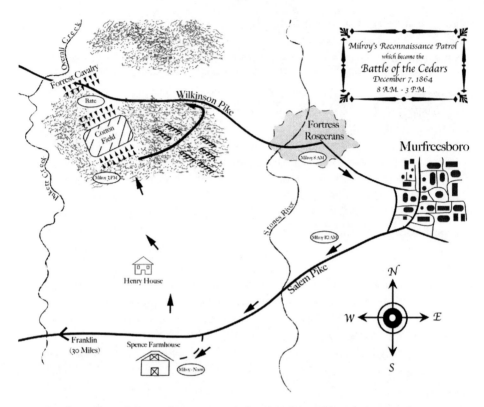

On the orders of General Rousseau, Colonel Robert Milroy led a reconnaissance patrol south out of Fortress Rosecrans at 8:00 A.M. They skirted the town of Murfreesboro, meeting a slight Rebel scouting party at 10:00 A.M. along the Salem Pike. After learning of the main Confederate body at the Spence House around noon, the Union forces headed north, where the main force of Bate's infantry awaited behind an open cotton field. Milroy moved his forces east though cedar ridges and reformed along the Wilkinson Pike, much to the surprise of Bate and Forrest. The Confederates, believing Milroy had retreated to Fortress Rosecrans, hurriedly reformed, but were out of position and stretched thin (Jennifer Dean).

Aligned at right angles to the Wilkinson Pike, Milroy placed the 174th Ohio on the left, the 181st Ohio in the center, and, just north of the Pike, the 8th Minnesota on the right. The second brigade, comprising the 177th and the 178th Ohio infantries, and the 12th Indiana cavalry, were placed just behind the first division in reserve.[41]

    "Taking the 181st Ohio Infantry, Magee sallied out of the works, and rushed upon a battery posted on an eminence hard by. The charge was made most gallantly, but the fire of the enemy was resistless, and slowly the column fell back. But the intrepid orderly did not for a moment falter in his purpose."[42]

Robert Milroy had placed Colonel Minor Thomas in charge of the first brigade, and he picked the right man. Thomas had been the colonel of the 8th Minnesota since 1862 and his unit was one of the North's best regiments. They had fought Indians as far west as Yellowstone, and later would inflict heavy damage on the Confederates in North Carolina. The 8th was hardy and tough, and was not about to run from anybody, including Nathan Bedford Forrest.[43]

As the firefight was about to begin, where was Will McGee? Though the heavily depleted 61st Illinois was down to only 200 men, it is not likely McGee was one of the skirmishers, as he was still only fifteen and had not fired a gun in action for at least a year — if ever. Surely the Illinois regiment would not need more drummers, especially on a "reconnaissance mission."[44] On the Union flanks were the two newly formed Ohio regiments, both raised within the past few months and close to full strength, and neither would need convalescents filling their ranks. Back at Rosecrans, there were still almost 5,000 men, so the Federals were definitely not desperate to fill in the ranks. As the battle was about to be joined, Willie would have had to have been somewhere in the rear — if he were present at all — with one of the two other new Ohio regiments, the 177th or 178th, also at full complement, or the 12th Indiana cavalry, as a convalescent substitute. The only other possibility was that McGee was on the field as an orderly for General Van Cleve, who never left the fort. The fifteen-year-old drummer boy was, by his later accounts — and Van Cleve's — an orderly only for the general.[45]

Wherever Willie was, Colonel Minor Thomas unleashed his first brigade at the temporarily unaligned Confederates at two hundred yards sometime after three P.M. on a bitterly cold but clear Tennessee day. While the Confederate commanders Bate and Forrest struggled to plug their gaps by moving men laterally, the three Union regiments attacked straight on with withering fire. For fifteen minutes the action was as vicious as can be found in war, and just when it appeared the Confederates might be able to regroup and hold their own, Milroy's front line made a spontaneous rush at the enemy's works, which included the Louisiana six-gun batteries. Within minutes, it was over. Forrest and his cavalry would be too late, as Bate's infantry, perhaps with the memory of Franklin in their minds, broke and ran back toward Overall Creek.[46] The Florida regiments stampeded wildly, and with some justification. Bedford Forrest's cavalry, attempting to reform lines and support the riflemen, had been firing at the rear of the Floridian units, mistaking as Union soldiers the blue coats many of Colonel Finley's boys (under the temporary command of Major Jacob Lash) had grabbed from the Federal dead after Franklin.[47]

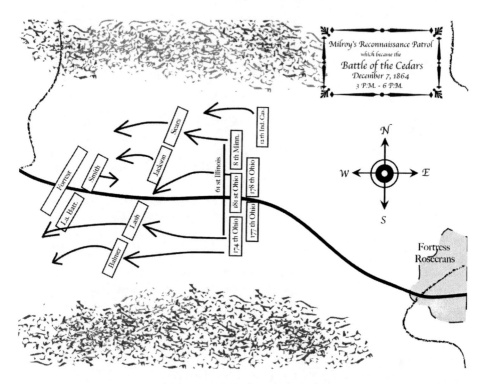

Milroy's forces were in control of Wilkinson Pike as the Confederates scrambled either too wide or not at all, leaving gaps everywhere, especially in the center. Palmer and Lash's Florida troops, facing fire from the 61st Illinois and the 174th Ohio, as well as friendly fire from the rear by Forrest's men, were the first to run. Following a fifteen-minute firefight, the Confederate front line caved, and Milroy's six brigades began a half-mile rout of the rebels, capturing two guns and almost 200 prisoners. By 6:00 P.M. all Union forces were safely back at Fortress Rosecrans (Jennifer Dean).

The terrified Floridians could not be stopped, even after Forrest himself chased down, shot and killed a color bearer in the head at point blank range in an attempt to stem the wild retreat. "They could not be moved by any entreaty or appeal to their patriotism," wrote an angry Forrest in a later report (or by shooting color bearers, he did *not* add).[48] Forrest had no choice but to order the rest of the cavalry to rescue the remainder of Bate's infantry to the safety of Overall Creek. "He stood in the stirrups, eyes blazing, face gone red with rage," wrote the historian Shelby Foote.[49]

"Accordingly selecting the 174th Ohio, Willie again moved out, charged the foe, again met their withering fire, still, however, pressing on until at last the victory was his."[50]

In the initial Union charge, Companies C and K of the veteran 8th Minnesota "blazed away at the rebel Washington Artillery, and a number of the Louisianans horses had been killed or wounded." Though the Louisiana boys gallantly attempted to save their guns by adding new horses, they were shot down by Minnesota or Ohio minie balls. In the end, the Confederates were able to save only one of their guns, leaving two on the field, "where they were claimed by men of the 174th Ohio Regiment, Company A." [51] As the Confederates gave up the fight, the first and second brigades charged through the hastily abandoned Rebel fortifications and chased Bate's men a half mile, capturing almost 200 prisoners, a Florida flag, and the two twelve-pound Napoleon guns.[52] The battle lasted forty-five minutes, including the vicious fifteen-minute firestorm, with the chase of the greycoats going another half-hour. Milroy, receiving a message from Rousseau back at Fortress Rosecrans about possible Rebel activity north of Murfreesboro, recalled his men in fine order, and all Union troops were safely within the fort by 6:00 P.M. Milroy assembled his troops and thanked them, and they "were then dismissed and permitted to return to their quarters."[53]

"This signal success at once dispiriting the enemy and reviving the hopes of our own men proved the first in a series of victories which resulted, finally, in driving Hood from Tennessee and restoring the whole section to Federal control. The army and the nation rang with the praises of the boy hero."[54]

Inside Fortress Rosecrans, Milroy met with his officers and Rousseau. Though Federal casualties had been light, the 8th Minnesota, in the center of the action, had lost thirteen killed and seventy-seven wounded. The three other regiments of the lead brigade, the 61st Illinois, the 181st Ohio, and the 174th Ohio, had a total of 8 killed and 159 wounded. There was barely a scratch on the rear guard brigade, but all in the fort felt the pain of the loss of twenty-five-year-old Major Benjamin C.G. Reid of the 174th Ohio, who was shot in the head and killed, on his horse as he led a charge early in the fight.[55] Reid, or Reed, whose story has never been told, had enlisted as a twenty-one-year-old sergeant in Zanesville, Ohio, immediately after hostilities broke out in April of 1861. He fought and was wounded while with the 3rd Ohio before being captured and confined as a POW in Georgia. Reid escaped from his captivity in March of 1864 but was recaptured in April in North Carolina. After being paroled and mustered out, he reenlisted as a major in the newly formed 174th in September, where he led his regiment to Murfreesboro. Promoted four times in three years, Major Ben Reid is buried at the Stones River National Cemetery in Murfreesboro.[56]

Forrest, besides the humiliation of a shameful retreat, the shooting of some of his fellow Confederates, and seeing 197 others be escorted to Fortress

Rosecrans as prisoners of war, lost thirty killed and another 175 wounded.[57] Both Bate's infantry and Forrest's cavalry were recalled to Nashville, and the threat to Murfreesboro was over, an event most historians call either "a minor irritation," or "a small action."[58] Forrest never blamed himself for his own miscalculation, failing to admit that Milroy had outwitted him, or that, by keeping all his cavalry with him instead of allowing some to scout, he had allowed Milroy to reform and attack quickly and successfully.[59] Though Bate and his men had been less than courageous in retreat, it was Forrest who was most to blame. Following the Cedars, Confederate troops were barely visible, and one week later, after the Battle of Nashville, armed Rebels would be scarce in all of Tennessee, as George Thomas swept John Bell Hood into ignominious obscurity.

Almost a year later to the day, Kentucky Congressman Lovell Rousseau, the general of Fortress Rosecrans for three weeks, recalled the following with just a hint of self-importance: "While General Hood was between my command in Murfreesborough in December 1864 we had several battles with the rebel Generals Bates and Forrest on one of which we captured many prisoners and two new 12 pdrs. Napoleon guns, in a charge upon the enemy."[60] Up to this point Rousseau is correct, but he failed to mention that at this particular action he was not present at Fortress Rosecrans. While Milroy was in

Nathan Bedford Forrest, one of the most brilliant, courageous, and enigmatic cavalrymen in U.S. history, was outmaneuvered at the Battle of the Cedars. Though a "minor irritation," it was still a defeat for Forrest, a rare occurrence (U.S. Army Military History Institute).

the process of returning victoriously to the fort, Rousseau himself had taken a regiment and marched just northeast of the post to attack a cavalry of Confederate colonel Buford, who had been reconnoitering with his men and some small artillery east of the fort, in the vicinity of Murfreesboro town.[61] Rousseau completed his remembrance of the role of drummer boy Willie McGee and the Cedars with the following two sentences: "The lad was amongst the first who got to the guns and he and one or two others, all mere boys, mounted the Artillery horses and took the guns into Fortress Rosecrans. Magee's behavior was very gallant and meritorious and he richly deserves the medal asked for him."[62]

If indeed Rousseau was not present when Milroy and his 3,300 troops returned, who told him about the gallant Magee? There were several reports, letters, and studies made

Major General Robert Milroy, "The Gray Eagle," who had been banished from high command for two years, was either lucky or smarter than Forrest, and his realignment along the Wilkinson Pike resulted in a quick Union victory on December 7, 1864, one week after the bloody massacre at Franklin, thirty miles away. Milroy, whose victory helped restore his reputation, never mentioned Drummer McGee and most likely never knew of his existence (U.S. Army Military History Institute).

about the minor irritation of what would become known as the Cedars, Wilkinson's Pike, or Murfreesboro II, and they must be investigated to discover the role of the drummer boy on December 7, 1864, in particular regarding the capture of the two artillery guns from the Louisiana battery.

Starting with the officers, General Rousseau wrote one report to George

Thomas in Nashville, adding only "the rout was complete, infantry and cavalry running in every direction."[63] Rousseau mentioned nothing else in his report that illuminates in any way the capture of the guns, and never mentioned Willie Magee, or any enlisted man in his report. "The readiness and gallantry displayed by young Magee in this affair very naturally attracted the attention of those around him, and he received the hearty commendation of Generals Rousseau, Milroy, and other officers in command."[64]

Major General Robert Milroy in several official reports, besides noting the capture of the guns, did not add any specifics, and the closest he came was the statement, "The gallant regiments composing the first line (174th and 181st Ohio, 61st Illinois, and the 8th Minnesota) seeing themselves supported, advanced with a yell and darted over the enemy's works.... A rapid pursuit of half a mile resulted in the capture of many more prisoners, one battle-flag, and two fine pieces of artillery with their caissons." Milroy also praised his troops in general, and several officers in particular, especially Major Reed: "The history of his services and adversities in the present war is stranger than fiction."[65] Milroy was effusive in his praise in all of his reports of men, supplies, decisions, subordinates, and superiors. It was his first heady action since his semi-disgrace two years before at Winchester, Virginia, when at the hands of Ewell's corps of Lee's Army he lost most of his troops, all his artillery, and a large quantity of supplies. If there had been a great story about heroism with young soldiers and a drummer boy it seems he would have been mentioned them — everybody else was. In General Milroy's collected papers in Jasper, Indiana, neither Willie nor his act of heroism is ever mentioned.[66]

The most specific account of the gun capture occurs in *The History of Fortress Rosecrans:* "On the right, the soldiers of Companies C and K, 8th Minnesota blazed away at the 5th Company, Washington Artillery. A number of the Louisianans horses had been killed or wounded. When the cannoneers sought to lead up additional horses to withdraw their guns, they were likewise cut down. In the end, the cannoneers succeeded in saving one of their guns; the others had to be abandoned. But as the fortunes of war would have it, soldiers from the 174th Ohio reached the two 12-pounder Napoleons first and claimed their captive."[67]

Major George Camp of the 8th Minnesota portrays this account almost verbatim in an official report on December 7, no doubt only hours after the battle had concluded: "During the charge, Companies C and K, on my left, opened a severe fire on the enemy's battery in front of the center of our line of battle, killing the enemy's horses, which they attempted to replace with others, but were driven back, and their horses killed or disabled by the fire of my men."[68]

A letter written by a soldier of the 174th Ohio, while not confirming the above, adds credence to its validity. Private Kosciusko (Kos) Elliott, of Company E, sent a letter home to his sister Mary on December 14, 1864, from Murfreesboro, just one week after the Cedars. "On the 7th," wrote Kos, "while I was on Picket the Regiment was ordered out again with the 177th, 178th & 181st O.V.I. & 8th Minnesota on a Reconnaissance in force they marched about 12 miles when they cam upon the rebels behind some breastworks of logs these they charged Co. 'C' being deployed as skirmishers they went in and on over them capturing a good many prisoners. Co. A got two guns & the battle flag of the first and fourth Florida that had 'Murfreesboro' inscribed on it."[69]

What makes Kos Elliott's story more believable is the proof that this Ohio unit captured the Florida battle flag, which was still in Ohio from 1865 until at least 1971, when it was returned to Florida. Could he be so wrong about one thing — the guns — and so right about the other, especially considering that it was written just a week after the event?

Colonel John Jones of the 174th Ohio, in his December 8 report, said, "The regiment made a gallant charge against the rebel breastworks and captured two guns, a stand of Rebel colors, and about 200 prisoners.... Major B.C.G. Reid of Zanesville, was shot through the head while leading his men on a charge."[70]

Another eyewitness to the account of the Cedars was 22-year-old Edson Dean Washburne, of Company E of the 8th Minnesota. In an autobiography written in 1907 at the age of 65, Washburne recounted his war experiences with the 8th Minnesota. While Private Washburne does not mention the guns, his recollection is worth noting:

> But on the 7th of December, 1864, our two brigades under General Milroy, numbering about 2,800 marched out on the Winslow [Wilkinson] Pike, some two or three miles from Fortress Rosecrans, where our battery was soon engaged with the Rebel battery. We lay concealed in a corn field between the two while they threw shells over us. This continued for about 2 hours when our battery spent their ammunition and retired for more back at the fort.[71]
>
> We silently slipped out of the corn and swung around to the right, some two miles on the double quick. As we came near their left flank, we were in an open cotton field, exposed to a most galling fire of shell and musketry. A number of the Regt. Went down among whom was our gallant Lieut. Col. Rodgers, wounded from the effects he never fully recovered and died a few years later. When we got to within 30 or 40 rods of the Rebel works, we were ordered to lay down.... Here for ten minutes we were exposed to as terrific a musketry fire as soldiers ever met. It was here that brother Eldridge was instantly killed as was also Elliott Poncher and 12 others wounded. We saw that to lay there exposed as we were, was to be shot down like cattle, and with one impulse we arose and with fixed bayonets we charged their works. When we reached the shelter of the

woods, we slipped from tree to tree whooping like Indians (We were called the Indian Regiment). We pored in a most deadly shower of Minnie balls."[72]

This they could not stand and soon broke and ran and we after them. I had the satisfaction of capturing three Rebels from behind a log, sending them to the rear where someone who had sulked in the first of the fight took them to the Fort and claimed the honor of capturing them. (Such is fate.) With our Battery far in the rear and no cavalry we found that we could not overtake them and we returned to the Fort with 250 prisoners and one battle flag. We rejoiced over the victory, but were saddened by the thought of the death of 14 brave boys and 200 wounded.[73] The next day I went and found my brother, and he with 11 others were buried in one large grave.

It is difficult to imagine a more poignant remembrance of the day his brother was shot and killed; Washburne had most details correct, yet at no time does he mention the gallant deeds of a drummer boy, or even the guns being driven by "mere lads" like himself. Interestingly, Edson mentions how "sulkers" took credit for his captured Confederates.[74]

One soldier of the second brigade at the Cedars left a voluminous memoir, but there is no mention of any gallant action by a drummer boy or soldier from New Jersey. Malachi Pool, 12th Indiana cavalry, was a rear guard reserve who would have seen all the action in front of him; following the battle, he was assigned as the rear guard and security for the two brigades as they returned to Fortress Rosecrans. Neither Malachi nor a lieutenant colonel in his regiment records any heroic duties near the guns.[75]

The official reports from every other commander involved in the Cedars are silent regarding Willie Magee, or heroism by young soldiers, or unusual bravery regarding the gun capture, with the singular exception of Colonel John O'Dowd of the 181st Ohio. O'Dowd, a thirty-three-year-old native of County Roscommon, Ireland, who would die at thirty-nine in Cincinnati in 1871, was the only commander involved in the action other than the 8th Minnesota or the 174th Ohio, who would claim responsibility for the capture of the guns on December 7. O'Dowd says plainly in his official report of December 8, "I charged these works and captured them, killing Colonel Weaver and capturing 2 commissioned officers and 33 men. I formed my command immediately, executing in a northwesterly direction with the intention of capturing a section of artillery that was to my right and rear. The enemy, seeing this movement, commenced falling back as I advanced. My men shot the artillery horses and captured the guns."[76] Allowing for the self-promotion of O'Dowd, which stands alone, at least the 181st Ohio was in the front line and could have claimed the guns with their action in the battle. Even O'Dowd, however, never mentioned Willie Magee. The official reports from all three rear guard commanders made no mention of any gun capture or serious action whatsoever.[77]

Within weeks of the Cedars, Lovell Rousseau was transferred out of Murfreesboro. Robert Milroy, though he felt grateful for the opportunity the Battle of the Cedars afforded him and his reputation, finished the last months of the war in Tennessee and left the army embittered at the West Point establishment he felt held him back throughout the war.[78] General Horatio Van Cleve maintained his post as commander of Fortress Rosecrans until war's end, while General George Thomas, the hero of the Army of the Cumberland and one of the most ingenious leader the United States Army had ever produced, has never been truly appreciated, an irony the only Southern-born Union general would have understood.[79]

General John White Geary, who was not in Tennessee in December 1864; General Thomas, who was in charge of 60,000 plus Union soldiers in Nashville at the time of the Cedars; and General Lovell Rousseau, who was not physically present at the action which earned Willie a Medal of Honor, all assisted McGee in his pursuit of fame.[80] General Robert Milroy, the actual commander of the reconnaissance-in-force which evolved into the Battle of the Cedars, and General Horatio Van Cleve, who knew Willie McGee intimately, never helped at all, and were never mentioned-ever-by McGee, an inveterate name dropper in his postwar life.[81]

While the published reports of McGee's heroism are nothing short of fabricated untruths regarding the murky circumstances of Willie McGee at the Battle of the Cedars, there seem to be three real possibilities: one, that the drummer boy was somewhere in the rear of the fight for unknown reasons, and when the first brigade chased the Confederates a half mile beyond the abandoned guns, Willie and some "other mere boys" claimed the prize, hooked up some horses, and rode the two guns back to Fortress Rosecrans,[82] second, that Willie was inside Rosecrans the entire day and made up the entire story when he left Tennessee; or third, that the New Jersey boy had heard something about the guns, and simply added himself to the story. McGee, who valued his letters of recommendation from the service above all his worldly possessions, never mentioned one from Milroy, Rousseau, or Van Cleve, the three people most in the know about the Battle of the Cedars. Willie also never mentioned once that he was acting in concert with any of the regiments, only that he was Van Cleve's orderly, and General Horatio Van Cleve would not be heard from until 1878.

In the spring of 1865, with the war almost over, a sixteen-year-old drummer boy from Newark, William H. McGee, was allowed to leave Fortress Rosecrans and rejoin his regiment, the New Jersey 33rd Infantry, in Virginia. He would never return to Tennessee, but back home in New Jersey he became a Tennessee hero.

CHAPTER SEVEN

The Court-Martial

Sooner or later everybody sits down
to a banquet of consequences.
— Robert L. Stevenson

It took the United States Army less than three weeks in Baton Rouge to convene the court-martial of Lieutenant William McGee in December 1869.[1] The 20th U.S. Infantry was prepared to show Willie, and perhaps Baton Rouge, its own special definition of honor and justice. Retribution, however, it was not. General Sykes began an investigation into the shooting of Dr. Braman while the smoke from Willie's borrowed pistol was still thick in the doctor's room.[2] The army had turned McGee over to the sheriff one week after the murder, but had continued its intention of a court-martial.[3] Andrew Herron in early September petitioned the court that dual prosecutions would only muddy the waters, and General Sykes agreed to postpone the military trial until after the outcome of the civil criminal case.[4]

Thus, when Will McGee was freed on Wednesday, November 25, it is possible, indeed highly likely, that he was placed under rearrest and sent to the brig. Importantly, there was no concern about double jeopardy, a ruse Willie would attempt to use for a long time. Andrew Herron and his firm were well aware of the two separate trials and never raised a single objection. During the court-martial, Herron made the statement, "The killing of Doctor Braman has already been the subject of judicial investigation and he [McGee] had a fair and impartial trial, and has been acquitted. However, this is not urged as a bar to your right to try him, for it is conceded that you are

92

trying him, not for the same offence, but for another offence growing out of the same act, and connected with it."[5]

Under Special Orders No. 98 a General Court Martial convened December 17, 1868, at ten in the morning. Seven officers were chosen as judges:

> Lt. Col. Romeyn B. Ayres — President
> Captain Robert Offley
> Captain Kinzie Bates
> Captain Isaac DeRussy
> Captain Leslie Smith
> Captain Edward Parry
> 1st Lieut. Henry Miller

The standard bearer for proper order and thorough and efficient protocol, Captain Septimus Carncross, was chosen as the judge advocate. Carncross, intimately involved in the actions both before and after the shooting of Chandler Braman, as well as a witness in the civil trial, would be a guarantee that Willie McGee was in for a tough fight. Most ironic of all, the U.S. Army commander who signed off for the approval of the court-martial was none other than Brevet Major General Lovell Rousseau, the very man most responsible for drummer boy Willie McGee being awarded the Medal of Honor three years prior.[6]

As Lieut. McGee was brought before the court and asked if he had any objections to the members named above, he replied "in the negative."[7] Even the captivating and magnetic Willie must have sensed this was a different ball game. After being seated, Will McGee was arraigned on three charges, each charge carrying multiple specifications.[8] McGee, as the trial began, had no representation. For a man with so many friends, it must have been a shock to be so alone. Perhaps he was waiting for the Louisiana Tigers, led by "Major" Andrew Herron, to arrive.

The small, nineteen-year-old second lieutenant was charged with the following:

Charge One— Riotous and Disorderly conduct to the prejudice of good order and military discipline.

Specification 1. That Lieut. William McGee ... did borrow a loaded pistol ... for the purpose of using it in an intended altercation with Acting Assistant Surgeon Chandler B. Braman, on August 15, 1868.

Specification 2. That Lieut. William McGee, after borrowing said loaded pistol, entered the quarters of Chandler B. Braman, and when no one else was present, did assault and strike Dr. Braman with a whip, on the same August 15, 1868.

Specification 3. That Second Lieut. William McGee in continuation of the assault recited above, and when neither his life or person were in jeopardy, by reason of Dr. Braman being unarmed, did without cause or provocation, maliciously shoot at and kill with a revolving pistol, loaded with powder and ball, Acting Assistant Surgeon Chandler B. Braman, U.S. Army, at Baton Rouge, August 15, 1868.

Charge Two — Disobedience of Orders

Specification — That Lieut. William McGee, having received an official note from the Adjutant of his Regiment, Captain Septimus Carncross, about 10 o'clock A.M. in the 17th of October, 1868, in the following words and figures, to wit:

> Headqrs. 20th U.S. Infantry
> Baton Rouge, La.
> October 17, 1868

2nd Lieut. Wm McGee
     20th Infantry
Sir:
   The Brvt. Major General Commanding the Regiment desires to see you at his office at once.
         I am Sir,
             Very Respectfully
                 Your Obedient Servant
(Signed) Septimus Carncross
             1st Lieut & Adjt. 20th Infantry
                 Brvt. Capt. USA

McGee did fail to comply with the requirements of said note, or offer any excuse therefore until noon of the 19th day of October, 1868, when he informed his Commanding Officer, Bvt. Major General George Sykes, U.S. Army, in writing that he was confined to his bed, and unable to report in person. This at Baton Rouge on or about the dates specified.

Charge Three — Conduct Unbecoming an Officer and a Gentleman.

Specification 1 — In this that Second Lieutenant William McGee ... did address a letter to his Commanding Officer, Brevet Major General George Sykes, U.S. Army in the following words, and figures, to wit:

> Baton Rouge, La.
> October 19th, 1868

Bvt. Major Gen George Sykes, USA
Comdg Post Baton Rouge, La.
Sir,
   In compliance with your order of the 14th inst. I am compelled to report by bed, and unable to report in person. As soon as I am well enough, I will report in person at your office.
   I have the honor, to be
             Very Respectfully
             (Signed) Wm McGee
             2nd Lieut. 20th Inf.

Which letter was intended to deceive his Commanding Officer, Bvt. Major General George Sykes, U.S. Army, and convey the impression that he, Lieut. Wm McGee, was too sick to comply with the letter of the Regt. Adjutant when in fact he, Lieut. McGee was on the streets of Baton Rouge, La. about 6 o'clock P.M. on the 17th day of October, 1868, and again in the streets of same city with a party of noisy and boisterous citizens about 8:30 o'clock P.M. on the 18th day of October, 1868.

Specification 2 — In this that Second Lieutenant William McGee, 20th U.S. Infantry, having been met on the streets of Baton Rouge, La. About 6 o'clock P.M. October 17, 1868, and asked by Bvt. Capt. Septimus Carncross, Adjt. 20th Infantry, why he had not complied with the tenor of the note sent him in the morning, did falsely state "that he had written to his commanding officer, and that General Sykes had sent him a very polite answer" he Second Lieutenant McGee, well knowing that he had neither written to, or received any communication from his commanding officer as avowed. This at the time and place certified.

Specification 3 — In this that Lieut. McGee (to the great disgrace of the service) was intoxicated in the streets of Baton Rouge, La. in the presence of citizens, and while wearing his uniform. This on or about October 16th day of October, 1868, at the place specified.

Specification 4 — In this that 2nd Lieut. William McGee (to the great disgrace of the service) was drunk and disorderly on the streets of Baton Rouge, La. in the presence of citizens, and while wearing his uniform. This on or about the 18th of October, 1868, at the place specified.[9]

Willie McGee, without an attorney, pleaded not guilty to each and every charge. At first review it seemed Willie had misread the Army. Later, in letters, he writes after the civil trial that he thought the court-martial was just a formality and "everything would be the same," and truly thought he could resume his regular duties in a very short time.[10] Perhaps that is why he did not have any legal representation. Whatever the reason, reading the charges and seeing the makeup of the court, it was obvious Willie had really raised the hackles of the United States Army, 20th Infantry.

Though the first charge was certainly the most serious, the mood of the court may be best judged by charges two and three. While on bail for murder, McGee had been charged with lying — to a General and his adjutant — and been caught red-handed, with the implication he had been partying. In charge three, again while out on bail, he had been drunk in uniform at least twice. Not the brightest behavior for a young man looking for sympathy in a self-defense plea. It appeared on the surface the army believed Willie was spitting in their face, and the two words in the charges, "lying" and "drunk," seem to follow Willie forever.

The court prosecuted each charge separately, and the presiding judge,

Septimus Carncross, called Sergeant William Jones. Jones testified at length, telling the panel Willie not only borrowed his loaded pistol, he also told his sergeant, "It is just the thing I want." Sgt. Jones also told the court that a half hour after giving Willie his pistol, he saw McGee go up to the room of Dr. Braman and then "heard a shot from that direction," and saw Lt. McGee come out and walk down the stairs, "very excited." Jones ran from his quarters and saw a "crowd running toward the hospital. I went in and saw Dr. Braman dead."[11]

Jones testified, under very specific questioning by Carncross, that he next saw the same gun in General Sykes possession on August 17, when "I identified it as the one I gave to Lt. McGee, and one barrel was discharged." Acting as his own attorney, proving he was not prepared for the severity of this day, Willie asked Jones several questions, none of which were relevant. The sergeant concluded his testimony by saying Dr. Braman died while lying face down on the cot with blood on his shirt.[12]

The second witness for the prosecution was the top man, Commanding Officer General George Sykes. Lt. Carncross directed to his boss one statement: "Please tell the Court all the facts within your knowledge connected with the original arrest of the accused." [13] This time around, George Sykes was not to be denied. Whether he felt justice delayed was justice denied, or whether it was emotional sympathy for the victim's family, or disappointment, or worse, disappointment in Willie; or whether he needed to regain control of his post, General George Sykes was ready.

The first sentence almost flies off the transcript: "On August 15th, McGee was arrested because I believed him to have killed Acting Assistant Surgeon Chandler B. Braman, U.S. Army, who was then acting as medical officer at this Post." Sykes proceeded to say that "trouble of a personal character" began between the Doctor and McGee and he had interviews with them both. The general then recounted the events, starting with the forged note brought to him on Friday, August 14. Sykes continued with actions taken on Saturday morning, when he met first with Dr. Braman and then with Willie McGee. The general added that he "received a note from Dr. Braman at a later period in the day and he informed me he had an interview with Lt. McGee and he [Braman] had made it all right."[14]

General Sykes additionally stated that about 5:00 P.M. Willie came back to him, asking for the penciled note, and threatened to hurt Braman with a whip. An hour later, according to the general's testimony, while he and Major Todd were sitting on the steps at Todd's quarters, they heard a pistol shot "followed by a scream." The general said he immediately ran to Dr. Braman's room and from there to the hospital tents, where "I found him dead."

Sykes continued and said he immediately sent for McGee by an adjutant (Carncross). When Lt. McGee arrived Sykes said Willie admitted he "fired at Dr. Braman." The pistol was brought to Sykes' office and he said, "I was satisfied Dr. Braman was killed by Lieut. McGee, and I thus ordered his arrest."[15]

After Sykes had completed his long but thorough account of August 14 and 15, Willie McGee, way in over his head as an attorney, asked the general six questions, all regarding Lt. Clark, the forged note, and the defamation Dr. Braman committed against him. General Sykes patiently responded, several times repeating things he had just testified about. Not one question dealt with the shooting or the actions Willie had taken in the doctor's room. The advocate general finally cut off this line of questioning by asking General Sykes, "What did the Doctor die of?" Sykes said simply, "From the effects of a pistol shot," and added that he ordered a post mortem to be conducted as soon as possible.[16]

Willie McGee came back at the general and asked, for whatever reason, if the general knew of any meeting that had taken place between Dr. Braman and himself that Saturday, August 15. Sykes responded that McGee himself had told him that such a meeting took place, and "the Doctor confirmed such a meeting in writing." Judge Carncross ended the Sykes testimony by asking how old Willie McGee was. "He is about twenty or twenty-one, I should so judge," Sykes responded. Willie was then only nineteen, commissioned an officer at eighteen, another McGee lie unknown to authorities.[17]

The third and last witness the first day was Chelsea Walker, whose civil trial testimony was challenged and then critiqued because he was "colored." Even without Herron's cross-examination, Chelsea's time on the stand was lengthy. Lieut. Latchford's servant told the court the same story he had given in the civil trial, only in more detail. After talking with and delivering messages from McGee and Braman, Chelsea said he followed Willie right up to the door, "Where I stopped and looked in the window." Walker then repeated exactly what he said in the county courthouse about the whipping and the shooting, ending with Willie McGee coming out of the front door yelling at Braman, "I'll make you howl if you say that about me!"[18]

The judge advocate asked Chelsea why he followed Willie up the stairs. "I thought Lieut. McGee was going to do something," he replied plainly. Carncross again asked, "Was Dr. Braman facing Lieut. McGee, or was his back to him, at the time you say McGee fired?" Walker said, "His back was towards Lieut. McGee." When asked by Judge Carncross to explain the shooting in more detail, Walker said he was not sure in what hand McGee held the gun, but that his hand was extended about four feet from the floor, and three feet from the doctor. Just before the shooting, Walker said, Dr. Braman was sitting in his chair, and when the whipping began, he tried to rise and turn, and as he did so Willie shot him in the back.[19]

McGee attempted to cross-examine Walker but each question was explained with clarity, and Willie gave up the effort. A member of the court asked Walker if the doctor had any arms in his possession at the time "you saw Lieut. McGee fire at him." Chelsea replied, "Not that I know of." With no further questions from Willie or the court, the first day was adjourned at 3:00 P.M. until the next morning.[20]

The sun may or may not have risen brightly in Baton Rouge the next day, but it surely did for Willie McGee. After he found out the old adage "a man who defends himself has a fool for a client," was true, the Louisiana Tiger cavalry arrived for him in the form of Andrew Herron. Willie made a quick application for Herron to be his counsel, and the court accepted.[21]

The initial witness the second day was Dr. Reynaud, who described his autopsy, and added at one point, "He was shot in the back." Questions by the judge advocate and Andrew Herron peppered the doctor about entry spots, standing up, sitting down, one or two hands on the pistol, until finally Judge Carncross asked, "Could the wound described by you have been inflicted while Dr. Braman was in the act of rising from his chair?" Reynaud answered, "Yes, Sir." Andrew Herron was silent and Dr. Reynaud was excused.[22]

Next up was 1st Lieutenant Louis Morris. Morris gave a detailed account of the time period between 5:00 P.M. and 7:30 P.M., Saturday, August 15, when he and Captain William Fletcher first encountered Willie on the barracks gallery, where the two men were resting. Morris, listed as a prosecution witness at the civil trial but never called to the stand, recounted how the two men tried to calm Willie McGee down, but as the hours wore on, they observed him almost plotting his course of action, until finally both Morris and Fletcher heard the fatal pistol shot. Morris added that as he ran towards Dr. Braman's room he met Willie McGee coming toward him. Louis Morris asked McGee what he had done, and Willie replied, "I have laid the doctor out." Morris then told the court he continued to the hospital tent where he saw Dr. Braman die, with blood running from his mouth.[23] There were no questions — not one — from Andrew Herron. The witness was excused, with observers perhaps wondering why Morris was not called in the first trial. More cynical people might wonder if it would have made any difference, given the political climate in Baton Rouge during Reconstruction.

The third witness was Lieutenant Thomas Latchford, who had appeared as a prosecution witness earlier in November. Latchford provided the same damaging testimony he gave the first time, and again there were no questions from Andrew Herron.[24] It did not look promising for Lieut. McGee, at least on the first and most serious charge of riotous and disorderly conduct.

Private George Mayhew then appeared before the court, and, like Latchford, was not a good witness for the defense table. Mayhew told the court Dr. Braman was afraid of Willie and anticipated trouble with him. Mayhew gave perhaps the best account of Dr. Braman's time from the moment he was shot until, mortally wounded, he expired on a cot in the hospital tent.[25]

The defense called one witness, Dr. Thomas Buffington of Baton Rouge. Buffington reprised his very short testimony from the civil trial, but the longer he talked in this one the worse it got for Willie McGee. Buffington was supposed to bolster the defense theory of the mysterious McGee hand injury, proving it was possible the shooting was an accident. Under questioning by Herron and the judge advocate, Dr. Buffington revealed he never removed any gunpowder from Willie's hand, and in fact did not even remember which hand was injured. Buffington admitted to the court he did not exactly remember when he had examined Willie except that it was in the city jail, "some days" after the shooting.[26]

The good doctor also told the panel he was requested to examine Willie but couldn't remember who made the request and that there was "some inflammation" which had "the appearance" of having been done recently.[27] Buffington was no help except to dreamers, and these army officials, and Herron as well, were certainly not dreamers. Andrew Herron must have sensed he wasn't going to get lucky twice. Whatever Willie McGee believed is unknown, but it would get worse before it got better for our young hero turned assassin.

Testimony ended on the first charge, and Carncross finished off day two by swearing in a few Baton Rouge citizens. They all testified to Willie's boisterous, alcoholic behavior in the streets of town while he was on bail and dressed in military garb. One man, Charles Thiel, even told the panel of judges McGee threatened a group of men with a whipping of his cowhide while out on bail for shooting Dr. Braman. The court adjourned about 2:00 P.M., and agreed to meet after the weekend on December 21.[28]

On Monday, more local citizens were ushered into court testifying to Willie's public drinking habits and behavior, which politely could be called immature.[29] How badly did the 20th U.S. Infantry want to punish Willie McGee? Badly enough that Judge Advocate Septimus Carncross switched hats and was sworn in as a prosecution witness, and then, after testifying, returned to his role as judge advocate. General Sykes and Carncross testified that McGee lied to them both when he was ordered to report to the general, and Carncross added that when Willie was supposed to be sick in his quarters he

Adjutant General E.D. Townsend's written record of Willie McGee's court-martial conviction, April 9, 1869, sentenced the ex-lieutenant to five years in the Stillwater, Minnesota, prison (author collection).

observed him partying and drinking in downtown Baton Rouge.[30] It was difficult, if not nearly impossible, for the past Baton Rouge war hero and future congressman Andrew Herron to go after Sykes and Carncross. These career United States soldiers were clearly in charge of this venue, so Herron passed on attacking these two leaders of the 20th United States Infantry.

As the third day fell, Herron followed the same pattern that was successful in the civil trial. Once again, Lieut. William McGee did not take the stand to defend himself. Instead Andrew Herron submitted several letters of support for Willie. The letters describing past character and valor came from two governors and two ex-generals, as well as McGee's Medal of Honor Citation, which was labeled Exhibit F. Each letter was at least a year old, some two or more. Not one current show of support was entered as evidence, suggesting either Willie was ashamed to tell his high-placed friends of his present predicament, or his friends were deliberately distancing themselves.[31]

McGee also submitted, word for word, the written statement he presented at the civil trial, and Herron, not Willie, read even this. Attorney Herron was also allowed to give his own verbal statement, and it was a tour de force, the Louisiana Tiger at his best.[32] Upon receipt of all defense documents, but no personal appearance by Lieut. Willie McGee, the judge advocate submitted the case to the court "upon its merits and without further remarks."[33] William Fletcher, whose civil trial testimony was so beneficial to McGee — and likely perjurous — was never called as a witness, and his name was never mentioned in the court martial.

On Tuesday, December 22, the panel of seven judges, "after due deliberation and having maturely considered the evidence submitted," found William McGee guilty on all three charges, and guilty of five of the seven specifications. McGee was thrown a bone on charge three, specifications three and four, and found not guilty. These were the ones connected to public drunkenness in the streets of Baton Rouge while out on bail.[34]

Three days before Christmas 1868, Judge Advocate Septimus Carncross sentenced Second Lieutenant William H. McGee, perhaps the youngest officer ever commissioned in the history of peacetime in the United States Army, to five years in a federal prison. It also marked the first time in United States history that a Medal of Honor soldier was convicted of shooting a man in the back and dismissed from the service forever.[35] We can surmise that General George Sykes found some small solace in his letter, maybe his last letter, to the Braman family in Massachusetts. Dr. Isaac Braman no doubt received the general's letter in the spirit of kindness with which he lived his life, but no solace, peace, or modern word like "closure" would ever embrace his heart again.

Will McGee, whose past was turning out to be better than his prospects, would have five years of another kind of closure — behind a cellblock door. To his great discredit, McGee would never admit guilt of any kind, never apologize, and never spell the word "Braman" correctly for fifteen years.[36] Willie McGee became a professional victim, and never figured it out.

CHAPTER EIGHT

McGee, Magee, and the President

> There is a time in youth, lads, when all is clear, an unruffled lake,
> a stream pellucid as crystal. Time stirs up the mud.
> Later on we live in dirt — we do the best we can,
> but there are the bare bones of the matter.
> — Thomas Flanagan,
> *The Tenants of Time*

The year 1866 was a wonderful one for seventeen-year-old Willie McGee; he had arrived in Muskegon, Michigan, to start a new life after the war, and within weeks had surprisingly been awarded a Medal of Honor.[1] McGee's new father, Holmes Pattison, was a minister and attorney, a male role model Willie had missed since the death or disappearance of his father when he was just an infant. In the fall of the year, McGee was interviewed by John Y. Foster, who was researching a book on the history of New Jersey in the Civil War. But just when life was looking up in Michigan, Willie would be pulled back home to New Jersey in 1867, and, in a whirlwind year no one could have anticipated, the drummer boy would be lionized by a governor and meet the president.[2]

Early in the year, Foster's *New Jersey in the Rebellion* was published to acclaim in the Garden State.[3] One of the revelations was the previously unpublished but wonderful human interest story of a Newark drummer boy who played such a magnificent role in a pivotal battle in Tennessee late in 1864.

No less a personage than Governor Marcus Ward, himself a Newark native, was taken by the tale of little Willie McGee. On April 12, 1867, McGee accepted an invitation to return to New Jersey and meet with Ward, the grateful "soldiers friend," who held a reception for many of those portrayed in Foster's book, a work commissioned by the New Jersey legislature. Whether Governor Ward had planned to reward Willie because of the fame garnered by the Irish teenager or was swept off his feet by the force of the McGee personality there is no record, but reward the drummer boy Ward did, and quickly. Before April was over, both Ward and his Republican friend, Governor John White Geary of Pennsylvania, had written letters of recommendation to the secretary of war, Edwin Stanton, as had General George Thomas.[4] Geary's letter was typical of each:

> Harrisburg, Pa.
> April 26, 1867
>
> Sir:
> I take great pleasure in recommending to you for an appointment in the U.S. Army Mr. William Magee, formerly a drummer boy in the 33rd New Jersey Volunteers, and who throughout the war distinguished himself for his exemplary and gallant conduct. He served in my command, and from personal observation I can speak unreservedly in his behalf. For his conduct in the actions at Murfreesboro he was presented with the "Medal of Honor" awarded by your department under the Act of Congress of July, 1862. You may rely upon his being in all respects a worthy candidate.
>
> With great regard
> I am, truly yours
> John W. Geary[5]

Any recommendation or reference from Geary was taken seriously. John W. was a true Irish-American legend. Born in a log cabin in Westmoreland County, Pennsylvania, in 1819, Geary was forced to leave college when his father died, having lost his property and savings in the process. Assuming his dad's debts, Geary taught school and worked as a civil engineer before returning to college and graduating at age twenty-two. Four years later, he joined the service at the outbreak of the Mexican War. The huge (6' 6"), 250 pounder was twice wounded and highly decorated, ending his service as a colonel. After the war, he went to California, where he was elected the first mayor of San Francisco.[6] Tiring of the West, Geary returned to Pennsylvania, where he became a gentleman farmer in his hometown. Like so many other thousands of Americans, his life changed forever when Fort Sumter fell in 1861. In the next four years, John White Geary would be wounded three more times in action, rise to brigadier general, and have a son die in his arms at Lookout Mountain, Tennessee.[7] The last two years of the war Geary was a commander of the XX Corps of the Army of the Cumberland, under which the 33rd New Jersey Infantry fought its way through the South.[8]

Following the war, John Geary served two consecutive terms as the governor of Pennsylvania, from 1867 to 1873, and he would die three weeks after leaving office in his beloved home state.[9] Of all the military leaders and politicians in the Civil War era, John White Geary was one of the more unblemished at its conclusion. His recommendation of Willie McGee as an officer for the regular army in 1867 would carry great weight and obviously helped the drummer boy. Four days after Geary's letter was sent to Stanton, another was sent from the governor's office in Trenton, New Jersey:

April 30, 1867

Hon. E.M. Stanton
    Sec. of War
Sir:
    William Magee, late a drummer boy in the 33rd Regt. N.J. Vols., is desirous of an appointment in the regular army, and won the praise and good will of his officers. I am personally acquainted with him, and know his widowed mother, a highly respectable lady, whose residence is near my home in Newark.
    I commend his application to favorable consideration.

Very respectfully yours,
Marcus Ward[10]

Marcus Ward, unlike John Geary, was never a war hero, and in fact never served in the military at all. A lifelong Republican, Ward, a native of Newark, was a large-scale merchant who entered politics in 1862 and was governor from 1865 to 1868.[11] Ward was considered, as was Geary, a friend of the common man and as governor and a close political ally of President Grant, his recommendations carried great substance, just as any New Jersey governor's does today.

These two letters, and a similar one by General Thomas, who never met drummer McGee, had the desired effect, and Willie was quickly sent to Louisville, Kentucky, to receive his appointment and be tested. On May 16, Willie, as was the protocol, responded in writing to his nomination, just three days after his eighteenth birthday:

Louisville, Ky
May 16, 1867

Adj Genl USA
    Washington
I have the honor to acknowledge the receipt of my appointment as 2 Lt. 20th Infy and to accept the same. I was born in Newark N. Jersey May 13th 1849. New Jersey is the state of which I am a permanent resident.
            Yr. Obd. Svt.
                    William Magee 2nd Lt. 20th Infy.[12]

There remained only two final steps before Lieutenant William H. Magee would be confirmed by the army and assigned to a post, making him the youngest officer in United States Army peacetime history. Seated before an examination board of five senior officers in Louisville, Kentucky, the applicant wrote a one-page history, which shows some of the deficiencies of his self-acknowledged lack of schooling:

> I was born in Newark N.J. on the 13th May 1849 previous to the rebellion I attended school until the death of my father in 1861. I then engaged a clerkship for the support of my mother. In August 1861 I enlisted in the 33rd N.J. Vol. Infy. I was in the battle of Missionary Ridge, and in the Atlanta campaign as far as Tenesah mountain. There I was taken sick and was sent back to Murfreesboro and when that town was attacked by Forest I led a party and captured two guns. I served with my Regiment until its muster out in August 1865.
> Respectfully
> William Magee[13]

After completing the history, brief and as inaccurate as it was, Willie sat before the board and faced the question and answer session, which would determine his army career. The test was recorded, and then signed by the applicant as "William Magee":

Ques. What are the Articles of War?
Ans. I cannot answer it.
Ques. What is the form of our Government?
Ans. A free government.
Ques. Into what three branches is it divided?
Ans. Legislature, Executive, and Supreme Court.
Ques. What is the number of Senators?
Ans. Two from each state.
Ques. How are senators elected?
Ans. Elected by the people.
Ques. What determines the number of Representatives from each state?
Ans. I cannot answer it.
Ques. How is the President elected?
Ans. By the people.
Ques. How is he elected if he does not receive a majority of electoral votes?
Ans. House of Representatives.
Ques. What is Treason?
Ans. Any act against the government.
Ques. What are the rules of arithmetic?
Ans. I cannot answer it.
Ques. Add $\frac{1}{3}$ and $\frac{1}{2}$.
Ans. I cannot do it.
Ques. Subtract $\frac{1}{3}$ from $\frac{2}{3}$.
Ans. I cannot do it.
Ques. Multiply $\frac{1}{3} \times \frac{2}{3}$

Ans. I cannot do it.
Ques. Into what general divisions is the earth divided?
Ans. Eastern and Western Hemisphere.
Ques. What are the names of the oceans?
Ans. Artic, Atlantic, Pacific, Indian, and Southern.
Ques. What are the principal kingdoms of Europe?
Ans. Sweden, Russia, Prussia, Spain, Austria, Germany, Italy.
Ques. What are the Republics of Europe?
Ans. I do not know.
Ques. What sea separates Europe and Africa?
Ans. Red Sea
Ques. What is the most southern cape of Africa?
Ans. I do not know.
Ques. What that of America?
Ans. I do not know.
Ques. What are the boundaries of the United States?
Ans. On the north Russian America and Canada. On the east by Atlantic
     Ocean. On the south by Mexico and the Gulf of Mexico. On the west
     by Pacific Ocean.
Ques. How many degrees of longitude are there?
Ans. 360.
Ques. How many of north or south latitude?
Ans. 90
Ques. How many motions has the earth?
Ans. One
Ques. What is the period of the moon's revolution around its axis?
Ans. I cannot answer.
Ques. What are the summer months at Cape Horn?
Ans. I cannot answer.
Ques. Where were the first settlements made in the United States?
Ans. Jamestown
Ques. Where was the first bloodshed during the Revolutionary war?
Ans. Lexington.

William Magee[14]

Following the examination, it was little surprise that 2nd Lieutenant
William Magee, 20th Infantry, presented himself before the board of examiners, and was told, "You have not passed a satisfactory examination, and the
proceedings in this case are herewith terminated." This had to be a shock to
Willie and his supporters, who may have seen McGee's vibrant verbal presence as a sign of his education, not realizing that the power of his personality masked serious educational faults. Most amazing was the board's
recommendation, which read, in a sentence sure to give pause, "We find the
applicant almost totally uneducated, but being only eighteen years of age, the
Board suggests him as a worthy subject ... for the Military Academy."[15]

McGee had to have an entourage of handlers and supporters, for two days after his disastrous exam the young Irishman penned a lengthy letter from Louisville to Secretary of War Edwin Stanton, no doubt with assistance:

> Louisville, Ky.
> May 18, 1867
>
> Hon. Ed. Stanton,
>
> In compliance with the appointment you so kindly gave me as 2nd Lt. 20th Infy I reported to the Board in this city for examination. With shame and confusion I have to acknowledge that I have just received a statement from the [Board] President of the same that I had failed to pass a satisfactory examination. This would seem to end my bright hopes for the future and with it the means to provide for my poor widowed mother and little sister. I am left their only support, my two elder brothers having given up their lives on the altar of this country. You were kind enough to recognize my services by giving me a medal of honor and this appointment for my services during the war. I was just a poor drummer boy but — I did service that commended the admiration of my officers. I am now only eighteen and if you will be so kind as to give me an appointment where I will not have to be examined I will promise you to apply myself and learn enough to satisfy you that I can be a man and that your kindness has not been mis-placed. If I cannot get in an old regt. can you not assign me to duty in the 20th Infy without examination? Sir, the soldiers friend, you shall never have cause to regret your favorable and kind treatment of a widows son.
>
> Yr Obd. Svt.
> Wm Magee[16]

That same day General George Thomas also sent a letter to Stanton asking for another chance for McGee, a rare occurrence in the army. With powerful political cachet, Marcus Ward only could have orchestrated the campaign for a second chance for McGee. After his return to New Jersey from Louisville, Ward played a bigger card, an actual audience with President Andrew Johnson.[17] On June 20, Willie and Governor Ward were in Washington, and McGee, after his audience with the president, sent the following specific request for a second chance to the White House, as directed by President Johnson.

> Washington, D.C. June 20, 1867
> His Excellency, Andrew Johnson
>   President of the United States;
>   Sir;
>   I have the honor to state that I was appointed by Your Excellency a Lieutenant in the Army upon the recommendations of Governors Geary and Ward. I was ordered before the Louisville Board for examination and failed to pass. I am now but eighteen and was thirteen when I entered the army having a widowed mother dependent upon me for support I have had no opportunity to fit myself as I might.

General Thomas addressed a letter in my behalf to the Honorable Secretary of War, asking that my appointment be not revoked and that I have time to prepare.

I therefore ask Your Excellency to direct that my appointment as Second Lieutenant in the Twentieth Infantry, being dated the 8th of May, 1867, be revised and not revoked, and that I may delay my examination before the Louisville Board for three months from this date. I am further recommended in this matter by Generals Rousseau and Meade.

Trusting that the generosity of this request may not be incompatible with the interests of the public service.

I remain Your Obd. Servt.

William Magee[18]

Written in a much neater hand than any of Willie's previous letters, the letter was handed to Andrew Johnson, and, after meeting with Marcus Ward, President Johnson directed the secretary of war to direct "a second examination in this case," and signed the memo, "Andrew Johnson."[19] Drummer boy McGee returned to New Jersey, and within days a Ward-induced arrangement was reached where Willie was sent to live with the Trenton superintendent of schools, Elias Cook, to be tutored by Cook and a Professor Elijah Apgar, who also lived with Cook.[20] Nobody seemed to notice the untruths of Willie's early letters, especially regarding his family. President Johnson surely was privy to the Stanton letter and the question might also be asked, if Willie McGee was willing at eighteen to lie to the secretary of war and the president, to what else might he succumb? Cook and Apgar did their job well, and Willie McGee was apparently an able student. Marcus Ward sent the young hero back to Louisville armed with the following:

Executive Office
Trenton, New Jersey
September 13, 1867
Sir:

I have read, and take pleasure in endorsing the statement of Prof. Apgar in his letter to you of September 13, 1867, in relation to Lieutenant William McGee. The young man has shown remarkable energy in pursuing his studies here, and I have the testimony of Elias Cook, Esq. of this city, a gentleman of the highest respectability, and in whose family young McGee has resided, that he has found him in all respects a most worthy and exemplary young man. I heartily commend him to favorable consideration.

Very respectfully yours

Marcus Ward[21]

On September 21, Willie sat for his second-chance examination and wrote once again his background paper. The effects of his New Jersey tutoring are evident:

Louisville, Ky. Sept. 20, 1867
Brevet Brigadier Genl Cady
President of Examining Board,
    General:
        I have the honor to submit herewith my military history:
On the 28th of July, 1863, I was mustered in to the U.S. service in Co. "C,"
33rd Regt N.J. Vols. The Regiment was soon after ordered to Washington D.C.
and thence with the 12th Army Corps: to reinforce Genl Rousseau at Chattanooga. I was in the engagement at Lookout Mountain, Missionary Ridge, and
the assault on Murfreesboro in the latter fight Dec. 8, 1864 for leading a charge
and capturing two pieces of artillery from the enemy. I was awarded under
order of Congress, July 12, 1862 a "Medal of Honor" by the Secretary of War.
I was honorably discharged at close of war, July 17, 1865.

                                    With great respect yours,
                                    William McGee[22]

President Andrew Johnson gave Willie
McGee a rare second opportunity for an
officer's commission after a personal interview with the eighteen-year-old ex-drummer
boy (U.S. Army Military History Institute).

The examination session followed, Willie performed to the satisfaction of the five officers on the board, and his appointment was finally secured. After five months in New Jersey, including a side trip to Washington, D.C., the new 2nd lieutenant, William Henry McGee, continued to surprise by, incredibly, going immediately to Muskegon, Michigan, and Holmes Pattison.[23] Despite all the work done by his fellow Jerseyans, there was no celebration with his family, no appreciative dinner for Ward, Cook, or Apgar. Not one letter of appreciation to Ward or anyone connected with the governor can be found in the Marcus Ward Collection at either the New Jersey Historical Society or the Alexander Library at Rutgers. From Muskegon, on October 4, Lieutenant McGee confirmed his appointment:

Muskegon, Mich. Oct. 4, 1867
Genl U.S. Grant
Secty of War
    Genl I have just recd my appointment as a second lieutenant in the 20th
Regiment of Infantry in the service of the United States, dated September 25th,
1867 (now 9 o'clock A.M. Oct. 4, 1867).
    It gives me great pleasure to say that I accept the said appointment, and
enclose herewith the required oath. My age is twenty-one years, my birthplace
is Newark, N.J. My permanent residence is Muskegon, Michigan.
                                    Yours Respectfully
                                    William McGee
                                    2nd Lieut 20th Infantry[24]

    With this simple letter of acceptance, Will McGee is on the threshold
of an incredible future. The fact that he has lied again about his age, this
time to a general, indeed the next president, U.S. Grant, seems a minor matter, but it is becoming a pattern. For the moment it was forgotten, but not
by everybody. An unidentified paymaster somewhere in the bureaucracy
alerted Asst. Adjutant General John Kelton of questions and discrepancies
regarding the new lieutenant from New Jersey, or Michigan, named McGee,
or Magee. A memo was sent to Willie and he responded to some obvious
questions:

Oct. 15 Muskegon, Mich
To the Adjt Genl U.S.A.
    Sir — In reply to your note of the 10th inst. I would say that I was born on
the 13th day of April 1846 at Newark New Jersey. My age is 21 years last birthday. My place of residence when appointed is Muskegon, Michigan. My full
name correctly written is William McGee.
                    I am sir very respectfully
                        Your obt servt
                            William McGee 2nd Lieut 20th Infty, USA[25]

    Simultaneously, the army conducted a check of the muster rolls of the
33rd New Jersey Infantry.[26] Though nothing major turned up, official army
rolls showed that there was no William McGee, or even Magee. The army
determined that the spelling on Willie's enlistment papers read "Megee." They
did, however, admit that the Medal of Honor read "Magee." Kelton, the assistant adjutant general, was concerned enough to order a hearing in Louisville,
and once again Willie McGee was summoned to the Board of Military Examiners. The memorandum from Kelton, on October 21, is direct and forceful,
and all points of emphasis are Kelton's:

                    War Department
                    Adjutant Generals Office
                    Washington City, D.C October 21, 1867

Memorandum

William Magee (formerly of Newark, 33rd N.J. Vols.) accepted an appoint-ment of 2nd Lieut 20th Infantry, May 16, '67, reporting the date of his birth as May 13, 1849. (18 years of age)

He appeared before the Board at Louisville, failed the examination and his appointment was cancelled May 28, '67. On the 20 June 67, he addressed the President, and an application for reexamination was ordered, and a letter authorizing him to appear before the Board at Louisville, on or before Septem-ber 21, 1867. This was given to Wm McGee who reported his age to be "twenty one."

The discrepancies both in the name and in the age, reported in the accept-ances of the first & second appointments having been noticed, a letter was sent calling upon him for the date of his birth. The answer to this McGee reports his date of birth as April 13, 1846, whereas Magee stated his to have been May 13, 1849.

This seemed to prove not only that the parties are different persons, but also leads to the belief that the appointment given to Wm Magee had been fraudu-lently disposed of to one Wm McGee and it is therefore recommended that McGee (the party holding appointment) be ordered to the Adjutant General, and that failing to prove himself the person to whom the appointment was given, that the appointment be cancelled. It is also suggested that the paymaster general be directed to suspend all payments to Liut. McGee.

Respectfully submitted to the Adjutant General

John Kelton, Asst Adj General[27]

The orders were given and the hearing was held at Louisville in Novem-ber, and by this time Willie McGee could be excused if he wondered whether the reward for his bravery in Tennessee was worth the effort. But Willie, fac-ing the board for the third time, gave a simple but dazzling performance, blaming several famous people, including Congressman Lovell Rousseau and President Andrew Johnson, without one ounce of blame on himself:

Ques. How do you spell your name?

Ans. William McGee

Ques. What is your exact age as near as you can give it?

Ans. I was born on the 13th of April 1847, so recorded in our family bible.

Ques. In your first examination, and in your letter of acceptance of May 16, 1867, you signed your name as "Magee"; explain why you followed this mode of your spelling?

Ans. I do not know why until I was at the time looking at my letter of appointment as it was written as "Magee' and I supposed it should be written the same way by me.

Ques. In your application for a re-examination you also used the same spelling; how did that happen?

Ans. When I went to see the President about getting an appointment to West Point he said that all the appointments were full. He told General Rousseau that he would give me three or six months to go to school to prepare for a

re-examination before the Board, and he said to send in an application making the request and he [President Johnson] would direct the Secy of War to
extend the time. Genl Rousseau requested Mr. Dodd submit the application,
who he [Genl Rousseau] dictated it — Mr. Dodd signed my name to it.

Ques. In your letter of May 16th, to the Adjutant General, and your letter for
re-examination you state your age to be eighteen years. How do you account
for the discrepancies?

Ans. I told in General Rousseau's letter the year I was born in, and I do not
think it was my mistake, as I am certain I told him 1847. My letter was
written from Louisville, Ky., May 16, 1867 was written by Genl R.W. Johnson, who made the mistake in regards to my age. I signed that as "Magee,"
but I cannot account for it further than I have already given. The same
explanation holds as to my signature to the oath of office, dated May 16,
1867.

Ques. In your letter of October 4, 1867, you state your age as twenty-one, and
in that of October 15, 1867, you say you were born April 13, 1867. How do
you account for this discrepancy?

Ans. I did say that I was near twenty-one to Mr. Pattison who wrote the letters.
In the first one he stated that I was twenty-one. In the second one he gave
the date of my birth as born in April 13, 1846, which error he committed, as
I am certain I told him 1847.

I would further state that as I have used the assistance of others in my
communications with the Board and the Adj. General. I am sure that the
discrepancies as regards my age and name I have explained.[28]

Willie McGee may have learned a lot from his tutoring in Trenton, but
the lessons he learned in deflecting all blame before the Board of Military
Examiners was either in the genes or learned on the streets of Newark. Five
senior career officers, trained to ferret out the suspicious and the untrue, did
not hesitate before rendering the following decision: "The Board deems it
proper to say that in its opinion McGee has had no purpose at any time to
give an incorrect statement in regards his name or age, but that the discrepancies noted have arisen in great part from his inexperience."[29] As Christmas
1867 approached, there is no record that Willie McGee, all decked out in his
new officer's uniform, and alone in his quarters in Baton Rouge, ever quietly
reflected on the last two glorious years of his young life. But even if he had,
Willie McGee could never have predicted how life could turn on a dime, even
for a hero.

CHAPTER NINE

Prison

> If you are going to live life on your own terms,
> there need to be terms,
> and somehow you need to live up to them.
> — Spenser, Private Detective
> (Robert Parker, *Back Story*)

In one of the many ironies of Willie McGee's young life, General E.D. Townsend, the assistant adjutant general, approved and signed Willie's General Court Martial papers on April 9, 1869.[1] Three years before, Townsend approved and signed McGee's Medal of Honor application.[2] This time, Townsend's signature sent Willie to the Louisiana State Penitentiary for five years. In addition to the "nickel" hard time, the court-martial papers expressly stated that Second Lieutenant William McGee, 20th U.S. Infantry, "accordingly ceases to be an officer of the Army from the date of this order."[3] In years to come, McGee would use extreme selective memory not only of this statement but also of the admission by his attorney, Andrew Herron, regarding the army's right to try him. Herron, at the court-martial, said, "It is conceded that you [the Army] are trying him, not for the same offence, but for another offence growing out of the same act."[4]

Why did the paperwork incarcerating Willie take so long? There can be no question the military brass was being very careful with imprisoning a Medal of Honor soldier, especially one with political heavyweights in his corner. The Bureau of Military Justice studied the case for a full month before completing its review on January 22, 1869, in Washington. To the surprise of nobody, Marcus Ward had another chip to play. None other than the army's top legal officer, Judge Advocate General Joseph Holt, conducted the bureau review. Holt was no lightweight and was a major figure before, during, and after the Civil War. In September 1862, Abraham Lincoln named him the nation's first Judge Advocate General of the Army. Holt was an extreme opponent of slavery, and very loyal to Lincoln and the cause of the Union.

General Holt investigated disloyalty in the North throughout the war for Secretary of War Edwin Stanton, and after Lincoln was assassinated Holt joined with Stanton in calling for prosecution of the conspirators. The Lincoln trial, with Joseph Holt as the lead prosecutor, was over by July 1865 and eight conspirators were found guilty and four hanged, including Mary Surratt, the first woman executed in American history. Holt stayed in office until 1875 and died in 1894.[5] Joseph Holt was not to be trifled with, and his review was thorough, professional, and complete. He handled the case himself, not giving it to an assistant and signing off on it later. Each witness's testimony was highlighted and often quoted. Holt's understanding of the case seems fair and objective, and the report itself is twenty pages long, with no wasted editorializing.[6] The only real surprise was in the beginning of the review, and it has the fingerprints of Marcus Ward, the ultimate, some would say typical, New Jersey politician all over it.

On page four, immediately after outlining the charges and specifications against McGee, Holt opened his case review with a letter from General Robert C. Buchanan, the civilian commander of the Department of Louisiana from January 1868 to January 1869.[7] Robert Christie Buchanan was a political hack who would not have known Willie McGee if he had been his own orderly. A nephew by marriage of President John Quincy Adams, Buchanan was an 1830 graduate of West Point and most famous for forcing U.S. Grant to resign from the army in 1854. In another of many amazing interactions between the famous and powerful in the life of Willie McGee, Robert Buchanan had the nerve to fire Ulysses Grant from the U.S. Army for being "under the influence"— not drunk — during a payroll disbursement in 1854; then fourteen years later in an empty suit job in Reconstruction Louisiana, he defended and asked for clemency for Willie McGee, a man he most likely never met, who murdered an unarmed doctor and was cashiered from the service.[8]

Grant, a man's man, never forgave the patrician mentality of his old enemy and felt it was the military softness of men like Buchanan which caused the war to be so needlessly prolonged. Grant, and others like him (Kearny and Sherman to name two), decried the fact that politicians and the socially prominent became military leaders and then led men into battle like politicians.[9] Buchanan always held high positions of little worth, among them commander of the Fort Delaware POW post, and then later the commander of New Orleans, from 1864 to the war's end in 1865, a city which had been under Union control since 1862.[10] Robert Christie Buchanan was not a mover or shaker, but he was in the loop of people who were.

Buchanan approved the verdict of Willie's court-martial — he had no jurisdiction or choice — but nonetheless said to ask the Bureau of Military Justice, "In consideration of the youth and inexperience of the accused, and of the testimonials appended to the record, as to his good conduct in the field during the war ... I have the honor to recommend him no imprisonment and the clemency of the Executive."[11] Somebody got to

Judge Advocate General Joseph Holt was one of the few men in power not to fall for the McGee charm. Holt reviewed Willie's court-martial and pardon requests, and was both times convinced McGee was lucky to receive only five years; he recommended against a pardon (author collection).

Robert Buchanan, and it would not have been someone low on the food chain of the Republican Party. No widowed Irish domestic servant from Newark; no brother or sister in Connecticut or New Jersey; no officer in the Baton Rouge Post — with the exception of Sykes or Carncross, and it wouldn't be them based on their previous testimony; not even Holmes Pattison, the attorney and minister from Muskegon; none would have the standing for Buchanan to recommend — in effect — an overturning of the verdict for a young man he had never met. This effrontery has all the earmarks of Marcus Ward, the New Jersey governor and a chairman of President Grant's reelection campaign. In later letters by Ward himself, even some of the exact phrasing used by Buchanan becomes mantras Ward will use to assist and enable McGee for years.[12]

Holt opens his review with the charges and the testimonials before swiftly getting to the meat of the case. After weighing all the evidence, in what amounts to a third trial, including Willie's self-defense statement and the acknowledgement that Willie had been tried and acquitted of manslaughter by a civil court, Holt terminated the inquiry and arrived at the following conclusions:

> It will be seen that the only fact offered during the trial which tends in the slightest degree to sustain accused's theory of defence, namely the accidental discharge of the pistol in his hands, is the lodging of a few grains of powder under the skin of the palm of his left hand. This fact cannot in the opinion of this Bureau, outweigh the proofs that establish the deliberate character of his crime. This is shown by unrefuted testimony to have borrowed a pistol immediately before the homicide; to have remarked to a brother officer that he intended to kill Dr. Braman; to have gone to the latter's room at once, armed with a cowhide and the borrowed pistol; to have assaulted Dr. Braman with the first named weapon, and then to have shot him with the pistol in the back, as he rose from his chair to escape the blows of the cowhide.[13]
>
> The testimony of the colored servant, who saw the homicide through the window, is confirmed by the place and direction of the bullet; to have entered Dr. Braman's back near the spine and ranged upward; stopping under the skin of the breast nearly a foot higher, as it is testified by the surgeon.... So far, moreover, from the accused having made to suppose that Dr. Braman was in a condition to resist his attack, it is shown that the pistols belonging to the latter were not only not in sight, but were shut in and put away, in a drawer opposite to, and distant by the width of the room, from the mantle place towards which Dr. Braman turned when rising from his chair.[14]
>
> So convincing [said the man who prosecuted John Wilkes Booth's coconspirators] are the elected proofs of McGee's intent to murder, so utterly feeble his defence, that it is felt that to punish by mere dismissal from the service a crime so heinous, would be a mockery of justice, which would encourage, rather than tend to check, the perpetration of similar acts of violence in the future. It is therefore advised that the sentence be enforced to its full extent. [A note from Holt is attached at the bottom of the review.] A letter from the father of the murdered man, which was referred to the Bureau by the Adjutant General of the Army in December last, is respectfully returned with this report.[15]

When Holt's signature was dry, it was passed to General Townsend, and it appeared the shooting and killing of Dr. Chandler Braman on August 15, 1868, had come to its final legal conclusion. Willie McGee, who gave Chandler Braman one shot, was himself given three shots at justice; now he walked in chains from the post brig in the barracks to the downtown state penitentiary. But he wasn't there long. Willie was transferred almost the day he arrived and sent to the federal prison in Stillwater, Minnesota, 1,000 miles away, even though the verdict called for him to be imprisoned in the Louisiana State Prison.[16] If General George Sykes truly appreciated the bind Willie

McGee was in, he may have transferred McGee to Minnesota to save his life. A Yankee held in a Louisiana prison during Reconstruction would not last long. For whatever reason, Willie became a resident of Minnesota in April 1869.[17]

Stillwater, sitting on the west bank of the St. Croix River, just northeast of Minneapolis, was more than remote. When Minnesota was accepted as a state just twenty years previously, in 1848, Stillwater had high hopes of becoming the state capital, but all the lumber and mill town got was the first Minnesota prison. When McGee arrived in April, there was room for 158 convicts, but it was only at half capacity.[18]

Entering his cell, William McGee could be forgiven if he shuddered at more than the Minnesota weather. All cells were alike in their discomfort. The disgraced ex-lieutenant had grown to 5' 8" and he, like all the prisoners, felt the isolation a 5 × 7 foot room offered. McGee's cell had a bed, a washstand with one piece of soap, a basin, a spoon, a water jug, and one wooden chair. Near the floor was a small closet, large enough to hold a small commode. For the next five years this would be Willie's home. If the cell was depressing, the lifestyle was much worse. This was 1869, and prison life was vastly different from the real or imagined routine of the present. There were no weight rooms, lawyer visits, or conjugal visits.[19]

The seventy-two prisoners, when Willie received his standard issue zebra suit, would arise at 5:30 A.M. and have breakfast and coffee at 6:00 A.M. Each prisoner would be served food in tin plates, then they had to be at their assigned workplace at 6:30. They would stay at work until 6:00 P.M. with only a half hour of lunch in between. Dinner was served only with water, and after a half hour of eating in total silence, all prisoners would return to their "rooms" for the night. The social life was simple — one letter sent per week, one visitor a month.[20]

But "hard time" meant more than hard work. The rules at Stillwater were spelled out in capital letters and enforced stringently. Isolation and arduous work were difficult but expected by anyone sentenced to time in a federal prison. Few first timers however, would be prepared for what they faced in Stillwater. There would be two distinct sets of rules, the first regarding the dining hall, the other general discipline. It might be difficult for the modern reader to fathom that the following rules were not only adopted but also enforced. Regarding general discipline, there were eight main rules, three of which were as follows:

1. You must observe strict silence in all departments of the prison while marching through the yard.
2. You must not speak to, give or receive from visitors anything except by

permission of the Warden or Deputy Warden. Gazing at visitors or strangers passing through the prison is strictly forbidden.

3. You must approach an officer in a respectful manner. Always salute him before speaking. You must confine your conversation with him strictly to the business at hand. You must not address an officer on matters outside the prison. Insolence in any form will not be tolerated.[21]

Though corporal punishment was prohibited, the following are a dozen of the principal offenses for which prisoners could be reported:

1. Talking in chapel
2. Talking in line
3. Talking in school
4. Talking at work
5. Talking from cell to cell
6. Talking in corridor
7. Laughing and fooling
8. Staring at visitors
9. Hands in pockets
10. Impertinence to visitors
11. Communicating by signs
12. Loud reading in cells[22]

The Dining Hall rules were just as demanding.

1. On entering the dining hall take your seat promptly — position erect — arms folded, with eyes to the front until the signal is given to commence eating.
2. Strict silence must be observed during the meal.
3. Eating or drinking before or after the gong sounds, using vinegar in your drinking water, or putting meat on the table, is prohibited.
4. Crusts and small pieces of bread must not be left on your plate.
5. In passing to and from the dining hall, you must not gaze into cells or loiter on the gallery. Walk erect with eyes to the front. It is strictly against the rules to carry out any of the dining hall furnishings or to carry out food to or from the dining hall at any time except on Sundays and holidays, when you will be allowed to carry lunch to your cell for the evening meal.[23]

Whoever was responsible for sending Willie McGee to the Stillwater Federal Prison surely meant him to be punished. It is therefore no surprise the transfer had to shock McGee both physically and mentally. Since he had left New Jersey to fight in the war as a fourteen-year-old, he had spent time in Tennessee, Louisiana, New Jersey, and seven spring and summer months in lower Michigan. But being ensconced in the frigid North Country, living behind fourteen-foot stone walls with no family, friends, or even acquaintances was hard, and meant to be.

Days after arriving in Minneapolis and making the short trip to Stillwater, Willie reverted to what he knew best, and befriended, or attempted to, the prison chaplain, Edward Wright. A native of Ohio, Wright was descended from two generations of country preachers, and was ordained in the Presbyterian order at age twenty-nine.[24] The Murfreesboro routine worked with Wright temporarily, as the reverend sent the following note to Methodist minister Holmes Pattison in Michigan, on May 4, 1869:

A lithograph circa 1870 of the Stillwater Prison, home to the court-martialed William H. McGee in April 1869 (Minnesota Historical Society).

Dear Sir:

Lieutenant McGee, who is now in confinement at the Minnesota State Prison, at this place, desires me to write to you and inform you of the result of his trial by court-martial. He is sentenced for five years. His opportunities for writing are limited, but he will soon write and give you particulars and get you to collect money due him.

He desires to have you write him a long letter and also to hear from his mother. Any favors that I can extend to him consistent with the discipline of the Prison shall be gladly rendered.

In writing to him direct to the

Minnesota State Prison
Stillwater, Minnesota

Respectfully yours

Edw B Wright
Chaplain of State Prison[25]

This would be the first and last correspondence from the Reverend Wright regarding Willie McGee. Wright remained in Stillwater for several more years, but there was no apparent continued connection with Willie. Perhaps he resigned the prison job, or maybe he gave up any relationship with McGee, but by 1875 Rev. Wright would move to Austin, Texas, where he preached the gospel for more than thirty-five years.[26]

Looking at the letter itself, there are hints one may draw about Willie's last six months. Holmes Pattison was well aware of the civil trial, and according to one of General Sykes' letters, Pattison was thinking of attending the trial in person, but did not, and it appears in Wright's letter that Willie had not been in any contact with his adoptive father since the civil trial ended in late November.[27] In the entangled web of McGee's family life, it is now certain that Holmes Pattison knew of Willie's mother, Margaret, but no correspondence survives. His brothers' and sister's very existence and names are not mentioned except in the letter to Secretary of War Stanton in May 1867, and then falsely.[28] Third, Willie requests — or will soon request — money "due him," a theme which will recur as long as McGee lives. Lastly, in what would become another familiar tactic, Willie had someone else write for him; when he did so they were usually chaplains.[29]

Could Willie McGee, the twenty-year-old federal prisoner, survive such a life, even for the relatively short period of five years? Surely it would not be easy, but it might be exactly what he needed the most. Though the prison was infamous for bedbugs for decades, and while talking was forbidden except on holidays, this very isolation and silence might be just what the personable, deceitful, alcohol loving Medal of Honor recipient unconsciously craved. Warden Henry Jackman, writing in 1872, knew the absence of alcohol was crucial. "Nine tenths of the crimes which sent men to this prison are the direct or indirect consequences of liquor," said Jackman.[30] Five years off the bottle had to help McGee, and might be the jumpstart Willie would need to overcome his self-denial in the shooting of Chandler Balch Braman; and five years of relative silence might direct the obvious outward charm our hero possessed into inner strength and maturity. We do not have any idea what the Reverend Pattison thought of his adopted son, but the silence was deafening. After behaving like the ultimate pushy stage parent, Pattison remained quiet, at least for a while. The Rev. Wright's letter was unsuccessful, for on September 14, almost ten months after the criminal trial ended in acquittal, another chaplain, the Reverend Robert Langley, wrote again to Holmes.

Stillwater, September 14,
Dear Sir
    I am requested by Lieut Wm McGee of the U.S. Army; he has not I think written to you of his present circumstances and asks me to say to you that, he is contented with his lot as far as he can be under the circumstances; he had some

difficulty with a brother officer and accidentally his friend died. He was tried by a jury in a civil court and acquitted; and then tried by a court martial and sentenced to the State Prison for five years! (I think). He is in good health and spirits and feels it is right he should suffer some for his errors; and hopes when a proper time has been spent in suffering that efforts will be made by which he will be pardoned, and seems to be seeking an interest in the atonement of his Redeemer; for he is a gentleman even in prison. I hope you will write to him or me and encourage him all you can as he thinks much of you.

When you write address him at Stillwater, Minnesota; care of the warden of the Prison or to my care

> I am Dear Sir
> Respectfully yours
> R Langley
> Chaplain State Prison[31]

Willie had apparently still not heard from anyone, and had been behind bars since Christmas 1868. Contradictions abound. It was the first time Willie had shown any signs of remorse, though the words are Langley's, not McGee's. On the other hand, his lack of honesty regarding the shooting of Braman continued. "Had some difficulty with a brother officer and accidentally his friend died," is not very remorseful.[32] Was Willie milking another chaplain, or just ecumenically attached to them all? Robert Langley was, unlike Wright, an elderly man of 70, who like Pattison had been a chaplain in the war.[33] All three were Protestant, each a different denomination.

It seemed the now twenty-year-old is in good health, and it was more than possible the ten months without alcohol had served him well. This second letter from a prison chaplain appeared to have penetrated Holmes Pattison's paternal — or whatever — instincts. Perhaps it was the religious tone, or maybe it was Willie not mentioning money, but on September 28, 1869, two weeks after Langley's letter, Langley sent another to Holmes, and there is definite movement in the affairs of Willie McGee.

Dear Sir

Enclosed please find proceeding in the court martial in which Lieutenant William McGee was tried, and sentenced. I have said nothing to him about your letter; and hope you will write him soon, as I know he is very anxious to hear from you and your Lady whom he loves much.

> Please write him
> I am deare Sir
> Yours Respectfully
> R Langley
> Chaplain of the Prison[34]

Pattison had at least written to Langley and obviously asked for the court-martial papers. He had also told Langley not to let Willie know about his letter. Across the country, the Braman family did not want to hear about Willie's adjustments to prison. While McGee was reaching out to Pattison — and presumably others — the Bramans were searching for peace, peace they would never and could never have again. Dr. Isaac Braman wrote to General Townsend in October, asking for "a full copy of all the evidence taken at a Court Martial, convened at Baton Rouge, La. For the trial of 2nd Lieutenant Wm McGee, who murdered my son the late C.B. Braman, on the 15th of August, 1868."[35] Dr. Braman was in possession of the case review by Joseph Holt. Now he was working backward for as much information as he could get. Braman's request worked its way rather swiftly up the Army chain, and the Bramans had their paperwork by mid–November, just about the same time Willie McGee heard from Governor Marcus Ward of New Jersey.

Holmes Pattison and Marcus Ward may have done much before, during, and after the trials to assist Willie, but once he was sent to prison all communication from them stopped for almost a year. Each man separately was charmed and manipulated in one way or another by young Will McGee, but now, in November 1869, Marcus Ward stepped out of the shadows:

> Newark, NJ Nov 29, 1869
>
> Lieut William McGee
>
> Dear Sir:
>
> I have heard of your misfortune and most heartily regret that you have been in so much trouble. I have looked into the matter somewhat at Washington — and am anxious to hear your story concerning the transaction for which you are suffering punishment. I feel a deep interest in your welfare — your brave and glorious career in the war commends you to the admiration of any house of this country and I am desirous of doing all in my power to help you out of your difficulty.
>
> Tell me the whole story — just how it all happened —<u>Of course you will tell me the truth.</u> If I find upon reading your letter, as I have no doubt I will, that the circumstances would justify me in laying the case before the President and asking his clemency I will surely do so — meanwhile take the best of care of yourself <u>attend faithfully to your duties.</u>
>
> As opportunity occurs study hard and fit yourself for the duties of life when you leave your present place. Keep up your courage do not dispond —
>
> If your statement compounds with my understanding of the case, they would not think anything less of you for having been imprisoned.
>
> Truly Yours
>
> Marcus Ward[36]

Opposite: "Of course you will tell me the truth," were the words of Marcus Ward to McGee in this November 29, 1869, letter. This was the first contact Marcus Ward had with Willie McGee in over a year (New Jersey Historical Society Archives).

Newark N J Nov 29. 1869

Lin William McGee,

Dear Sir:

I have heard of your mis-
fortune and most heartily regret that you
have been in so much trouble — I have
looked into the matter somewhat at Washington — and am anxious to hear your story
concerning the transaction for which you are
suffering punishment — I feel a deep
interest in your welfare — your brave
and glorious career in the war commends you
to the admiration of every honest hearted Country,
and I am desirous of doing all in my power
to help you out of your difficulty.

Tell me the whole story — just how it
all happened — Of course you will tell me
the truth. If I find upon reading your
letter, as I have no doubt I will, that the
circumstances would justify me in laying
the case before the President and asking
his clemency I will surely do so — meanwhile take the best of care of yourself attend
faithfully to every duty. As opportunity occurs
study hard and fit yourself for the duties
of life when you leave your present
place. keep up your courage do not
dispond — If your statement corresponds with my understanding of the case, the
world will not think any thing less of you
for having been imprisoned —

Truly your &c

Marcus L Ward

Could Ward's letter to Willie, coming on the heels of Langley's letter to Pattison, be just a coincidence? It appears so, but the timing for Willie could not have been more serendipitous. In 1869, four years after meeting Willie in New Jersey, Marcus Ward opened the door himself.

There are still many questions about Willie McGee, but as Christmas approached in 1869 in the cold state of Minnesota, the wonderment is why the Governor of New Jersey would be willing to go to the president of the United States on the word of a twenty year old convicted murderer, a young man to which he had only recently made acquaintance. We await McGee's response to Ward's entreaty, "Tell me the whole story — just how it happened.... Of course you will tell me the truth."[37]

Willie McGee was many things, but he was not, at twenty years, an innocent. If he could sell Marcus Ward, Ward would go to the top to gain McGee's freedom. One wonders at the gullibility of Marcus Ward, who had read each of the court verdicts, including the review by Joseph Holt, a political friend of some years. Whatever charms Willie McGee possessed, they were considerable, and Marcus Ward is the proof. This promised carrot of assistance by Ward was just what the convict William McGee needed to return to society, a society that pampered and enabled our young Irish-American. Unfortunately, it might also have been the worst thing that could happen to Co. C drummer Willie McGee — the young man filled with immaturity, denial, and anger, who may have needed the five years of prison to grow and change into the strong adult so many people had predicted for him not so many years before.

Willie wasted no time responding to the opening given him by Marcus Ward. McGee, after a year of apparent abandonment by family and friends, was given an early Christmas present he could never have imagined. Though allowed by prison regulations to write one letter a week, it seems Willie had either chosen to tell nobody of his plight or his entreaties had fallen on deaf ears. After trying unsuccessfully for months to get the attention of his adoptive father, and not even telling his own mother, two brothers, or sister what had become of him, Willie woke up one bitter Minnesota December morning and was handed a letter with an offer too good to refuse from one of the most powerful political presences in the United States.[38] This influential ex-governor, who had just left office, was one of the prime campaign leaders in the Ulysses S. Grant drive to the presidency.[39] Not only would Grant be on a first name basis with Marcus Ward, but every leading Republican in Washington would also recognize and respect the word of Marcus Ward. The Republicans, make no mistake, were totally in charge.

When Marcus Ward told Willie McGee, in writing, that he would go straight to the president for clemency if Willie told him "the truth," it would not be an idle boast. Ward added, "I am desirous of doing all in my power to help you out of your difficulty."[40] Why Ward would go to such measures is unknown, but Willie McGee, behind very cold iron bars, didn't care about why, only how. Could McGee convince Marcus Ward? Willie, just before Christmas 1869, gave it his best effort, and never let the truth get in the way of his goal. In reality, it would not take much to reel in Marcus Ward, because New Jersey's most powerful man handed him the rod. After reading McGee's version of an August in Louisiana, a version which would become Willie's standard for the rest of his life, it is clear that while he may have been awarded the Medal of Honor for heroism on the battlefield, he would never be awarded medals for moral heroism:

Stillwater Dec. 16th, 1869
To His Excellency
      Marcus Ward
        Dear Sir:
    In answer to your letter I would state that late on the evening of the 15th day of August 1868 Gen. Sykes commanding officer sent for me and exhibited a note which note accused me of forgery and theft on Lieut. Clark of the 20th Regt. U.S.A. he also informed me that the note was in the handwriting of the acting assistant Surgeon and that he, Brayman had placed it in the hands of an irresponsible person as a detective and that he had placed the paper in the hands of the Mayor of the city of Baton Rouge. General Sykes also informed me that it was known in the town and was, or would be a town gossip attacking my good name and character. I of course, became indignant and exasperated and I went to him for an explanation, showed him the note and asked him if he had written it. He said he had. I then drew a small cowhide and undertook to chastise him when he raised and turned towards his revolver and said McGee I will make short work of you. I of course drew my revolver in self defence, while in the act of holding it in my left hand with both of my hands the pistol discharged not intending but accidentally shattering my left hand badly. Previous to this I went to Gen. Sykes and asked him to give his advice as I was young and inexperienced and did not know how to proceed in such matters. He told me it was a personal difficulty between Dr. Brayman and myself, that he being my commanding officer he could not give me any advice but he knew what he would do if a gentleman and an officer should attack him in that manner. I went to other brother officers and asked them what I should do and they told me that they would certainly inflict chastisement upon him, if I had the proof that he had accused me of such conduct. I said I had the proof and went back to Gen. Sykes for the note which he gave me and on my second return to Gen. Sykes he told me to give him the note as he wanted to take steps in the matter himself. He also informed me that he had a conversation with Lieut. Clark that he asked Clark if I had ever forged an order on him, he Clark said My God! No, but that he gave an order for me for five dollars which I owed him that Brayman had no grounds whatever to make such a statement. I was turned over to

the Civil Authorities by the proper military authorities and tried for manslaughter and acquitted by that tribunal.

After being acquitted by the civil court I reported to Gen. Sykes, who informed me that my life or liberty was in no further jeopardy though I would be tried by a military court as a matter of form as they would be governed by the proceedings of the civil court. I was then tried for "Riotous and disorderly conduct to the prejudice of good order and military discipline." And the same testimony was introduced on which I had been previously acquitted, and sentenced to be dismissed from the service of the U.S. Army and to be imprisoned in Military prison for five years. I asked Gen. Sykes as a witness on my trial what he meant by telling me he knew what he would do if an officer or gentleman had insulted him as I had been. He replied that he meant he would as officer and gentlemen usually did, that he would inflict a public disgrace or personal chastisement. Doctor Braheman or Brayman had got a private soldier to watch my movements and had him clean and load his pistols and told him that he anticipated trouble with me. He also directed him to listen when I was conversing with any fellow officer and inform him what I said, and if I approached his quarters to let him know and to be on hand as there would be probably be fun. I believe there was a conspiracy to gotten up by some enemy of mine. Dr. Brahman was in the habit of bullying other officers in a similar manner. At the time that this unfortunate affair occurred I was deeply engaged in study to qualify myself for the performance of my duty, with credit to myself and country, and in my young heart hoped to be an honor to my country, and show those noble men of the land like yourself and Gen. Thomas that their confidence in me had not been misplaced. I give you a copy of Gen. Thomas' letter to the Secy. Of War simply to show that he was desirous that I should be appointed in the army, that it would be advantageous to myself and support my widowed mother & educate my little brother & sister. As I failed in my first examination he wrote this letter to Secy Stanton requesting my appointment be not revoked and advised me to go to Gov. Ward as you know I did. I studied hard to pass the second examination and since I have been in the army I have received several letters from Gen. Thomas encouraging me to study hard, as he said my future looked bright. I think if Gen. Grant knew my past life he would not deprive a fatherless boy of that name earned so dearly. This is my first offence against any law, civil or military even to the trifling offence of a soldier. I would not have cared a particle had I not been advised by my brother officers to do as I did, and I knew that Dr. Brahman would use violence towards me and my safety depended on my being armed. Please send me the history of my life as published. Send it to the chaplain who will give it to me. Below find copy of Gen. Thomas letter to Secy Stanton.

Respectfully,

Wm McGee[41]

It does not sound as if Willie felt any longer "it is right he should suffer some for his errors." Willie had taken the offensive, and had left the "suffering and remorse" lessons of Rev. Langley a distant memory.[42]

Just in case, Willie took no chances with "His Excellency," and sent a follow-up note two days before Christmas. The letter, which purported to be from the Reverend Langley, was written by Willie in his own handwriting. A copy of the letter, written and dated the same day, is also found among Ward's papers.[43] Either Langley wrote the original and McGee copied it, or Willie wrote the first and Langley was the copier. The vocabulary and phrasing are without question McGee's, so it is difficult to believe the letter was Langley's idea. How both ended up with Ward is another matter. Langley was seventy at the time and a man who portrayed himself—accurately—as an unwell, poor preacher with a huge heart but little education.[44] The Methodist pastor did not even know Ward's name was Marcus, and wrote "William" in his version. The other copy, written by McGee, had the name Marcus correct, but is signed "Langly," not the correct "Langley." The Reverend's version was full of misspellings and though Willie was not a scholar, his writing was neater, generally spelled correctly, and legible. It is possible both men composed the note together, with Langley writing the original as Willie dictated the words. McGee easily may have realized the Reverend's version would not do, and copied it, signed Langley's name incorrectly, and sent both. In any case, the follow-up cannot have been more flattering to Willie McGee. In the chaplain's version it reads:

Stillwater, Dec. 23, 1869
To his Exclency William Ward
        Dere Sir,
    Having written the letter at the request of Lieutenant McGee, I now address you in my own name; and in his behalf McGee is a Gentleman of fine qualities and I think has been Treated badly and should be Pardoned out of the Prison where most of his associates are felons. It seems to me to be an unparaeled case in Military Law; havng bene in the army myself during the Late War I became somewhat acquainted with the Regulations of the army and I do most earnestly hope you will use your Influence with the President in his behalf. He is very industrious and faithfull young man and attends to his Duties Punctually, and is highly Estemed by all the officers at the Prison. I think if the President is mad acquainted with the fact that he had bene tried by the civil authoriety and acquitted and then by a Court martial he will pardon him out of it.
    Please send him the history of your State that is of the war.
                                    Yours Truly
                                    R Langley
                                    Chaplain of the Prison
P.S. I find that I have written your name William in Stead of Marcus. I had not your name written and hence the mistake.
                                    R. Langley[45]

Langley, though a poor writer, surely believed in Willie McGee, and he was working feverishly to gain an audience for his new friend. After sending the letter to Ward, he sent another to Holmes Pattison, fellow minister, and Willie's foster son:

Feb. 28, 1870
Stillwater, Minn
H.A. Pattison
        Dere Sir

    Lt McGee requests me to ask you if you have heard anything from Gov Ward or from the Department at Washington in relation to his case as he had heard nothing from you or Gov Ward. He is in good health and spirits, and is getting along very well in his present condition. He is respected by all the officers of the Prison as a steady and industrious man making the best of his condition.... I think he is a changed man.

                              I am Dere Sir
                              Very yours
                              Respectfully
                              R Langley
                              Prison Chaplain[46]

Marcus Ward, a very pious and religious man, was in possession on the New Year 1870, of a "true" confession of the poor victim, William McGee, and a most sincere and earnest plea from a man of God — the Reverend Langley — to believe in everything Willie says. But if Ward harbored any doubts whether he should further involve himself in the life of the supposed fatherless Newark drummer boy, fate stepped in again on the side of William McGee.

The Reverend Holmes Pattison, after more than a year of ignoring his adopted son, wrote to the powerful New Jersey politico and put the stamp of approval on the "Free McGee" parade. Had Pattison become convinced of his new son's innocence through his legal training, or had Christian charity and Holmes' religious background overcome his anger and disappointment of the past year? Maybe hearing from the two fellow ministers from Stillwater turned him around; or was it just a guilty conscience? Even more relevant than the letter of support to Ward, Holmes Pattison sent a package with every letter he has ever gotten in the past three years concerning Willie. Correspondence from Sykes, the military charges, Ward's own letters of recommendation, and of course the two pleas from the ministers at Stillwater. Pattison also played the legal angle, and sent it all with his professional letterhead:

H.A. PATTISON
ATTORNEY AT LAW, REAL ESTATE AGENT
and
U.S. COMMISSIONER
Muskegon, Mich.

March 21, 1870

Hon Marcus L Ward
New Ark, N.J.

Dear Sir. At the instance of Lieut. Wm McGee, I trouble you at this time, for the purpose of asking your aid in procuring for him a pardon at the hands of Prest. Grant. You know, I have no doubt the circumstances attending the confinement in the Minnesota State Prison. I have not the slightest doubt but that his conviction is the result of a second trial for the same offence to wit the shooting of Dr. Bramin at Baton Rouge La in Augst 1868. For this he was tried by the civil courts of the State of La & acquitted. He was subsequently tried by a Court martial & the result is imprisonment as stated.

I also send you the charges or rather a copy of the charges upon which he was tried by the Court Martial. I also send letters from Brevt. Maj Genl Sykes, Col 20th U.S Infty in relation to the whole transaction & his surrender to the civil authorities by order of Genl Buchanan at the time commanding the Dept of the Gulf. These letters were written at the time the unfortunate affair occurred, and put forth the worst features of the case, also McGee's letter as to trial & acquittal. Also letters of Chaplains of Prison as to his conduct since his confinement, hoping that they may be of some service.

His second trial, it strikes me was in violation of a very well settled principal of law, & in my judgment goes some ways towards jeopardizing the rights and liberties of citizens. As I regard the matter, as soon as he was surrendered to the civil authorities for trial, the Military Authorities relinquished all right to try the case, & the verdict of the jury in the civil court final. If the trial in the civil court had resulted in conviction, at the most all a court martial could have done, would have been to pronounce sentence of dismissal from the service, & that in my judgment would have been in view of *conviction* for an infamous crime, & not for the crime, but the civil court acquitting, should, it seems to me in all fairness have made an end of the whole matter. I take this interest in Lieut McGee 1st because I know the boy well. I took him from the very jaws of death in 1864 when as a drummer boy of the 33rd N.J. Infty Vols, he was in Hospital at Murfreesboro Tenn. I adopted him, having no children of my own. 2nd Knowing him as I do, I do not believe he would do an act of the kind in cold blood. 3rd I *know* him to be as brave a soldier as ever served a country & lastly because I am satisfied that his incarceration for crime is unjust.

Hopeing to hear from you at your earliest convenience I remain

Yours Truly

H.A. Pattison[47]

If Marcus Ward needed an ally, he now had one. Ward had an "innocent" young man's truthful story of victimization and slander, as well a man of God's word that our young victim was a great patriot deserving of freedom, and finally a professional lawyer/minister who was convinced our Medal of Honor hero had been railroaded by the United States Army. Thus armed to the teeth by the beauty of abused youth and a miscarriage of justice, Marcus Ward would do exactly what he promised Willie McGee the previous November when he wrote, "I am desirous of doing all in my power to help you out of your difficulty."[48] Marcus Ward was about to jump into the ring with both feet, and both hands swinging, for his fellow Newark hometown boy, Willie McGee.

CHAPTER TEN

The Push for Freedom

> Irish America is a story of many splendors.
> It is also a parable of shame about the past,
> of secrets kept to endure and deny that shame.
> — Maureen Dezell, *Irish America*
> *Coming into Clover*

After forming an alliance with Holmes Pattison, Marcus Ward began the push for a pardon.[1] Pattison's letter of March 21 no doubt took some days to arrive in New Jersey, but it did not sit long on Marcus Ward's desk, for on March 26, 1870, the former New Jersey governor sent a letter to McGee, and though it has not survived, it sent Willie's spirits soaring with anticipation. On June 9, Willie sent back a letter to the "soldier's friend." It is full of hope, anxiety, and, for the first time, some sensible maturity. McGee had by now been in Stillwater more than a year — a year with little or no alcohol, enabling, and pampering of a hero:

Stillwater Minn
       June 9, 1870
Hon M. L. Ward
       Newark N.J.
My Dear Sir.
    Your last favor to me of the date Mch 26th gave me such flattering hopes of a release from prison life that not until this last late day do I find myself attempting a reply to the generous sentiments contained therein. The delay has been occasioned by my having been anxiously waiting from day to day and week to week to see what might be the result of your application to the President.

Oh! My dear sir you cannot conceive what an agony of suspense I have experienced during that time, and yet not withstanding each successive day brought disappointment. I have been watching & hoping that the morrow might bring the long looked for glad tidings.

I am exceedingly anxious to know my fate whatever it is so that my mind may be at rest. When I came here I had no friends to do aught for me but thank God there are many here now who will do all in their power to obtain my release. Gov Austin was here a few days ago & had a long talk with me. He kindly offered his services to help me in every way he could & said he would write you & would cooperate with you in the matter. Perhaps you have had a letter from him by this time. He with the Warden [Webber] and other officers of the prison & the Contractors are all my friends & will do for me all they can, but of course they have not the influence at Washington you have & consequently their aid together cannot aid me so much as yours. Should all efforts fail to accomplish the desired end I shall not give up all hope nor despair but shall try to keep up my spirits and good courage till the last. I am applying myself to study as close as opportunity will possibly allow.

True my study moments are limited but I endeavor to derive a benefit from every spare moment & to write something in memory's page that may be of practical advantage to me in the future.

I regret most exceedingly that I have not more time in which to engage in the pursuit of knowledge. I begin to fully realize the many opportunities which I have had & that realization inspires me with a new degree of determined energy to make the future pay me a tenfold amount of knowledge for lost time now beyond reach. But my letter grows lengthy & I shall conclude by again saying that whatever may be the result of your efforts to help me I shall always know that you have done everything for me you possibly could. I shall hope to hear from you again as soon as your convenience will allow but shall I fear, be in a constant state of uneasiness & anxiety until that time arrives. Thanking you from the fullness of my heart for your multiplied kindnesses to me. I shall whatever fate awaits me remain ever

Your most grateful & obliging Servt
Wm Magee[2]

Clearly Marcus Ward pulled out all the stops. He wrote to Governor Horace Austin of Minnesota, and the governor trekked to his own prison and visited an inmate at length.[3] Austin did not send a staffer or even the lieutenant governor. The number one citizen was no doubt asked to personally attend McGee, and Austin appeared to have complied rather quickly. Once the governor paid his social call, it comes as no surprise that McGee mentioned that the Warden and other prison officials "are all my friends," and it certainly appears Willie had quickly evolved from just another convict to a semi-celebrity, almost overnight.[4]

Willie's response was intriguing. Did the incarcerated ex-lieutenant show true signs of maturity and personal growth, or did he once again reveal himself to be a master manipulator? At every stage of the game — since Tennessee -- he had reached out to men of the cloth, knowing they generally search for the goodness in every soul, and thus will fall for the "victim" ruse more often than not. This angle had worked to his advantage more than once and would continue to work for him for years. In the letter to Ward, was he playing on Ward's well-known love of education? Such phrasing as "I am applying myself to study as close as opportunity allows" and "I endeavor to derive a benefit from every spare moment.... I regret ... I have not had more time in which to engage in the pursuit of knowledge" paints a picture we have not heard or seen from Willie before.[5] Was he being honest, or was he telling Ward exactly what he believed the governor wanted to hear? Considering that for the past year Willie had worked in a prison job eleven hours a day in a striped prison suit, with lights out no later than 8:00 P.M., when and where would he have been he doing all this studying? Is it possible that the manipulation even extended to McGee signing his name "Magee" for the first time in years, simply because that was how the hero and Medal of Honor name was spelled?

Marcus Ward, an inherently compassionate man, could have easily sent Willie a positive, paternalistic letter, asked the local governor to visit as a favor and to write an obligatory politically correct letter to a bureaucrat in Washington, and feel he had done the right thing. Nobody, not even McGee, could possibly be upset if such was the case with Marcus Ward. The "soldier's friend" had done so much for so many, but Willie McGee was a hard case. This was not postage, nor a pension, nor even a burial. This was a convicted felon whose case had literally been heard three times. Despite his sincere promises, how much could Ward honestly do to help McGee? As it turned out — everything. On June 17, 1870, Marcus Ward wrote the following to Secretary of the Navy George Robeson in Washington. Robeson would be just one of the heavy hitters Ward used to try to free McGee. Republican Robeson was another son of New Jersey and the newly appointed secretary. He could be counted on to lend major support for any of Marcus Ward's plans:

Newark, N.J. June 17th, 1870
Hon. George M Robeson
    My dear Sir:
        When I last saw you in Washington you kindly consented to deliver into the hands of the Hon Secretary of War my petition for the release from prison of William McGee, now confined in the Minnesota State Prison. I now send you the papers in the case and beg you will immediately place them in Gen. Belknaps hands. I have no doubt the petition will receive the Secretarys favorable action, but if he should have doubts on the subject I beg he will not decide against me, so if he should decide adversely, it must be because I have

not properly laid the subject before him and I will
feel it to be my duty to
again visit Washington and
try and acquire the desired
object. I feel that the
young man has been
unduly punished, especially
when his extraordinary
services and gallantry are
taken into the account and
that every moment he is
detained in that horrid
prison under the circum-
stances of the case is a
wrong and an outrage
upon a poor and friendless,
but noble boy. Should his
release be granted the President and the Secretary will
have the thanks and gratitude of

Yours truly
Marcus Ward[6]

Minnesota governor Horace Austin personally visited Willie McGee twice in prison at the request of Marcus Ward, the New Jersey power broker. Austin helped pave the way for gentle treatment of the ex-lieutenant (Minnesota Historical Society).

If there was ever a question whether Marcus Ward was in this to win, that question was answered, and Willie McGee could not possibly realize how lucky he was. Governor Horace Austin on June 27 filled Ward in on his earlier visit. Austin told Marcus, "The warden has been informed of the interest you have taken in this case," and then the Minnesota governor added, "I am willing to do anything in my power to aid this man."[7] The coup de grace of Marcus Ward's power play was his petition to the secretary of war, William Belknap, referred to above. The seven page letter was a dangerous mixture of truths and half-truths, but it is forceful, passionate, and close to intimidating. In short, it was a powerful politician at his best and worst.

Newark N.J.   June 17th, 1870
Hon Wm. W. Belknap
     Secretary of War
My dear Sir:
     I beg leave respectfully to present to you most favorable consideration
the case of William McGee late Lieu 20th Regt U.S.A. now confined in the

Penitentiary at Stillwater in the State of Minnesota. I have carefully investigated the facts of the case and from the credible information acquired, and my own knowledge of the young man himself, am entirely satisfied that his pardon would be just and right. Aside from the unfortunate occurrence that resulted in his present imprisonment the history of the young man is a remarkable one and gives him, I think, the highest claims to executive clemency. The circumstances of the occurrence referred to were doubtless such as to expose him to merited censure, but it seems to me this criminality was greatly overestimated by the Military Court that tried him and that whatever criminality really existed has been amply atoned for in the punishment already inflicted.

He was born in this city. His early advantages were poor. At the age of 15 he enlisted in the 33rd Regt N.J. Vol. as a Drummer, leaving a widowed mother at home. His career was so striking, and meritorious, as to have gained for him an extended notice in the History of the New Jersey troops, which, since the close of the war, has been prepared and published by the authority of the State. It may be found in pages 857, 858, and 859 of that work. His conduct at Murfreesboro in leading two successive charges at the head of his Regiment, and capturing the enemy's guns and soldiers, was so signal a display of gallantry and skill as to have attracted the attention at once of the Generals in command and received their hearty commendation. He afterwards received from the War Department a medal inscribed, "The Congress to Drummer Wm McGee Co. C 33 Regt N.J. Vols.

At the close of the War he was appointed 2nd Lieutenant in the 20th Regt U.S. Infantry. To prepare himself for the examination required he was allowed extra time in consideration of his services and promising qualities of character. The recommendation of Maj Gen Thomas U.S.A., upon which this special allowance was in part based, bears strong testimony to the merits of Lieu. McGee. A copy of this letter is herewith annexed with other papers bearing upon the case. This preparation he made with assiduous application and supplied by native energy of mind the deficient opportunities of his earlier life. A high and useful career seemed open to him when he was unfortunately provoked by the unwarranted and insulting conduct of his surgeon, while stationed at Baton Rouge, La. in August 1868 into the rash conduct which resulted in the sentence of the Court Martial dismissing him from the service, and subjecting him to imprisonment for the term of five years. The facts of this occurrence are I believe undisputed and admitted. A letter was written by Doct Braman Acting Assistant Surgeon containing scandalous charges of theft and forging against young McGee which came to the possession of Brvt Maj. Gen Sykes, Col. of the Regiment, and was by him shown to McGee and produced in him, not unnaturally, such excitement and anger — the charges being untrue and without foundation. He consulted his fellow officers as to what he should do and among them Gen Sykes, and was so influenced especially by the latter that he resolved to put upon the surgeon the disgrace of a public chastisement. There is no dispute that the charges were false and it is needless to say that to an aspiring, high spirited and honorable young officer they seemed of a kind not to be borne. He called upon the surgeon, asked him if he wrote the letter, and being told that he did and receiving no retraction or apology, he proceeded to chastise the offender with a whip. The surgeon turned around to take up his revolver and said he should make short work of it. When McGee also drew his pistol and while holding it in both hands without meaning to shoot then, the pistol went off wounding McGee's hand and killing the Doctor. The shocking result was unexpected to the unfortunate Lieutenant who immediately gave himself up to the Civil Authorities, was tried for Manslaughter before a court and jury and acquitted by a verdict of NOT GUILTY. Having been tried by the civil courts, it was deemed by his friends that he could not properly be tried again — but in this they were mistaken, and he was afterwards arraigned and tried before a Court Martial upon the three charges of 1. Riotous & disorderly conduct, 2. Disobedience of orders and 3rd, Conduct unbecoming an officer and a gentleman and was found guilty under the first two charges and sentenced to be dismissed from the service and to be imprisoned for five years at such place as the Military Authorities might decide.

The foregoing is a brief outline of the circumstances of the case from which are necessarily excluded the particulars and details that verify and strengthen its claims to executive clemency. It is believed by his numerous friends who are acquainted with the facts, and who take a lively interest in his case — a belief and interest in which I strongly concur and participate — that his pardon is not only warranted by sound views of what is due to justice, but that a longer subjection of this young man, distinguished and promising youth to so severe a penalty as he has now undergone for more than a year would be injurious to the interests of public justice, as well as disastrous to the hopes and welfare of the young man himself. That he erred is not denied by his friends or himself. But the error such as it was has been heavily punished and will be a cause of life long regret, and of life long efforts to atone for and explain. It is proper to add as showing the influences and suggestions which acted on his mind while suffering under the supposed disgrace of Dr. Braman's charges, that when consulting Col. Sykes as to what he should do, Lieu McGee was told by that officer commanding — that he would not advise him, but he knew well what *he* should do if the case was his own. By this language, Col. Sykes when examined as a witness on the trial of the case, explicitly stated that he meant and had in his mind that he would inflict upon the surgeon the disgrace of a public chastisement. The error of Lieu McGee was one which a spirited young officer would under so great an affront, and under similar influences, be greatly in danger of making and which, having unfortunately made, he now profoundly regrets — and prays to be enabled by leading a pure and useful life to retrieve to the utmost of his power. I beg leave in conclusion respectfully to repeat my recommendation that the opportunity be afforded him to do so by the interposition of executive clemency in restoring him to his liberty.

> I am with great Respect
> Your Obedient Servant
> Marcus Ward[8]

In one letter, Marcus Ward, as compassionate a governor as New Jersey ever elected, gave credence to the old dictum, "Don't vote for politicians — it only encourages them." Marcus Ward was masterful in his defense of what he believed to be a New Jersey native hero, but he cruelly misrepresented the truth so often one doesn't know where to begin. His attack of the victim was expected, as that was Willie's defense cornerstone, and, after all, Braman was from Massachusetts, not New Jersey. One wonders what direction this case might have taken had Braman been from John White Geary's Pennsylvania, or Horace Austin's Minnesota, much less Newark, New Jersey. But you still have to wonder in the series of mistruths if Ward did not choke a little when he wrote, "The shocking result was unexpected to the unfortunate lieutenant, who immediately gave himself up to the Civil Authorities."[9]

The secretary of war realized this was not a decision he could make without backup. Within days, Belknap sent the petition and all the familiar paperwork to the man who hanged Mary Surrat and her fellow conspirators for killing President Abe Lincoln just five years before — and obviously Joseph Holt was not unfamiliar with the case of ex-Lieutenant William H. McGee.[10] The Bureau of Military Justice was about to review Willie's conviction one more time, and again Holt did not farm out the petition to a staffer or subordinate. Holt's name was on the first review a short year ago, and he knew the case well. It is no surprise that Holt's reply was succinct and quick, and on June 29, the United States judge advocate general replied to the secretary of war, with McGee's future in the balance, and Marcus Ward and Willie McGee would not like it.

War Department
Bureau of Military Justice
June 29, 1870
  Respectfully returned to the Secretary of War, with the original report of this Bureau upon the record of trial of <u>Lieut. McGee</u>, addressed to the Secretary of War on June 22, 1869. In this report it will be perceived that the opinion is expressed that the homicide committed by the accused was premeditated, and that his sentence of five years imprisonment should be fully enforced. The principal circumstances now urged in his favor was presented upon the trial or in connection with the review of this Bureau. The fact of the false charges that had been made against him by Surg. Braman (the officer killed) — the incitement supposed to be contained in the conversation between the accused and Genl Sykes — the previous record of accused, as exhibited by his having received a medal of honor and by testimonials in his behalf consisting of letters from Genl Buchanan, Genl Geary, and Governor Ward — all these are either set forth in the record or referred to in the report of this Bureau.
  In the present application it is particularly urged that the killing was not premeditated, but was the result of an accident the pistol having gone off in McGee's hands without his intending it. To prove this he himself avers in the within statement that while holding his pistol with both hands, it went off "shattering my left hand badly," and this view is adopted by Governor Ward. This statement, however, does not accord with the sworn testimony of a

Surgeon, in the record, as quoted in the former report — to the effect that the hand of the accused was examined by the witness a few days after and found to exhibit no injury calling for the "aid of a surgeon," but merely some "specks of powder beneath the skin"— a consequence which, as observed in the report, might have resulted in accused's retaining his left hand near the pistol when he fired.

On the other hand the evidence of premeditation on the part of the accused is of a marked character. His borrowing the pistol from a sergeant with the remark that it was "just the thing he wanted"— his statement to Capt. Morris shortly before the homicide "that he was going to shoot the Doctor"— and his remark to the same witness directly after the act "that he had laid him out"— are facts which certainly constitute strong evidence of intent.

The character and gravity of the crime are further illustrated by the fact that Doctor Braman was not armed. For though McGee now states that when he first struck the Doctor, the latter "turned toward his revolver," the testimony shows that the only pistols in the room, besides that held by McGee, were shut up in a drawer of a desk, and that the Doctor did not turn toward or approach this desk before being shot.

The evidence in the case is so fully stated in the previous report that it needs not be further recalled. The material facts of the record of the accused in the service have also been considered in that report, and although his military history is now more fully presented, the additional details are not deemed such as necessarily to modify the views already expressed in regards to the merits of the case.

It is for the Executive to determine how far the excellent military record of this young officer, added to the stinging sense of wrong by which he was maddened beyond self-control, shall support the appeal for clemency now made. The exasperation, under which the homicide was committed, was inspired by the accusation of an utterly degrading crime, of which he was innocent, and to an honorable and sensitive spirit, a greater outrage could scarcely have been offered. Treating the case however, from a strictly legal stand point, this Bureau can make no favorable recommendation.

J. Holt

Judge Advocate General[11]

Willie McGee, the magnificent little enchanter of both peasants and the famous, had never met Joseph Holt, and the Irish smile, the boyishly handsome face, would not be able to sway the tough advocate general. Maybe the charm wouldn't have worked on Holt like it did on most others, anyway. Holt condemned the only woman ever executed in the United States in a hundred years, and sentenced Dr. Samuel Mudd to life imprisonment, in the Dry Tortugas.[12] Joseph Holt was not falling for Irish charm, or for that matter, New Jersey political pressure, even from a man as connected as Marcus Ward. Holt forwarded his report — the second one in a year — and the secretary of war had all the information he needed and sent the following letter to Marcus Ward:

Secretary of War William Belknap's note to New Jersey's Marcus Ward, informing him of the presidential pardon to Willie McGee (New Jersey Historical Society Archives).

War Department
Washington City

July 13, 1870

Hon. Marcus L. Ward,
    Newark,
        New Jersey

Sir:
    I have the honor to inform you that, upon due consideration of all the

circumstances of the case, an Executive pardon has been granted to William McGee, of New Jersey, now undergoing a sentence of five years imprisonment imposed upon him by a general court-martial, while an officer of the Army, for certain offenses by him committed in violation of the rules and articles of war.

Very respectfully,

Your obedt. Servant,

Wm Belknap

Secretary of War[13]

Somewhere in Massachusetts on this summer night, Dr. Isaac Braman, who in all likelihood would never learn of Willie's pardon, went to bed believing that as educated as he was, as much as he had contributed to his country and his family, any wisdom he may have accumulated during his life was worthless. Isaac Braman would wake up each morning, as he did day after day until he died, remembering only that since August 15, 1868, his child was gone.

CHAPTER ELEVEN

New Life at Twenty-One

But while he caught high ecstasies,
Life slipped between the bars.
— Patrick Kavanagh,
The Great Hunger

While Willie awaited the results of Marcus Ward's petition, the ex-second lieutenant continued to arise at 5:30 A.M. each day and ready himself for an eleven-hour work detail, nine on the weekends. The vast majority of the seventy-two prisoners in July of 1870 worked for the Seymour, Sabin & Company, which specialized in lumber, wood and cooperage, in a political deal still seen in prisons throughout the United States.[1]

The prisoners at Stillwater were a mixture of Minnesota prisoners and those, like Willie, who were shipped in from out of state. They were natives of sixteen states, including Rhode Island, Alabama, and New York. Minnesota was a wide-open area in 1870 and attracted people from all over the world, including convicted felons. Irish, English and German would be expected, but Stillwater even had residents from Denmark and Prince Edward Island among its guests. Willie was the only ex-soldier, and most of the men were common laborers, cooks, tinsmiths, stonecutters; but there were a convicted barber, clergyman, and locomotive builder among the mix. All but seven of the men were white, and there was one counted as a "half-breed," Taylor Combs, of Missouri.[2]

Seymour, Sabin & Company, owned by local Congressman Dwight Sabin, was controlled prison labor — and prison affairs in general — for twenty years, starting with McGee's arrival in 1869. In 1870 the convicts produced barrels, tubs and wooden buckets worth $50,000 for the company, and tripled that the next year.[3] No records of Willie's time spent working tell us exactly what he did, but following prison Willie became a painter, so perhaps he spent time in that department.

Marcus Ward, meanwhile, had won the political if not the moral game. Ward was notified the very day of the decision by telegraph and wrote a thank you note to Secretary of War Belknap the following day, July 14, and more than a full week before Willie McGee was notified by Warden Webber:

Newark NJ July 14, 1870
Hon Wm W Belknap
        Secy War,
Sir:
   I am under the deepest obligation to you for your letter of 13th instant conveying the information of the Pardon of young Magie. God bless you for your humane and generous action. I feel that you have almost saved the life of the young man in dispensing him from that dreadful prison. I trust that his future life may be such to cause you no regret that you have given him his new liberty. Gratefully yours,

                              Marcus Ward[4]

What convinced Secretary Belknap to overturn the Bureau of Justice and the fairly emphatic opinion of the judge advocate general? No record survives except the formal one sentence announcement, but the lack of such an explanation creates questions. If there was no discernible reason to overturn Joseph Holt's second review in a year, we can only presume it was simply a political reversal. It certainly was possible Belknap went to President Grant prior to making the decision, aware of Grant's friendship with Ward, but even if the secretary of war had made the choice for a pardon independently of Grant, it had to be on a political basis, and not as Holt said, "from a strictly legal standpoint."[5] If that was the case, William W. Belknap's past and future cloud the decision.

Born just over the New Jersey border in Newburgh, New York, William Belknap graduated from Princeton University in 1848 and became a lawyer before the war. After the war he turned Republican and following his stint in Grant's cabinet he moved to Philadelphia. Thus we have a secretary of war with ties to both New Jersey and Pennsylvania states where heavy-hitting Republican governors, Geary and Ward, were also Willie McGee's most influential mentors. Six years after granting McGee a pardon, Secretary of War Belknap was accused of accepting more than $24,000—a huge fortune in 1875 — in bribes from a post trader in Indian country. Belknap was impeached by a unanimous vote of the Senate, but prior to the formal Senate trial, he

Marcus Ward's "thank you" response to Belknap following the pardon to Willie McGee in July 1870. Belknap helped override Joseph Holt's unfavorable recommendation (New Jersey Historical Society Archives).

resigned and the matter was, in effect, dropped. Though he lived another fourteen years, practicing law in Philadelphia and Washington, seeds of doubt would always be raised by suspicious minds.[6]

By any definition, Marcus Ward pulled off a miracle — a coup which took commitment, time (at least two trips to Washington), energy, and who knows what else to free Willie McGee from jail.[7] Willie understandably couldn't have cared less about whatever political machinations were at work in Washington; he had placed every ounce of trust in soldier's friend Marcus Ward and on July 20, 1870, the ex-lieutenant was called in to Warden Webber's office and told he was a free man.[8]

The twenty-one-year-old prisoner most definitely left

Secretary of War William Belknap, who bent to the wishes of his good friend Marcus Ward regarding the imprisonment of Willie McGee. Belknap would resign from his office in disgrace five years later in 1875 for accepting a bribe (author collection).

the cell he had occupied the past 449 days within hours, spending the first night of freedom since December 1869 in the town of Stillwater, staying with either local businessman Dwight Sabin or the Reverend Langley. The official record comes in the form of a note from Webber to Marcus Ward:

Office of the Warden
State Prison
Stillwater, Minn
July 21st, 1870
Hon Marcus L Ward
        Newark
            N J
        My Dear Sir:
    Yesterday, with unfeigned satisfaction, I restored to freedom your worthy young friend Wm McGee.
    His unexceptional [sic] demeanor in prison, and the unvarnished story of his

Office of WARDEN STATE PRISON,

Stillwater, Minn., *July 21st* 1870

Hon. Marcus L. Ward
　　　　Newark
　　　　　　N.J.
　　　　　　　My Dear Sir:

Yesterday, with unfeigned satisfaction,
I restored to freedom your worthy young
friend Wm. McGee.

His unexceptionable demeanor in prison,
and the unvarnished story of his unfortunate
troubles, at once, challenged my sympathy
and regard; and I had enlisted our good
Gov. Austin in his behalf.

To you alone, however, is he solely indebted
for his timely discharge.

He goes out with a light, happy heart, and
a character unimpaired. God bless him!
Rest assured he will never forget your unceasing kindness.　　Very Respectfully

　　　　　　　　A. B. Webber
　　　　　　　　　　warden

Warden Andrew Webber of Stillwater Prison had taken up McGee's cause at the
urging of his boss, Governor Horace Austin. Webber said he knew Willie was
innocent "because he told me so" (New Jersey Historical Society Archives).

unfortunate troubles, at once challenged my sympathy and regards; and I had
enlisted our good Gov. Austin in his behalf. To you alone, however, is he solely
indebted for his timely discharge.

He goes out with a light, happy heart, and a character unimpaired. God
bless him!

Rest assured he will never forget your unceasing kindness.

Very respectfully

A.B. Webber

Warden[9]

This note came, interestingly, from the man known as "Bull Beef" Webber, for his penchant for allowing convicted murderers to take hunting trips,
some even out of state. McGee himself wrote to Ward in New Jersey the following day, July 22.

His Excellency,   Stillwater
    Marcus L. Ward
    Ex Governor Newark N J

Dear Sir;

I can not express to you in words how grateful I am to you for your interest
and exertions in my behalf, your kind sympathy and counsels have changed me
in prison. I cannot tell you how much they may have been instrumental in my
continuing in good resolve; trusting in your well remembered kindness and
confidence in my worth, I feel assured, that my day of release could not be
far distant, and now I have to rejoice—while thanking you for the wonderful
assistance so that I am now once again a free man, and what is known; that
my fellow friends throughout the country will not worry about what led to my
imprisonment and do not look upon me with aversion, nor deem the act which
I deplore as censurable with imprisonment in the Penitentiary.

Thanks to you the duration of my stay in that hated place was shortened
beyond even *my* expectations and you may feel secure that no small measure
of gratitude can be felt towards you by an orphan boy with nothing but his
character and former good record to depend on in life. You have probably, dear
sir, not heard of the death of my dear mother, but she is gone, and I have no
one now to look to for counsel and sympathy, save you, who have seemed like
a father to me; and the few in this place besides who have taken an interest in
my past history, and who appears to feel for me as much as strangers can feel for
one in like misfortune. I have received an offer for work, and today, the third of
my release, feel quite unwell though hoping it may not continue.

My reinstatement in the army I can hardly hope for; but having no little
experience in the world outside of that profession, it causes me no little anxiety
to determine what I am to do. There is about three hundred dollars due me
with which to make a start, but that will go but a short way, should I not be
successful in finding steady employment.

Dear sir, write me whenever and as often as it may be convenient, for I am
lonely here, and your letters will be treasured and your advice taken to heart as
from a father.

I have omitted to mention that Governor Austin kindly sent me your letter to himself and I need not say how helpful and proud your praises of me to another were the means of rendering me, when gloom was taking possession of my mind. I will at the first opportunity and when I feel better devote more time to you and write a longer letter, but now with best wishes and in hopes that at some not far distant day I may be able to thank you in person for your many kindnesses.

I subscribe myself
With sincere respect
Your obedient servant
Wm McGee[10]

Willie McGee, in his abbreviated life, had fought in a civil war, survived typhoid, been awarded the Medal of Honor, honored in a book as a wonder-boy hero, commissioned as an officer, shot and killed a doctor, been tried and acquitted, court-martialed and convicted, spent a year and a half in prison, and pardoned by the president — and was barely twenty-one years old.[11]

But even with his new freedom, Willie McGee did not come clean. McGee says he does not "deem the act which I deplore as censurable with imprisonment"; but Willie never — and by now it was two years later — admit he did anything wrong in Baton Rouge.[12] He deplores the act, "an unfortunate affair," but not the punishment. This denial remained constant the rest of his life. Willie also referred to himself as "an orphan boy with nothing but his character and former good record."[13] Not only was McGee not an orphan, he had an adoptive foster father and mother, and two older brothers, a sister, and a large extended family.[14] As for his "character and good record," even his most ardent admirers would have to admit his shooting of Dr. Braman, and his lying about it, would tend to show his "character."[15]

Willie continued to pull on Ward's emotional sleeve: "I have no one now to look to for counsel and sympathy, save you, who have seemed like a father to me."[16] In truth, the hero of Murfreesboro did not meet Marcus Ward until at least the summer of 1865, and last saw him in September of 1867.[17] Was it possible, even likely, that Willie was totally unaware that Holmes Pattison, who is not mentioned in the letter, had been in frequent contact with Marcus Ward for months? Additionally, Willie also continued to talk about money: "There is about three hundred dollars due me." But he listed no basis for such a statement.[18] He was dismissed from the service and had been since December 1869. Since then he had been in jail, and at Stillwater he surely did not earn a salary. The pardon was his get-out-of-jail card, but there was no mention of a reinstatement, thus no back pay, yet it is a subject McGee would harp on for years.

Towards the conclusion, Willie again leaned on Ward, using the "father" angle again, and asked Marcus to write often, as the "victim" Willie McGee, was "lonely here."[19] The ex-lieutenant never mentioned his sister or brothers back in the East, or any family member, though they were numerous.[20] Despite the fact he was Willie's adoptive father, Holmes Pattison was never mentioned, nor was the Reverend Langley, who had worked extremely hard to connect Willie and Ward those last fifteen months.[21] The Newark ex-lieutenant had what law enforcement calls "selective memory," not a good trait for a man of "character and good record."[22]

McGee supporters, and there were always some, defended Willie. The poor boy had only been out of prison for two days, and was, by his own admission, sick.[23] McGee friends saw a reformed young man writing from the heart to the one person responsible for extricating him from a dreadful life in a dreadful place. Most importantly, McGee had won Marcus Ward to his side, who responded to his new best friend immediately:

> Newark N J July 27, 1870
>> Mr. Wm McGee
>>> My dear Sir:
>>>> I am glad to hear that you are again at liberty and am especially pleased to learn from various sources that you have conducted yourself well during your great trouble and that you have the sympathy and regard of those with whom you have come in contact and who have watched your course. Although I have the fullest confidence in you and believe you will always try and do right, I beg to urge upon you never, under any circumstances, to allow yourself to be drawn into low company — avoid strong drink — be honest, industrious and prudent and you will if governed by these rules have a happy and prosperous future.
>>>> I send you my check for $25, which though not a large sum may help to procure you some necessaries — I would be glad to add to this amount but the numerous calls upon me forbid it.
>>>>>> With best wishes
>>>>> I am
>>>>>> Your Friend
>>>>> Marcus L Ward[24]

Here was Ward at his paternalistic best, giving positive, wonderful advice that any father would be proud to give a son; thus the "soldier's friend" added to his legacy. William H. McGee should have taken the $25 — a goodly amount for 1870 — and rushed home to New Jersey, where he could have started fresh at twenty-one, and Marcus Ward could, and likely would, have mentored him forever. Willie McGee chose a different road, much to his eventual regret, and, as Robert Frost mused in a poem years later, that made all the difference. But not everybody in Stillwater was thrilled at McGee's release. Willie evoked strong sentiment wherever he resided, and the fact that he was a free man at the moment would not change anything. In mid–August the Stillwater *Republican* reprinted an article from the Newark *Advertiser*, and, following the reprint extolling Willie's release, added to it with opinions from the local populace:

THE STORY OF A DRUMMER BOY

A Convict in Our State Prison
[From the *Newark* (N.J.) *Advertiser*, July 18, 1870]

Through the long continued and well directed efforts of ex Governor Ward, the remainder of the sentence of William Magee, the famous drummer boy of Newark, who was about a year ago sentenced to five years, has been remitted, and the gallant young hero has by this time probably stepped forth from his prison doors into the free air, to take up his walk again among his fellow men, and, as his friends confidently trust, to lead a career as brilliantly honorable and useful in the future as in the past. The story of William Magee is so much like the romances of the days of knightly exploit and achievement that it would hardly be believed were it not attested by the published histories of the war and the official documents narrating the action of the government in his honor.

The son of a widow living in Beaver Street in this city, William Magee, then a mere lad of fifteen, enlisted as a drummer in the Thirty-Third New Jersey regiment. It was not long before his daring exploits in the presence of the enemy attracted the attention of his superior officers. While Hood, in the fall of 1864, with an army of 10,000 men, held Gen. Thomas imprisoned in Nashville, Gen. Milroy, with a handful of men, kept his communication open on the railroad at Murfreesboro, thirty miles away. This post was soon surrounded, and the isolated beleaguered men lost all hope of escape. But it was determined to strike one blow for deliverance, and a "forlorn hope" of a single regiment was organized.

William Magee was then only an orderly to Gen. Van Cleve, but the command of the forlorn hope was committed to him. He sallied forth, and dashed upon a rebel battery on the nearest eminence, the boyish commander's charge was a gallant one; but the fire of the enemy was resistless, and his column fell back. But his heroic spirit was not to be crushed by temporary mishap, nor was his superior's confidence in him shaken. Selecting a new regiment, he again rushed upon the foe, again met withering fire. Still pressing on, however, victory was at last his. It was no ordinary victory, but the turning point of the crisis, and the series for that signal of quickly succeeding battles that finally drove Hood from Tennessee.

Amid the commendations of all the leading officers of the department, the Newark boy of eighteen was decorated with a medal of honor from Congress, transmitted through the War Department. Upon the close of the war the young hero was appointed a Second Lieutenant in the Twentieth United States Infantry, but on examination he was deficient in several studies, having never enjoyed educational advantages. Through the aid of Gov. Ward he secured an extension of time, and applying himself to the books with the same intelligence and indomitable pluck that marked his conduct in the field, he was soon ready to appear again before the examining board, and this time passed triumphantly. At the age of nineteen the Newark drummer boy donned the uniform of an officer in the regular service.

But now came a disastrous turn in the tide of an extraordinary career. While with his regiment, which was lying at Baton Rouge, La. he was charged by the Assistant Surgeon of the regiment with stealing his watch. Magee sorely felt the grievous insult. It was the first blur which had ever been cast upon his honor. In a moment of anger he visited the quarters of the Surgeon and demanded retraction. This being refused, Liet. Magee struck his defamer with a cowhide which he brought for the purpose. The Surgeon started for his pistol, which was lying near, when Magee drew his own weapon and fired. The shot was fatal.

Magee was tried for manslaughter by a civil court and acquitted. Then the friends of the surgeon procured Magee's arraignment before a general court martial at Washington and by this tribunal found guilty of conduct prejudicial to the discipline of the army, he was sentenced to be dismissed from the service and imprisoned five years in the State Prison at Stillwater, Minnesota. One year and three months of his term have elapsed, during which Magee has conducted himself in such a manner as to gain the warm interest in behalf of the Governor of the State and all the prison authorities. Meanwhile his early and steadfast friend, Gov Ward, has been actively working at Washington, and the result is seen in the pardon that has just been transmitted to Stillwater. However just the sentence and condign the punishment, all rejoice that the young man is now free to begin over again a career in which he has displayed such remarkable talents.

Now for the facts of the case. With the first part of the story we have nothing to say for we have no doubt, but it is perfectly true, but in reference to the crime, for which he was sentenced, it was nothing more or less than down right murder and we can not but believe that the President, through Governor Ward, has been led to commit a serious mistake in turning loose upon society a dangerous man. The assistant surgeon did not accuse him of stealing his watch but of forging a note or something of the kind for the sum of five dollars. Something more was done, and said about it until McGee determined upon revenge, and to this end, went to the room of the assistant surgeon, as he claims, for the purpose of only cowhiding him, but at the same time going there armed with a revolver or pistol. He found the surgeon in bed, and told him that "he had come there to get satisfaction out of him," whereupon the surgeon attempted to get up to defend himself when McGee drew his revolver and shot him before he even knew what the surgeon was going to do. That is the sum and substance of the difficulty that caused his incarceration. He was sent to this place by order of his commanding General, in whose department this State is, and ever since he has been here he has been trying to foment some trouble. He made arrangements with one convict who was discharged to bring 15 men over here from his company or regiment, a portion of which it seems was stationed at Fort Snelling, in order to break him out. This, the members of his company refused to do, but stripped the blue soldier's clothes which the liberated convict wore off of him and forbade his wearing them anymore as he had disgraced them. Besides this, and in connection with this city, he has been circulating the charge that Mr. Davis, the Deputy Warden, had stolen three hundred dollars worth of clothing from him. He, or anyone else, had ought to have known better than to have circulated such charges against Mr. Davis. Mr Davis has occupied his present position for more than eleven years now and he has enjoyed the confidence of each administration. The trouble with the prisoner [McGee] was, he was tampered with, and we are told that parties here in town took a great interest in him, talked with him, told him he was a martyr, and all that until he got to thinking and believing that his sentence and punishment was unjust. Several ministers of the gospel made almost daily visits to him, and constantly held out to him the hope of an early pardon. It came. One of the clergymen furnished him with five dollars on his liberation which was spent in treating one of the guards of the penitentiary until last Tuesday, when with the aid of a couple more dollars, furnished by another sympathizing clergyman, he got drunk, picked a quarrel with one of our most peaceful citizens because he refused to drink with him, and got put in the lock-up, from which he was bailed out by a friend, and last Wednesday was fined $7.50 for disorderly conduct. His whole conduct since his release has been to show that his reformation is far from complete. Last Sunday a week ago, he visited the beer garden and with money furnished by his Christian friends of this city, visited the boat opposite of this city. He is one of the most innocent fellows you ever saw, to let him tell it, and lays his late troubles to the guard who treated him and drank with him.

We would have been pleased to have let this whole matter drop, but from the fact that there has been an underhanded game played in reference to some of the officers of the prison, we deem it no more than just that the whole facts should be known. We also hear Mr. Davis will be removed upon representations of this Magee, but we hope that the Governor will rest his verdict upon stronger evidence than that of a convict.[25]

Public inebriation, and causing disturbances on borrowed money was bad enough for the citizens of Stillwater, but using money lent by "Christian friends" in order to visit a brothel, "the boat opposite the city" (in the only proper language of the day) was too much for the local populace, as evidenced by the local paper.[26] But Willie knew he had friends among the politicians in Stillwater, despite the damning newspaper story. Governor Austin, Marcus Ward's Republican friend, had appointed "Captain" Alfred Webber the warden at Stillwater in March, just months before Willie's pardon. Webber was an occasional attorney and part-time politician, best known as a hotel keeper. Webber was a political appointee with few if any qualifications and in October, after Willie's pardon and two months after the above story appeared, Webber dismissed Deputy Warden Davis on the accusations of the drummer from Newark.[27] Nobody questioned how Willie McGee could have $300 worth of clothes, worth in today's market over $4,000. When it was later discovered Webber allowed convicts time to hunt in Wisconsin, sold prison food for his own benefit, allowed wives to sleep in their husbands' cells, and permitted prostitution to function within prison walls, he was fired in November, but it did not save Deputy Davis.[28] An argument can be made that Webber and McGee were kindred spirits who found each other useful in Stillwater.

But reading Willie's letters, you would never know it wasn't a perfect life. A month later, on August 21, thirty-one days after leaving his prison cell, Willie wrote again to his mentor, Marcus Ward, in a letter that tells us a little more about McGee's past life:

Stillwater August 21st, 1870
Hon Marcus L Ward
My Dear Sir,

I have just received your kind and thoughtful letter of the 27th July — the check for $25.00 was much needed, and your kindness deserves my thanks.

Since my release I have been staying at the Reverend Mr. Langley's house — he was a good friend to me while in confinement and he kindly offered me a room with him while I remain in this place.

I am merely waiting for my expected pay that is due me in order to go east and I have a strong intention of going to Europe, if the threatened war in that quarter becomes a reality. You know sir my reputation was all I had to boast of, and as that must be considered tarnished by the mere fact of my having been confined in a State Prison — many will totally ignore the fact that according to my education I have always tried to do what was right — I think it best under the circumstances to begin life anew in another country, free from the chance of my misfortune standing in the way of my advancement, and to continue in the profession of arms for which I am best suited, in both education and temperament. My sympathies are with Prussia as opposed to France — but, a temporary offer of my services to any foreign nation will not prevent my again enrolling myself under the Stars and Stripes should that dear old flag ever be assailed. Wherever I may be dear sir you will always have my grateful remembrance for your fatherly kindness and interest for which I can not be sufficiently thankful. My recent troubles will no doubt prove of benefit to me in one way at least — as a warning for the future — they were required, I must believe; and by his help who ordered them, I mean so to conduct myself in the future, in resolution and understanding, that those who are my friends and take an interest in me need not feel a pang of dread whenever my name is mentioned.

The check reached me just when it was most needed — another evidence of my possessing a good friend, and I hardly add the forethought which prompted the remittance at such a time deserved double thanks. I shall return the amt. so kindly sent as soon as I receive the money due me which I expect daily.

Excuse my writing further as it is late and please picture to yourself the change in my feelings after splendid bath in Lilly Lake to be able to go to bed with no jailor to overlook my movements but God and my own thoughts.

With highest and most grateful esteem, I remain
Sincerely Yours,
Wm McGee

P.S. If you have a likeness of yourself at hand it will give me great pleasure if you will enclose it to me at the first opportunity. Wm McGee[29]

Three weeks later, McGee wrote again to his new "father," from Stillwater, where Willie, for reasons we never learn, has remained following his release from prison.

Stillwater Sept 6 1870
Hon M L Ward
My dear sir
    Gratitude for your very great services and friendship to me prompts me to take the pen to tell you that I am trying to follow your good counsel, and endeavoring to be a man. I have gone into business here commencing with what little money I have just received from my back pay.
    All my friends tell me I have a splendid chance and are doing all they can to help me and I hope by preserving my integrity I shall demonstrate to everyone of them that I am worthy of confidence and respect.
    I never can forget your great kindness to me in my trouble, and I want my life to show you how much I appreciate the confidence you have had in me. I shall esteem it a great favor to hear from you often and to have your counsel and advice.[30]

Six weeks after leaving the Federal Prison, Willie, still in Stillwater, remained thankful to his New Jersey mentor, but now asked for another favor:

As you have done so much for me I am now going to have the confidence to ask a favor for a little friend of mine. It is for Willie Langley, son of Rev. Mr. Langley who has been such a good friend to me and of whom you have heard me speak.
    Willie is just 12 years old and a bright active intelligent boy and above all he is at the early age a Christian boy which act alone gives him a splendid founda-tion. His inclinations all seem to point toward the water and he would prefer a naval life to any other. I have thought perhaps there might be some vacancies in the Naval Academy at Annapolis and if you would use your influence, to secure him an appointment there, it would be a great favor to me, a well deserved effort for the boy's energy, and a kindness for which his people would always thank you.
    It is very late and I must retire but the memory of your great kindness follows me in the nighttime as well as the day and after we have all come forth from the night of sorrows and trouble which sooner or later comes to us on earth, I hope to meet you in heaven's unclouded day saved, and purified, a star in your crown of rejoicing.
Respectfully
Wm McGee[31]

If Marcus Ward, upon receipt of Willie's latest correspondence, felt he was being manipulated, it did not show in his actions. Ward incredibly acceded to every whim of McGee's. The *Stillwater Republican* issue of October 8 pub-lishes the following front page article:

FOR ANNAPOLIS — Willie Langley, son of Capt of this city, is likely to receive an appointment to the Naval School at Annapolis. We have seen a letter from Gov. Marcus L. Ward of New Jersey in which he promises to use his influence to secure his appointment. Willie is a bright boy and if physically strong enough he will doubtless pass the examination.[32]

Willie must have been giddy with the influence he had with Marcus Ward. As Christmas 1870 approached, Marcus Ward, now 58 and still a major figure in New Jersey, was sent a letter from little Willie Langley's father, the Reverend Bob. It contained some familiar refrains:

Stillwater December 10th 1870
Hon Marcus L Ward
Newark, NJ
Deare Sir
At the request of Lieutenant Wm McGee:

I write you this he made application immediately after his discharge from Prison for his back pay, but has not rec it as yet I enclose you a letter ... and he wishes you would please do him the favor to see that it is forwarded to him sooner as he is in grate need of some news as he has had no money but the $25 you sent him when he came out of prison and he is in a sad condition indeed, and if his sister or any of his friends can help him I hope they will do so: he has bene with me all the time since he came out of prison, and I have had to mortgage my home to do what I have for him.

I am a pore worn out preacher of the gospels and have tried to do as I would be done by, but I am unable to do more than I have done. If he could get his back pay it would be some help and unless something is done soon he will become a raveing maniac; for his mind is very much shattered. Now I wrote to Mr. Pattison his foster father, and he came here but done nothing for him, and he told me that Pattison has money belonging to him, and if you could induce him to help William he would thank you very much — all this letter except the request in the beginning is my own and I hope you will not let him or anyone els to know it as I felt it is my duty to inform you as I know you're his friend. He is trying to be a man and does deserve help in his greate time of need.... He knows nothing of this letter, if you can do anything to forward his pay I hope you will do so and do it soone.

Please write him a letter of encouragement and also please write to me if you can spare the time.

I am Deare Sir

Very respectfully

Your Obt servant
R Langley[33]

Attached to the letter is an official note from the Treasury Department dated December 5, 1870, informing William McGee his claim for back pay has been received and is in the process of investigation and has been forwarded to the judge advocate general, none other than Joseph Holt. McGee, the form stated, "will be fully informed of the result."[34]

There was no record of a response from Ward to Langley or a query to Washington regarding the application. Joseph Holt, as can be best determined, never acted on McGee's request, and the winter in Stillwater must have been hard for Willie McGee in more ways than one. A week before St.

Patrick's Day 1871, McGee had Langley write another letter to Ward, with a much more desperate tone. (Rev. Bob, in addition to his ministry, was also the Stillwater coroner and one of the town's most revered citizens):

Stillwater, March 10th, 1871
Hon. Marcus L. Ward
Deare Sir

At the request of Lieut William McGee, I wrote to you some time ago, but have not had an answer. I write now to say that you are his only friend, at least the only person that has manifested any friendship to him. Mr. Pattison has never done anything for him and does not even when asked send him any assistance.

William is a young man if he had a little help would be a good man, but he is (he thinks) a forsaken man by those that ought to be his friends. He tells me that Mr. H.A. Pattison has several hundred dollars of his and a valuable watch, but will not help him with one dollar. William wrote to him for money to get some clothing for the past cold winter but he has never rec any thing from him, all that he has since he left the prison is the 25 that you sent him. I have kept him at my house and boarded and clothed him. I am a pore man and have been confined with sickness for over five months, and am unable to do all that I would for him he is very anxious to leave this place and go to his friends in the East and if you could help him to get away he would leave and go to his friends, and be a man that would do honor to himself and his friends, he is not unwilling to work but if he could get anything to do he could earn a good living and would pay his debts, he is an excellent painter and can earn good wages, he has gone to day to St. Paul to try and get work but I feel it is to early in the Spring.

Now Deare Governor, do not advise him to come home for none of his friends have even asked him to come to them. Will you please write to me in answer to this and if possible give him some encouragement, I have done all that I can for him and he feels he ought to do for himself, but can get nothing to do here, and this is no place for him and unless he can get away from this city he must and will be ruined, for God's sake, do help him. If only writing letters to him, do say come home.

> Very respectfully
> Your Obt Servant
> Robert Langley

P.S. William has never recd a dollar from the government for the pay that was due him for services rendered previous to his confinement.[35]

Marcus Ward, like Robert Langley a man of Christian charity, sent another $25 to McGee as soon as he received Langley's letter.[36] Still Willie did not use it to return home. Perhaps he used it to pay debts Langley mentioned, but he likely spent it somewhere else. Again, reading between the lines, Langley, in his most kindly manner, seems to suggest Willie McGee had worn out his welcome in Minnesota, and that feeling is confirmed when Dwight Sabin, the Stillwater Congressman and prison contractor who knew Willie both in and out of prison, sent the following unsolicited note to Marcus Ward, just a week later:

Hon M L Ward
   Newark N J
      Dr Sir:
   As you have taken a lively interest in Wm McGee — I take the liberty to
advise you that if he has any friendship in New Jersey who will interest themselves in his welfare, and assist him to some permanent business I think it
would be greatly to his advantage to be with them, as he advises me today he
is out of funds, and cannot find employment at this season of the year. He will
remain at Stillwater for the present. He tells me his is trying to earn a living but
sees no chance for anything better, and I am of the opinion that he is not well
adapted to the struggles of life without the fostering assistance of friends.
      Very truly yours
         D M Sabin[37]

   William McGee, painter, may have found some work as the weather
improved, as no letters of assistance or anxiety from any of the central char-
acters appear on the record. But at some point before Christmas 1871, Will

McGee, after living in Stillwater
rent free at Rev. Langley's home for
a year and a half, left Minnesota
completely and would be found at
the home of his foster father and
mother, Rev. and Mrs. Pattison, in
Muskegon, Michigan.[38]

   The Reverend Pattison, who
by his own account saved Willie
from typhoid fever in 1864 and
then adopted him, seemed to have
a rocky relationship with Willie
since the shooting of Dr. Chandler
Braman. During the previous
two years Pattison had alternately
defended Willie and ignored him.
While there may be suspicions
about Holmes Pattison, there can
be no doubt he helped McGee
while he was sick in Tennessee;
that without him there would be
no Medal of Honor; and perhaps
most importantly, his connection
and intervention with Marcus
Ward greatly advanced the pardon

Congressman Dwight Sabin, whose lumber firm made a fortune through convict
labor at Stillwater, was anxious to jump
on the McGee bandwagon but would soon
tire of Willie's lifestyle (Minnesota Historical Society).

Willie received. At other times Willie — through Rev. Langley — had accused Pattison of neglect and theft of personal articles. Whether three years in Minnesota was wearing on McGee, or, more likely, Willie was wearing out his welcome physically, economically, and socially in Stillwater, the following letter from Holmes Pattison shows us Will McGee had taken a new direction in his still young life:

Ridgeway, Elk County, Pa.
Dec. 22, 1871
Hon. Marcus L. Ward
    Newark
        Dear Sir — My adopted son William McGee is now at home with us in this place, my wife's home. He came home this fall, and appears to be contented and happy. He wishes me to say to you for him that he is under life lasting obligations to you for the favors you have shown him in the time of his troubles especially the money you sent him when he was without any whatsoever and would have acknowledged it long since but for his unsettled condition and the fact that you were about to leave for Europe and did not learn of your return until recently. He will go into the Bakery business here at the earliest possible day. Allow me in conclusion to tender you my sincere thanks for your kind offices to Willie, and to acknowledge my obligations to you of the same.
                I remain yours truly,
                H.A. Pattison[39]

On December 27, 1871, Marcus Ward sent an apparent response to Holmes Pattison, with wonderful news for all concerned:

Newark N J Dec 27, 1871
H A Pattison, Esquire
    My dear Sir:
        Your kind letter of Dec 22nd is received — and I am required to learn that you son is with you — well and happy. He is young and has, I trust, many years before him and it will depend upon himself alone what his future shall be. I believe him to be well disposed.... Accept my thanks for your letter and the kind intentions therein expressed. Tell your son that he can but repay all trouble I have taken on his account by an honorable and true life. Remember me kindly to your son and family
                Yours truly
                Marcus Ward[40]

It was a long hard road for any young man, but for the still 21-year-old New Jersey war hero, harder than most.

CHAPTER TWELVE

Willie McGee, Family Man

Some lives there are that move in music, lucky lives,
and some, most, that do not.
— Thomas Flanagan,
The Tenants of Time

What singular moment in the fall of 1871 caused Willie McGee to leave Stillwater, Minnesota, never to return? Why he left behind the Reverend Bob Langley, who had been such a steadfast mentor for almost three years is a mystery, but Willie McGee, since the day he enlisted in 1863, had established a pattern of sudden changes of address.[1] Perhaps a better question would be why McGee stayed in Stillwater more than a year after being pardoned from its federal prison.

Stillwater, today a beautiful, gentrified colony of art and antiques, was vastly different in 1871. When Willie left Minnesota, the West was still very wild and five years away from Custer's stupidity at the Little Big Horn and the James and Younger brothers' equally unenlightened raid on the Northfield, Minnesota, bank (which act would result in prison for three of the gang in the prison Willie had just left).[2] Will McGee remained for more than a year in the very river town he had just spent almost two years in as a prisoner. Upon his release, McGee may, on some level, have been regarded as a local hero, flashing his Medal of Honor and with a presidential pardon — much different than the criminal careers of most of the other prisoners in Stillwater. Friendship with Marcus Ward gave Willie cachet with Governor Austin and Congressman Dwight Sabin, which carried him socially for a while. It was certainly possible Willie McGee walked the streets of Stillwater showing his Medal of Honor, passing his letters of recommendation from various governors and generals, and showing his "life story"—the chapter from John Y. Foster's *New Jersey in the Rebellion*, though it was unlikely he included the negative story from the *Stillwater Republican*.

At what juncture McGee's notoriety or popularity ran out is unknown, but both the Reverend Langley and Congressman Sabin could see a bad moon rising for Willie and said so in letters to Marcus Ward.[3] Hinted at indirectly—and sometimes pointedly—for several years, it was evident Willie had a problem with alcohol, so when Holmes Pattison wrote to Marcus Ward at Christmas in 1871 from Elk County, Pa., it is clear that Holmes and Minny Pattison had a plan for their adopted son. It would turn out to be their last, for Willie McGee was not cut out to be a baker.

Elk County, Pa., then and now a great place to raise a family, is as remote a locality as can be found east of the Mississippi, but it was never exciting enough for a legend like Willie McGee. Willie was placed by his adoptive parents in the bakery business as the New Year of 1872 approached. It is a good bet that the Pattisons recognized Willie's weakness, and had taken him to Minny's homeplace, leaving him with relatives to recuperate, strengthen, and make a plan for his future. It would be the Pattisons last good deed for Willie McGee.

Whether Willie liked Elk County, whose population today is only 35,000, is unknown, but it is unlikely that the secluded area kept him long. Within a year, and probably much sooner, Willie was on the road, working 145 miles east of Elk County in Northumberland, Pa., at the confluence of the two main branches of the beautiful Susquehanna River.[4] Willie may have felt very comfortable in Northumberland, for it was much like Stillwater, only in a better clime and without a federal prison.

Perhaps Willie was finally making his way home to the metropolitan area where his friend Marcus Ward could mentor him personally. Maybe he was headed for Connecticut, where he could be reunited with his brother John, sister Mary, or even his oldest brother, Mike, who was raising a family in Jersey City.[5] Though it is strange he had taken so long to finally head east, McGee would not be the first veteran of the war to roam the countryside searching for a fresh start, only to eventually find his way home.

But head east he did, stopping in Northumberland after apparently deciding the bakery business in isolated Elk County was not in his long- or short-range plans. Leaving Elk County would be the final break between Willie and Holmes Pattison. Neither would publicly acknowledge the other ever again, in what had been a bizarre seven-year relationship. Northumberland sits on the east bank of the northern branch of the Susquehanna, with the older Revolutionary village of Sunbury on the south side. The area had been settled early in the eighteenth century because of its strategic river location. As the two powerful branches of one of America's great rivers meets at Northumberland and Sunbury, the Susquehanna runs west and south to Harrisburg before heading east again and eventually rolling into the Chesapeake basin. By 1860, both the river and the railroad had made the area a prime player in lumber and manufacturing. Northumberland was originally known earlier in the century, after the canals were opened, for its breweries, tanneries, and boat building, much like Stillwater a century later in Minnesota. After the war, lumber mills became prosperous and together with the railroad boom jobs were plentiful for Willie when he arrived sometime in 1871.[6]

Whether McGee was just passing through or had permanent plans we do not know, but sometime in early 1872 his plans solidified when he fell in love with a local girl, Regina Faust. Pennsylvania records are scant, and there is little we know but her name and age. Willie and the twenty-one-year-old Regina were married in the summer of 1872, and in the fall of 1873 Regina gave birth to the couple's first child, a daughter they named Julia Ward Magee.[7]

By 1873, Willie was an old twenty-two when he left Elk County and arrived in Northumberland, and we can only wish and hope that our Irish drummer boy was finally ready to accept life's responsibilities, with a new town, a young wife, and a baby girl. Surely it has been a formula millions of young men throughout history have discovered en route to maturity.

It was a wonderful opportunity for the young man from Newark, but if Willie McGee was looking forward to a new life with Regina and baby Julia Ward Magee, life stepped in and slapped them — and more than a million other Americans — in the face and knocked many of them into a gutter of poverty, hunger, and death.

There are years Americans never forget: 1776, 1861, 1929, 1941, and, of course, 2001, but the panic of 1873 and the depression which followed our first industrial collapse is often overlooked, though it was truly disastrous.[8] If a national depression can be blamed on one man, it rested with Jay Cooke, a Philadelphia banker who issued millions of dollars of worthless railroad stock. The national economy, already on the precipice of overextension, collapsed completely in a domino effect. The New York Stock Exchange closed for ten days, and of the country's 364 railroads eighty-nine went bankrupt within a month. In the next two years, 18,000 businesses failed, and the entire country suffered, as unemployment in New York City went over twenty percent and millions across the country were thrown out of work. Americans, who habitually refuse to recognize hunger in their own land while trying to save countless others, watched famine boldly break down the doors of hundreds of thousands. People throughout the country slept outdoors after being evicted from their homes, tenements, and property.[9]

The government did little or nothing to stem the tide of depression or alleviate the suffering it caused. In truth, many Americans believed that government interference in the economy was wrong, and wealthy leaders argued that the growing gap between rich and poor was just the natural order of things, that the strong should be rewarded and the weak had only themselves to blame for their problems and poverty. During the decade when Willie married and started his first family, some early unions attempted to protect its workers, and strikes were common. But unionization was not yet ingrained in the American mind, and most failed miserably.[10]

Willie McGee, after beginning his young adult life with seriously poor, even disastrous decisions, started anew in Northumberland, unwittingly at the worst possible time for young people of the "humbler" class. Willie's early life as a married man is lost to us, but it wouldn't have mattered what he did to try to earn a living, once Jay Cooke's scheme failed. Northumberland's industries declined or dried up completely. The Chamberlain, Frick and Company lumber mill almost folded at this time, as did the huge blast furnace built by James Marsh. The Northumberland Car and Manufacturing Company suffered even more, folding totally less than a year after erecting large buildings near the site of the empty Marsh furnace, eventually to be sold at a sheriff's sale. The only construction in town that did not fail was the erection of the new school building, begun in 1870 and completed in 1872, just a year prior to depression.[11]

Even more dismal was the railroad industry, on which Northumberland, like so many hundreds of other river towns, was dependent. Local people believed early on that the railroad would transform the area, especially after the Sunbury & Erie line commenced operations and the Erie Lackawanna started carrying passengers in May of 1860; but when depression hit in 1873, rail life died along with industry, and the railroads would never become a factor in Northumberland life again, certainly not as far as passenger lines were concerned.[12] In many respects, Northumberland suffered lost hopes in a lost American decade, which saw hundreds of thousands of Americans sink into hopelessness and degradation.

Following Christmas 1873, Willie, now two years removed from Minnesota, was once again desperate for work, but eastern Pennsylvania was aflame with hunger, poverty, and hate. Between Northumberland and Pottsville, 40 miles to the southeast, 1874 was no place for an Irish-American looking for work, Medal of Honor or not. The entire area was mountainous and heavily wooded, but more importantly it was seething with ethnic tensions, especially among the Welsh and the Irish. This tension would result in decades-long violence both by and against Irish immigrants throughout eastern Pennsylvania. A clandestine organization attributed to the Irish and known as the Molly Maguires ruled by fear, intimidation, and murder, though these Irish were in truth more victimized by the business power structure led by railroad baron Franklin Gowen. More than one man would be hanged simply by a whisper of the word "Molly" mentioned in the same breath as his name. But the fear and violence was real, and Molly Maguire country, when Willie and Regina were struggling to build a new life together, saw twenty so-called Mollies hanged for murder just east of their home in Northumberland. Between 1870 and 1875 the area stretching along the anthracite mines saw fifty-five dead and 1,667 maimed and injured in the mines, strikes, and "related" activities.[13]

In January 1874, when Willie McGee was about to turn twenty-five, fully one third of the workers in Pennsylvania were "idle" and the Pennsylvania State Bureau of Industrial Statistics commented that the "community has suffered a degree of demoralization that twenty years of war could not have effected."[14] Later that same month, Willie and much of America were desperate, and McGee turned to the one man he felt he could count on — his old friend and mentor, Marcus Ward. Willie, who had disappeared from public view for just over two years and had apparently made a conscious decision to avoid family and old friends to make a new life, reverted to old form:

Northumberland, Jan 21st 1874
Hon Marcus L Ward
　　Dear sir you will no doubt be considerable surprised on receipt of this note from me your humble friend Wm McGee drummer boy of the 33rd. But circumstances have so dealt with me that I need the assistance of some friendly hand. Now Gov I ask it as a great favor that you will use your Influence in getting me some kind of Imployment as I have been out of work all this winter and being married and having a family to support, knowing your former kindnesses to me in time past I again take the liberty of writing to you.
　　Gov I have been married nearly two years and I have had a great deal to contend with as concerns myself and family sickness and other troubles has followed me all along so that I have been compelled to deny myself in many ways the necessities of life also I have been compelled to make a sackrific that my very feeling revolted against I speak of my MEDAL a merchant knowing the great value I placed on it for the necessities of life and I have not as yet been able to redeem it. And will not unless I get some thing to do since I left the army I have learned the painting trade as I thought it would be something the world could not take from me therefore I would like it if you would favor me and see Mr. Brown the architect at the capitol and with your influence give me

a job and if he can not will you please get me some thing to do where I can support my family this winter I care not what it is. Some time ago while in conversation with ex-Gov Pollick he told me that he would do all that was in his power he all so told me that he would speak to Gov Hartsranft for me a position I went to Harrisburg and seen the Governor the other day and he said at present he could think of nothing as the legislature had just assembled and the Philadelphia members have filled all vacant positions with their friends he wished me to remind him of it by writing to him weekly he advised me to go to Washington and see our Representative of this district that he would no doubt with knowing my past career get me some thing to do. But not being intamality acquainted with the Hon J.B. Packe I appeal to you for your influence in getting me some thing to do for I do not know what I will do if I do not — get — work of some kind soon Gov I do not know as you will care to mention of my family I will say that it consists of my wife and child a dear little girl I have given her your name in part so as to ever keep in remembrance of your more than fatherly kindness to me it has made a new man of me and if it had only been a boy it would have had the honor of your full name. I ask you to do if possible something for me if you can this is the hardes winter that I have ever seen I hope and pray that you will please take note of this humble epistle and anser me as soon as convient.

> Very Respt your Humble servant
> Wm McGee

Direct your letter to William McGee
Northumberland
 Northd Co. Pa.[15]

Just like that, Will McGee was out of the shadows and Marcus Ward had to decide if he wished to resume a relationship with his missing prodigal project or take the stance of Holmes Pattison — and perhaps the McGee family as well — that of benign, or deliberate, neglect. Ward, who had steadfastly been loyal to all sons of New Jersey who fought in the war, had himself resumed active participation in national politics these past two years. In 1872 he was elected to Congress and, because of his stellar reputation, selected as chairman to the Foreign Relations Committee. When the depression struck in 1874, Ward was renominated, but change was inevitably in the wind and he was defeated, though gathering more votes than any other New Jersey Republican.[16]

The congressman, warmly appreciated by President Grant, was offered several national positions, including that of Commissioner of Indian Affairs, but his good heart never left New Jersey. He returned to his hometown of Newark, deciding that at age sixty-two he would resume his love of history and art. Ward visited Europe extensively twice, but most of the last decade of his philanthropic life was spent managing his own estate, the Home for Disabled Soldiers, which he built and paid for personally, and the New Jersey Historical Society.[17]

How far would Marcus Ward go to maintain a serious relationship with Willie McGee, a man who always had a strange relationship with the truth? After two years of total silence, Willie wrote to Ward begging for help in much the same language he had used after shooting Dr. Chandler Braman. In addition to asking for assistance, Willie's most anxious complaint was the loss of his medal, which makes him much more agitated than talking about his wife and child. Regina was never mentioned by name, and young baby Julia Ward Magee was discussed only regarding her name. Would it be possible that Marcus Ward, one of the kindest men ever to grace the governorship of New Jersey, would fall again for the charm of William Henry McGee? Would there be any doubt?

One month after his first contact in more than two years, Willie wrote again to Ward, the letter revealing without question that Willie was in steady communication with Marcus, and in fact had visited the congressman in his Capitol Hill office; he was given another loan, this one perhaps enabling Willie to recoup his Medal of Honor, and perhaps a little to help at home with Regina and the baby. Written from Northumberland, Willie was once again Ward's best friend, and there can be no question the drummer boy had the "soldier's friend" firmly in his corner:

Northumberland   Feb. 25, 1874
Hon M L Ward
Dear sir:
   Having safely arrived home, all right, I thought and finding my family safe and well I thought it my duty to drop you a few lines to let you know that such was the case. I have not yet received my papers yet but am looking every day. You will please send them as soon as you can conviently. I might say that I sent Mr. Dubois the reporter of the National Republican a few lines a few days ago. Expect to hear from you soon.

Anxiously waiting
William McGee[18]

Was Marcus Ward pleased with what he saw in the "new" Willie McGee? Was he pleased to see what changes had taken place in his former drummer boy, a married young father he had not physically seen in seven years nor heard from in two? In a book titled *History of Newark*, published in 1878 by Joseph Atkinson, Willie McGee was described as a "bright, sharp-eyed, intelligent, full grown and very handsome lad."[19] In February of 1874 when the two met in Washington, Willie asked for his "papers," a recurring theme he pursued the rest of his life. These "papers," from what we can gather, included his Medal of Honor letter, the letters of recommendation for his army commission from General George Thomas, Governor John Geary, and Governor Marcus Ward, his letter of pardon from the secretary of war, and without question the four page "story of my life" from John Y. Foster's *New Jersey in the Rebellion*.[20]

We can only surmise that once again Willie was able to charm the prodigiously generous congressman from Newark. Is it also possible Will McGee was a changed man and Ward was properly thrilled at his maturity and impressed as well with his new life as a husband and father? Surely McGee's letter was a positive note with no hints the meeting was anything but a positive one between the two strange bedfellows.

In the coming months, Willie McGee wrote almost a dozen letters, which have been preserved in the Marcus Ward legacy; and based on Ward's history, Marcus must have answered all of them — or they would not have continued. Ward received hundreds of such letters, postcards, and notes from veterans from 1862 to 1882, maybe thousands, and the majority were saved but not responded to by the kindly Jersey philanthropist. There were however, about three dozen veterans over the years who maintained some continuity with the governor, but none lasted as long, or were as passionate, as the ones between Ward and McGee.[21]

Though Willie seemed poised for additional help from Marcus Ward (for at least the third time in his brief life), he was limited in his options. Even if Willie was closer to his family than can be discovered, it would have been difficult to relocate to the metropolitan area, as unemployment in 1874 was well over 20 percent in New York City.[22] It has never been explained, however, why at various times McGee never returned to his hometown of Newark, especially since it was the home power and political base of Marcus Ward.

Willie may have been settled and content in Northumberland, and it is certain Regina had family there as well; nonetheless, there was little margin for error in 1874. If unemployment was high in Northumberland, it was worse in the immediate area east to Scranton. The entire eastern half of Pennsylvania was awash with strikes and violence, most of which centered on the Irish and Irish-Americans. Willie McGee, a first generation Irish-American with both a military and convict past, would find it difficult — if not impossible — to find honest work without becoming involved in the anthracite violence that to the present day has not yet been forgotten or forgiven. In the next eighteen months, starting in January 1874, killings attributed to the Molly Maguires took place in the area just east of Northumberland including Shamokin, Mahanoy City, and Tamaqua.[23]

When Willie asked for help, Ward was thus only able to advise him to head for Philadelphia, where Ward's political influence and fellow Republicans might be of some assistance. It can come as no surprise, therefore, that

Willie's next letter to his old friend would be from Philadelphia, on March 8, 1874. Willie must have convinced Regina he must leave home for the family to survive, and he very well may have been right.

> Hon M L Ward
>   Dear Friend
>   You will see by the date of this that I am in Philadelphia I arrived here and reported for duty at the Navy Yard on Thursday morning and am well satisfied with my position. I would like to be certain of staying through the year. But as there is to be a reduction in a few days I am afraid they will try to turn me out with the rest. Pleas inform me if my appointment here is permininit. I thank you for the kind advise you have given me and shall make my future conduct prove my recent resolutions. Pleas accept this kind regards and obliges
>   Yours
>   Wm McGee
> Direct to me   No 28 Washington Av
>   Phila
>   Pa[24]

If there was any doubt that Marcus Ward still felt something for Will McGee — concern, obligation, sadness, or sympathy — those doubts were laid to rest. McGee left Northumberland and traveled through anthracite mining country to Philadelphia, where Marcus Ward had procured a position for him at the Navy Yard.[25] Three weeks later, on March 31, Willie again wrote to one of the most generous, caring leaders in New Jersey history. In a scene now too familiar, it was really two letters in one. The first was from McGee, the second from William Phoenix, a minister and businessman whom Willie had befriended and asked for assistance:

>   Philadelphia   Mar 31 1874
> Hon M L Ward
>   Dr Sir
>   I understand that there is to be a large discharge to be made in the Phila Navy Yard to-morrow & I am afraid that I will be one of the discharged (You know how much in need of employment I am) I wish that you would use your influence to have me retained as I have sent for my wife and child.
>   Yours truly
>   Wm McGee[26]
> Please address Phila P.O.

> Phila Mar 31, 1874
>   I have met Mr. McGee in this city & I have found him to be a steady honest man. Work is scarce here & he is in need of it. I wish that you would do what you can for him. I write this to almost a perfect stranger but your son & I used to be quite intimate. I am a Newark man & perhaps you can hear from my

Mead & Robbins,

MANUFACTURERS OF STANDARD

SILVER-PLATED GOODS,

N. E. Corner Ninth and Chestnut Streets,

Philadelphia, Mar 31ˢᵗ 1874

Hon M. L. Ward

D Sir

I understand that there is going to be a large discharge to be made in the Phila Navy Yard to-morrow & I am afraid that I will be one of the discharged (You know how much in need of employment I am) I wish that you would use your influence to have me retained as I have sent for my wife & child.

Yours truly,

Wm McGee

Please address Phila P.O.

In the midst of a national depression, Willie went on the road searching for work, and conducted a letter writing campaign with Marcus Ward, once again begging for help.

family if you will write to W.A. or J.C. Ludlum. Hoping you will receive this in time to be of use I subscribe myself.

Respty Yours
William E. Phoenix

NE Corner 9th and Chestnut
Formerly with Curtain Hawkins & Dodd
Newark NJ[27]

A week before sending this to Ward, Willie wrote to Regina telling her he wished to have both her and their daughter come to Philadelphia, but this letter has not survived. After an absence of three months from Northumberland, Willie received the following letter from his young wife, the only letter we have from Regina to Willie:

North   April 8th 1874
My Dear Husband
   Yours of the 6th came to hand on last eve and was anxiously received. I am ashured you for I did not know hardly what to think about it. But as you gave explanation I am satisfied I hope that you will have no more trouble about your work. You spoke of sending for me on the 25th you will have to send me some money as I cannot very well get along without now that Spring time is here and I would like to arrange the Babe clothing before hand. I am still patiently waiting on her Cloak as I cannot take her out without something to wrap her in.... Will, you say you wrote to me during your stay there well I never seen it this is the first I have heard from you in nearly five weeks. I hope it may not be so long the next time the babe has grown so you would be surprised to see her. She is so far well I give her a kiss every night for her <u>absent father</u>.
   Well when are you coming home it seems an age since I saw you I would so like to see you I can hardly wait for the time you may laugh at this but it is true Well I must close for this now for I have sutch a headache that can hardly see to write. So good by once more dear husband from your loving wife Regina.

Write soon
Good by[28]

Two weeks after Regina wrote to her absent husband in Philadelphia, Willie again contacted Marcus Ward:

Philadelphia   April 21, 1874
Hon M L Ward
Dear Sir
   I have been waiting in suspense ever since I recd a letter from you. You said that I would be reinstated if I had not been discharged for cause there were 200 thrown out with me so as to reduce the number of workmen. My papers have not come in yet therefore I do not know what to do as I cant get anything to do here, what is the cause of the delay perhaps I am forgotten or they have lain strewn aside I have some enemy here that will work against me & perhaps he is

the party who has written to you. I suppose it has been John Walefnoff the one who was my pardner in the Painting business.

If it is only as a laborer do get me something so I will have something to do. I am sure that I have been living a good sober life since I have been here & worked every day that I have had work & no one could say any different without they told a malicious falsehood. I wish that I knew who it was positively that wrote you so I could go to them & compel them to write you the truth. I hope that you will see that I am put back immediately as I am pretty low down in the pocket.

Enclosed please find a letter from my wife, I wrote her after I read one from you. Will you please answer me as soon as is possibly convient. You can write me care of W. E. Phoenix as before.

> Wm McGee
> Rev Wm E Phoenix
> NW Cor 9th & Chestnut Street[29]

Three weeks later on May 10, 1874, Regina McGee had still not heard from nor seen her husband, and is in panic mode:

Northd May 10, 1874
Hon M L Ward
Dear sir

I take the liberty of writing to you in order to ask if you know weather my husband is in the employ of the Philadelphia Navy Yard now or not. As I have not heard any word from him for near two months. Thinking you might know of him is why I write to you. Not knowing who else to seek information from I will be grateful to you for any news of him however brief. Anxiously waiting I remain   Respectfully yours
> Mrs. Wm McGee
> Northumberland, Northd Co.
> PO Box 241   Penna[30]

Regina had reason to be concerned, for Willie had indeed been released at the Navy Yard in late April.[31] McGee, along with thousands of other unemployed men, was desperate to feed not only himself but also his family. All over the land households were now being run by women, as uncounted numbers of men searched for work wherever they might find it. While many families survived, countless others did not, as husbands abandoned their wives and children rather than admit their inability to feed and care for them. Several years later, the 1880 census showed many thousands of women like Regina Magee listed as "head of household" (not widows), with no man at home.[32]

Willie McGee did not run from Regina and little Julia Ward in 1874, but he did roam, looking for work everywhere and anywhere, and the stress, heartache, and loneliness had to be taking a toll. Willie took pains to tell

Marcus Ward in his last letter he had been living a "sober life," and had his
newest minister sidekick William Phoenix confirm it, leading one to believe
Marcus Ward had put some stipulations on his assistance to the McGee family. In his next letter to Ward, dated May 16, Willie wrote from Bryn Mawr,
Pa., then, as now, a wealthy Philadelphia suburb where homeowners hired
help rather than do it themselves. In 1874, Willie and Civil War veterans who
had fought a brutal war found themselves facing misery and hunger a decade
after surviving cannons, gunshots, and bayonets. The letter of May 16 read:

> Bryn Mawr May 16 1874
> Hon M L Ward
> My Dear Sir
> As I have been feeling so bad of late and since you wrot me your last letter
> I have not written home since for those who think I was discharged for cause
> which was not for when I was discharged theur was 200 men went out with me
> now Gov will you be so kind as to let me know what if any thing that I have
> done for Gods sake that I have tried but to write and Gov it troubles me so that
> I do not know what to do and when I look back up from my past life and thing
> what you have don for me I would freely lay my life down for you for you ar all
> the friend on earth that I have for both my parents ar dead. After I got your
> letter I went to the yard every day for three weeks and as my papers had not
> got thear and as I could not get employment in Phil I came to this place and
> got a gentleman house to paint and I will have work hear for about one month
> Gov do you think that I could get back in the yard in July when the new appro-
> priations begins as they will take on about 500 men and they tell me that if I
> could get in there that provided be shour of work till Spring and if I could get
> stead work for that time it would give me a start for I think things will not be
> much better this Summer and then things are now Gov excuse bad writing and
> spelling for as you know I was taking from school at the age of eleven and set
> earning a living for my mother and self Gov I will send you the money that you
> let me have when I was in Washington please let me know if you can get me in
> the nave yard in July if you would speake to John Kelley for me he could put
> me in as I'm in his district Gov pleas ancer this for if you know how bad I feel
> and a letter from you will cheur me up so good night Dear Gov
>
> Wm McGee
> Bryn Mawr
> Montgomery Co. Pa.[33]

McGee, though not an honest man in past lives, and perhaps not at the
time of this letter, still must be given credit for his recent attempts. Though
continuing to beg for assistance, his pleas were for work, not straight requests
for loans, pardons, gifts, or no-show jobs. True to his word — a major step
for Willie — he worked a month in Bryn Mawr, but when the work ended,
he traveled to Henry Clay, Delaware, and wrote again to Marcus Ward, still
the "soldier's friend."

Henry Clay, Del
    June 18, 1874
Hon M L Ward
    Dear Sir

I am now out of the job I had when you wrote me and have been traveling about the country hunting employment ever since but have failed in every until I came here when I got a week's employment; more from Charity than otherwise; with E. J. DuPont & Co. Powder Manufacturers — but it is but a week; after which time I am wholly at a loss where to go and what to do, as so many are in a similar state just now; Therefore I hope you may use your utmost endeavors to secure something for me to do anything in fact — work is as scarce now, it seems, as in midwinter — so that if you can get me the place in the Navy yard you will be doing something for me I can never forget!

One more favor. I possess two recommendations I received while in the Army. They were sent with my case to Judge Holt. One is from the late Gov Geary of Pa and one from yourself. If you will get them for me you will confer a great favor — as I would very much like to have them. One being from my dead General and therefore being valuable to me on that account. As I can only remain here a week and know not where to go afterwards, I hope you will reply as soon as possible.

            Very truly yours
            Wm McGee
Address   Henry Clay,   P.O. Delaware[34]

Where Will McGee roamed the rest of the summer and fall of 1874 is a mystery, as no correspondence survives. Did he return to Northumberland and find work, or was Marcus Ward successful — again — at helping Willie in the Philadelphia Navy Yard? Or did McGee roam with so many other thousands surviving day to day, week to week? There are no letters found in the Ward collection from Regina, so we can surmise Willie was in touch with his wife, either by letter or in person, especially considering Regina was pregnant in October. As Christmas 1874 approached, Willie wrote once again to his mentor, and now ex-congressman, Marcus Ward:

Dec. 21, 1874
    Phila Pa
Dear Gov

I saw Gov Mindle this morning and he informed me that he had received a letter from you, stating that you had seen the Secy of the Navy and used your influence to have me retained at the Philad Yard, I was discharged a couple of days after Gov Mindle had written to you. I went to the Navy yard this morning after seeing the Genl and found there had been no order for my reinstatement.

I am out of a situation at present and convinced that it will be hard to get a situation at any trade or anything else in Phila this winter. Do you think it possible to have me returned to the Navy yard or could you get me with architect Brown at the Capitol as he employs painters the year round.

I think if you saw General Negley he would cooperate with you in my behalf. Also if you get recommendations of mine which are in possession of Judge Holt, you would greatly oblige me.

Thankful for past favors recd

> I remain
> Very truly yours
> William McGee

913 Bainbridge Street　　　Phila Pa.[35]

In the course of the year 1874, Willie McGee left no stone unturned in his search for honest work. He reconnected with Marcus Ward, perhaps swallowing some pride, if he still had any, and met with him in Washington, securing gifts or loans, as well as promises of future help. Was Willie just a lifelong leech, or a changed family man? The drummer boy wrote with frequency throughout the year to the New Jersey humanitarian, who found work for him in Philadelphia, and loaned him money.[36] In addition the "soldier's friend" continued to spend much time corresponding not only with Willie directly but with those who were on the periphery of McGee's life. As the depression continued, Willie McGee worked extremely hard finding work on his own as well, and his letters to Ward show some definite maturity heretofore not seen in the Medal of Honor recipient. McGee never lost his lifelong penchant for the direct approach, and in 1874 he traveled to Harrisburg and Philadelphia to meet with Governor John Hartranft; former Governor James Pollack, a native of Northumberland; Pennsylvania congressman James Negley, a former Union army general, each a staunch friend of veterans; and any other politician he could try to charm and manipulate.[37]

In all his letters Willie's mind appeared sharp, and, because he worked at several jobs with no hint of dismissal other than the work ending, he may very well have been in good physical and mental condition — and sober — as he more than once mentioned to Marcus Ward. As New Year 1875 approached, the national depression continued, and in the Northumberland area it worsened. Franklin Gowen, one of the most despicable industrialists of the nineteenth, or any, century, was by 1870 president of the Philadelphia and Reading Railroad. In late 1874, when Willie was returning home to Northumberland, Gowen arbitrarily cut the mine wages of the area by half in violation of an existing contract. The move ignited "The Long Strike," where workers in the eastern anthracite mining area refused to work. The strike was a disaster, and when it ended in June of 1875, violence escalated in the region and eight more assassinations occurred, including that of Frederick Hesser at Shamokin, a short ten miles from Northumberland.[38] Two Irish brothers, Columbus and Michael McGee, natives of "The Rosses" in West Donegal County, Ireland, were among the many Molly Maguires tried for murder that year.[39] These

McGee brothers, with no hint of relation to Willie, were acquitted of the charge.

There is absolutely no evidence for the possibility McGee was involved, but all of 1875 is a mystery regarding William H. McGee. There are no letters in the Ward collection at either Rutgers University or the New Jersey Historical Society regarding Will McGee for the years 1875–1879. Was Willie given a full-time permanent position at the Philadelphia Navy Yard through the largesse of Marcus Ward which might have helped him into becoming a respectable citizen? It is possible, but if this were the case, it would seem there would have been more positive correspondence between the two men. Did Willie continue to roam the East Coast searching for work wherever it could be found? Another possibility, but when this happened in 1874, Willie was unrelenting in asking — begging — for help from the New Jersey philanthropist.

The only known fact of 1875 for McGee is the birth in Northumberland of Willie and Regina's second child, Mary Alene Magee, born on July 29.[40] With the exception of the birth of this baby, who would eventually grow into a beautiful and pious young woman, marry a minister and leave a large and respected family still found in Pennsylvania, nothing is known of what happened to Will McGee.

That there was another break with Marcus Ward is obvious, but what caused the rift? The only hint comes from the descendants of Mary Alene Magee, whose oral family history tells a familiar story. Mary Alene, left a true orphan as a teenager, married the Reverend Charles F. Kulp in 1903, at age 27, in her hometown of Northumberland. The couple and their children settled down in Phillipsburg, Pennsylvania, where both Mary and Charles became revered citizens. Mary Kulp passed down to her family only two memories of her father, Willie McGee, who left home when she was one year old. The first was that William Magee served in the army during the Civil War and was awarded a Medal of Honor by Abraham Lincoln as a very young soldier of fifteen on February 7, 1866. Like so much of oral history, it is based on solid truth and small misconceptions or exaggerations. Mary Alene Kulp had everything right except the part about Lincoln.

The other Magee memory passed down for more than a hundred years was less positive but known to all of Mary Alene's descendants. "After Willy got out of the army he worked for the Pennsylvania Railroad and regularly on payday headed for the saloon," remembers Diane Bretz, Willie and Regina McGee's great-granddaughter. "His wife, short of money for home and kids, wrote to the president of the railroad. He wrote back telling her he had instructed the payroll department to deliver Willy's pay only to her, his wife, and not to Willy." Diane's aunt remembers the letter being shown and read at family gatherings, "but it has not been seen for some years."[41]

This Magee oral history may be as close to understanding the missing years 1875 and 1876 as we can manage. Willie, no doubt hesitant to reveal aspects of his postwar life, nonetheless hid his Medal of Honor fame and notoriety from nobody, and we know from his letters to Marcus Ward that he had hocked the medal at least temporarily with a Northumberland merchant.[42] Certainly Pennsylvania Magee descendants had the truth about Willie and his serious problems with alcohol without knowing any other part of his history. There can be little doubt a letter from a railroad executive — perhaps even the president — existed, as many members of the family saw it for decades.[43] Can we with probability believe Willie worked, at least for a reasonable period between 1875 and the following year, for the railroad? Is it also likely Marcus Ward held back some support for Willie either because he had at last a steady job or, worse, because he had sunk deeper into the bottle? The letter enabling Regina to receive Willie's paycheck would be a wonderful victory for a woman in an 1875 man's world, but it would turn out to be a battle Regina would win only to lose the war.

We will never know exactly when or why, but in the summer of 1876 Willie McGee of Northumberland, Pa., abandoned his loved ones, leaving his twenty-five-year-old wife and two baby daughters, aged three and one. For sure Willie was not the only man in that terrible time to run, but perhaps the humiliation of his pay being sent directly home was

Mary Alene Magee, the only surviving child of the marriage between Regina and Willie, was left to be raised by an aunt in Northumberland, Pennsylvania. Mary would marry a minister and raise a family, in central Pennsylvania, still known for their kindness and generosity (Diane Bretz Collection).

the final straw. Magee oral history only proves how often families have some selective memory. Regina Magee, who raised two baby girls and had two sons who died in childhood, with an alcoholic, runaway husband during a dark depression, was remembered only as "Willy's wife," even her name forgotten, and the desertion of the family by Willie had been repressed in family memory. Mary Alene, the only surviving Northumberland Magee by 1886, raised by an aunt, would pass on to future generations two great stories: Her father's supposed magnificent military career and her mother's truly heroic battle of survival.[44] This Pennsylvania wife of Will McGee has been sadly forgotten while Willie's medal is remembered, but the true hero of the Northumberland Magee's would be Regina Magee, dead at 35 and buried in an unmarked grave in her hometown of Northumberland, Pa., along with three children who never made it to adulthood. [45]

Though Marcus Ward's collection is strangely silent, it would be impossible to believe he was unaware of Willie's decline and desertion. In a long forgotten work by Joseph Atkinson entitled *History of Newark* published in 1878, Willie's career is highlighted, and the ending is unflattering: "It is charity to draw a veil over his [McGee's] after-life. The iron of shame and disgrace entered into his spirit, and the proud hero of Murfreesboro became a moral wreck."[46] Marcus Ward not only had copies of this book in his beloved New Jersey Historical Society, but he himself would be a likely source for most of the chapter on Willie's career.

Willie McGee ran west. He had bold new ideas, proven old formulas, but no Marcus Ward, whose direct correspondence with Willie now ended permanently. McGee lost one nemesis during this pivotal year of 1877. Dr. Isaac Braman found the only closure any parent of murdered children can receive — his own death. The good doctor died of pneumonia in Boston at 63, eight years after the shooting of his son Chandler in Baton Rouge.[47] Dr. Isaac fought to bring Willie to justice as hard as Marcus Ward did to pardon him, but in the end power, money, and politics won the day.

CHAPTER THIRTEEN

Exposed

Temptation waits for all, and ills will come;
but some go out and ask the Devil home.
— John Boyle O'Reilly

When Willie McGee went on the run at age twenty-eight, he was not alone. By the end of 1877 three million people across the nation were unemployed, an unknown number abandoning homes and families just like Willie, and suicide was a viable option for many. Andreas Fuchs of Manhattan, a 40-year-old shoemaker, epitomized untold thousands when he shot himself to death in Central Park, leaving a note saying, "I have no work and do not know what to do."[1] In fact the depression of 1873 lasted until 1879, and the misery it caused has been glossed over in many of our history books.

Willie was not just running, he was running out of options. Throughout his young life, McGee's personality always found him friends, but he would not likely be welcomed in Baton Rouge, Minnesota, or Pennsylvania, and he had not been back to Newark for a decade. Where was he to go? Despite the fact Regina was of the "humbler" class, Willie had to pick somewhere he would not be recognized readily. Had McGee hit rock bottom? He had lost, by his own bad decisions, his military career, his family, and his best and most powerful friend. Desperation in Willie had been building for more than two years, and, when backed into a corner, he reverted to an old formula, the gathering of his "papers," which he treated as his legacy and proof of his unique history.

The Christmas prior to his abandoning Regina, Willie found the time to travel to Washington, D.C., and personally asked the secretary of war, J.D. Cameron, for his past letters of recommendation from Governors Ward and Geary and General George Thomas, and his Medal of Honor certificate, all dating from 1866–67. This was at least the third time in ten years Willie had requested these records, and it would not be the last. The ex-lieutenant claimed, "These documents, which were introduced in evidence, on my trial, as to character, are of great value and importance to me," though he specifically mentioned he did not want the court-martial copies.[2] McGee's plea for this correspondence may have included the plan to fly from home, and have a copy of his papers on hand as proof of the recognition he had gained. A hint of McGee's future may be gleaned from an August letter he sent to Marcus Ward in 1870, just after Willie received his pardon. When McGee was asked by the New Jersey mentor his intentions for the future, Willie replied, "I think it best under the circumstances to begin life anew ... and to continue in the profession of arms which I am best suited in both education and temperament."[3]

Though Willie had spent the six years following these sentiments on a different path, the need to escape his marriage and find a job at a proficient skill made the ex-soldier desperate. In an August 1870 letter to Ward, McGee wrote, "But a temporary offer of my services ... will not prevent my again enrolling myself under the Stars and Stripes."[4] With those thoughts as a possible precursor, William McGee, following a long one-day rail journey to Quincy, Illinois, enrolled on September 11, 1876, in the United States Cavalry. The western service, strapped for manpower, and fighting Indians following the June disaster at the Little Big Horn, eagerly accepted the twenty-seven-year-old recruit — who knew his way around horses, weapons, and the army — without any questions.[5] Hundreds of other men in similar circumstances joined Willie in the West. "Painters, bookkeepers, bakers, bankers, gardeners, miners, jewelers, and musicians would be found in the ranks of the Seventh Cavalry," wrote Bruce Hampton in *Children of Grace,* a study of the Nez Perce War in 1877. What had made these men join? Like McGee, Hampton said, "Some were simply down on their luck, trying to escape poverty or the drudgery of farm life, or simply felt they had no other skills after long years of fighting in the Civil War."[6]

The army did little or no background checking during this period. Some officers referred to this as the "Army's Dark Ages," where the skeleton force was widely felt to lack the mental, physical, and moral compass of Civil War volunteers. The numbers were astounding. From a million man army in 1865, there were in 1876 less than 25,000 men in the entire Untied States wearing army blue, 16,000 of these being privates.[7] Taking no chances the military bureaucracy would discover him, McGee simply changed his date and place of birth, said he was the 22-year-old youngest son of a widowed mother, born in Ludlow, Kentucky, but gave his correct name, William H. McGee.[8] The local history archivist of Kenton County, Kentucky, said there was no record of any William McGee by any spelling in Ludlow born between 1850 and 1860, though records were well kept during that time period.[9]

Willie originally enlisted for five years in this third stint as a military man, but spent only fifteen months fighting in Company K of the Seventh Cavalry as a private. Though he would later exaggerate his experiences — much as he did at Murfreesboro — McGee would suffer a legitimate minor leg wound at the Battle of Bear Paw Mountain, Montana, on June 30, 1877, in the fight against the Nez Perce.[10] Sent soon afterward to the hospital at Fort Abraham Lincoln as a minor convalescent, McGee was honorably discharged on January 22, 1878, the Army never realizing — or caring — that their private was a former disgraced second lieutenant.[11] Running away from a marriage and unemployed in the East, Willie went west partially to make a living, but he and all soldiers in 1877 would be bitterly disappointed. At the conclusion of the Civil War in 1865, privates earned $16 a month; in 1877 the pay was $13 for the Seventh Cavalrymen, and when Congress delayed an appropriations bill, no soldier was paid for five months.[12] It was an easy decision to leave the army again, but returning home to Regina and the girls must have been a hard pill to swallow. Alcohol, however, again stepped in the way, and William McGee, Indian fighter and Civil War drummer boy, was either escorted or thrown off the train on the way east at the railroad station in Sidney, Illinois, 800 miles west of Northumberland. He would remain two years, afraid or unwilling to face Regina.[13]

Willie, a sight to behold, had been beaten, bruised, and robbed of his clothes and money. He found a refuge with the widow Mary Van Brunt, who managed a farm on the outskirts of town, where he worked as a laborer for Mary and her spinster daughter, Jane Van Brunt, where he would remain for the next two years. In March of 1878, just months after Willie was deposited in town, Jane wrote a letter to Marcus Ward on behalf of the poor victim, Willie McGee. Following old tracks, Willie had someone else write for him, requesting money, and waving the flag of patriotism:

Sidney, Cham Co Ill   Mar 10 '78
Go Ward
     Deare sir you remember Will Magee the Drummer Boy how he urnt the government medell of youre stat.... he came here and hadent a change of close and no money he had bin robed of his clos and money.... he has aplide fore a pencen I think your state aut to donate to him fore his brave condent to new jersey. They aut to give him ten thousand dollars the government one thousand a yeare fore his is a good boy since he came here cant you make him a present of

one hundred dollars till he gets a start again.... I think he is beter on a farm if he had five thousand dollars he could by mye land here he wod all ways be sateds fide Pleas come and sea him so you will be shure he is the man pleas don't tell or rite to him I rote to you consurning him he don't want you to know he is so bad off Pleas write to him as soon as you get pleas don't fale.

Please direct youre letter to Will Magee

> Sidney, Cham. Co. Ill. My name is
> Je. E. Van Brunt[14]

How much trouble can one man be in, or handle? Now twenty-nine, McGee could not accept responsibility, pressure, stress, or alcohol. Willie had been beaten and robbed 130 miles south of Chicago.[15] Sidney, whose population has seldom risen to 1,000, even today, possesses some of the best farmland in America, but when Willie arrived in 1878, only the railroad competed with the farms.

Jane Van Brunt was, at Willie's arrival, a thirty-four-year-old single daughter of widow Mary Van Brunt, who ran the 176-acre family farm after her husband, Tom, had died.[16] The area around Champaign County was extremely patriotic and active during the war, and Jane's brother Henry served three years in the 10th Illinois Cavalry.[17] After cleaning himself up — or being cleaned up — Willie McGee would have found a very sympathetic populace with which to share his "history," no doubt brandishing the story of his Medal of Honor.[18] Within months after being in Champaign County, Willie had already convinced Jane, and who knows how many other people in Sidney, of his past heroism and importance, as well as his relationship with Marcus Ward.[19] Strangely, Jane wrote a second letter to Governor Ward just four days after the first. Though similar in content, both letters were found in the Ward collection, so the two were mailed and received in Newark:

March 14, 78

Gr Ward

Deare Sir I suppose you remember William Magee don't you he was the Drummer boy of new Jersey.... he came here with out money and no close fitt to poot on to gain company it is so he has bin here every sence couldent your State offerers donate to him foure ore five Thousan Dollars nexe wek ore the weak folling the reson I speak now is this he can get one hundred and sixty achors of Land fore $25.00 Dollars an achor.... when times was good were offered sixtey Dollars an achor now will haft to take lest I wod not ask you but he seams to try to do what is right. He ses he hant don right but he can live right here he cant spend his money out here he ses there is so meney temptation back home in the sitey. He is good to my staff and seams to take interest in every thing and try to do what is right he ses you have binn a father to him all his life he don't fore get you I think the state and the goverement aut to give him a prise. fiftene ore twenty thousand dollars corden to history of youre state

don't you he has binn a nobell boy do the best you can for him if you could
spare him $100 Dollars till the wether gets so he can go to work fore he wants
close so bad he is shame to ask off you fore money

    Pleas don't tell him I rote to you but you can rite to him and ask him if he
hant stopping at the widers van brunt here hes ben came from youre state one
you can all so sea I have told you the truth by asken if he hant aplide for a pen-
cion he neads it badley youre friend

    J.E. Vanbrunt

        Sidney   Chaim Ill

Pleas dont speak my name to Billey if you please come and sea him fore youre
self and then you will now the truth.[20]

According to the two badly written letters, Jane was offering her family
farm for sale, hoping that Marcus Ward would ante up enough money to buy
the farm and take care of Willie McGee. Though Jane was delusional in her
request that Willie be granted 5,000, 10,000, or 20,000 dollars, it was clear
the ex-lieutenant had found sympathetic ears in Illinois. The most intriguing
item in the Van Brunt letters was the mention of McGee's application for a
pension.[21] Always looking for income, Willie must have seen in the government pension system a chance to have monthly income for life. He was not
alone, as thousands of veterans applied long after leaving the service, especially during the depression. Because of the great number of requests, the government pension board had to be very thorough in checking each application.

Months into his Illinois persona, and after Jane's letters to Marcus Ward
(there is no record of a reply), William Magee, aged twenty-nine, applied for
an "invalid Army pension."[22] On April 10, 1878, Willie swore he was the same
Willie Magee that enlisted in Newark, New Jersey, in 1863 as a musician in
Company C of the 33rd New Jersey Volunteers.[23] After identifying himself
properly, Willie, unable to receive a pension for his Indian War wound, stated
that while in the line of duty, he had received his disability in Tennessee, which
could bring him as much as $6–12 per month for life. In his own hand, he
wrote, "At the battle of Murfreesboro Tenn on or about Dec 8th, 1864, I
received a shell wound in action.... Also at the same time a gun shot wound
in action ... while acting as an orderly for Gen Van Cleve comdg Brig Div
Corps." Willie also said he did not serve or enlist in the military naval or
marine service of the United States from the date of discharge until May 3,
1867, at which time he was appointed 2nd Lieut, 20th U.S. Inf."[24]

McGee also said that since his discharge he had resided at Muskegon,
Michigan, Philadelphia, Pa., and Sidney, Illinois (conveniently forgetting
Northumberland), and had been employed as a painter. He listed his post
office address as Sidney, Illinois, and signed the application as William Magee,
his 33rd New Jersey Infantry name. The witnesses were Henry Van Brunt

(Jane's brother) and Aaron Pressly. Just to be sure the Pension Office knew they were not dealing with just any soldier, Willie wrote along the side of the application, "I was awarded the Medal of Honor by the Sec. of War under a Resolution approved July 12, 1862 for distinguished conduct in battle given to him by the Adj. Gen, USA, under date Feb. 9, 1866."[25]

As all applications had to be filed with an attorney, Willie reached back to his New Jersey days and contacted E.L. Campbell of Trenton, a close friend of Marcus Ward who had known Willie when he had spent a year in Trenton being tutored for the army test in 1867 prior to Willie's commission. McGee might have been down and out, but he always knew how to contact his high-placed friends. Campbell, likely unaware of Willie's break with Ward, might simply have done the easy pro bono work, sending the application forward to Washington.[26] Perhaps Willie thought ten years' passage of time and his Medal of Honor, which had given him so many advantages, would speed his request through and be rubber-stamped. But the entire process was now in the hands of bureaucrats, and pension request no. 253.747 would now be duly processed. Attorney Campbell forwarded McGee's paperwork on May 1, 1878, with the following cover letter:

> E.L. Campbell
> Counsellor at Law
> 14 East State Street
> Sir
> I enclose the claim of Wm Magee Mus. "C" 33rd N.J.V.
> His wounds were received as his declaration will show, whilst he was detached as an orderly on a Brigade Staff & he has no idea where his officers can be found. As he was awarded the Medal of Honor (see his bio) I fancy all the necessary proof is on file somewhere.
> Very truly
> E.L. Campbell[27]

Willie McGee had asked an old Trenton, New Jersey, connection for some help and received it. Little did Willie know that in Campbell's eagerness to aid the drummer boy's chances for a pension, he would send the John Y. Foster version of the Battle of the Cedars, from the book *New Jersey in the Rebellion*, called by Willie and Foster the Battle of Murfreesboro. What Willie had successfully avoided these twelve years was a thorough and efficient examination of what exactly took place that cold Medal of Honor day in Tennessee.

The Department of the Interior, with thousands of pension applications to review, finally got around to the McGee case in the summer. In 1878 alone 18,000 pensions were filed, just like Willie's, and thousands more were filed by widows. Upon review of Willie's application there was only one problem, but it was a crucial one. The Pension Office replied to E.L. Campbell they would be happy to consider Willie's case as soon as he could state when, where, and the circumstances under which "the alleged wounds were received."[28] Seventy-five percent of all claims were allowed that year, and in the Pension Office's preliminary review, all of Willie's enlistment records were checked as well as the muster rolls, which read as follows: "From enrollment to Dec. 31st, 1863, McGee was present for duty. Jan. & Feb. 1864 absent sick in Hospital — Murfreesboro Tenn since Jan. 25, 1864. Same report to April 30, 1865. May & June 1865, present. Company M.O.R. dated July 17th, 1865 — Drummer honorably mustered out with company.[29] Regt returns from Dec. 1864 reports him absent — sick. Jan. 27th, 1865. No evidence of actions or of wounds received as alleged at Murfreesboro Tenn Dec. 8th, 1864 on rolls or returns."[30]

E.L. Campbell was smart enough as a veteran himself to know the muster rolls did not tell the whole story in any pension application. Not in one case out of twenty were there any War Department records showing what the Pension Office needed, but Willie McGee, in order to receive his pension, had to provide some proof of that December when he became a New Jersey hero. Campbell wrote to Willie and asked for his response. Willie replied:

> I was wounded at Murfreesboro on the 8th day of December 1864, in leading a charge and capturing two Brass guns from the Enemy. For corroboration of this fact I would respectfully refer to the reports of Genl Rousseau's who was the Commanding General in that engagement. I presume the report contains the facts of my being wounded as he was the person who instigated the procuring of my medal from Congress after he was elected in Kentucky.[31]
>
> Also for proofs Wm W Bowlby asst surgeon of the 33rd could furnish a certificate of my disability having sent me back from Look Out Valley to the Hospital at Murfreesboro. I am not in possession of the whereabouts of Wm W Bowlby. I was at Hospital No 2 at Murfreesboro while Dr. Titall and Dr. Franklin were in charge who could also give my certificates of my disability Can you with those facts do anything for me no If so let me hear from you at your earliest opportunity.
>
> Respy yours
>
> Wm Magee[32]

Campbell saw the dilemma more clearly than Willie. McGee had little or no proof in his application or follow-up note regarding his wounds, nor even much more than a general outline of the battle itself. Campbell thus sought to assist his client. Armed with the John Foster "biography of my life," which stated that McGee was the darling of General Van Cleve, who entrusted him with the regiment, and with Willie having mentioned he was an orderly to General Van Cleve the day of the famous battle, attorney Campbell did the sensible thing and wrote a note to Horatio Van Cleve himself.[33] Campbell was no doubt certain the old general would help his old orderly; it was, after all, in the history books. Campbell himself was extremely active in statewide Civil War reunions and dinners, as well serving as an officer in the New Jersey Historical Society with Marcus Ward. Campbell knew that witnesses were slow to answer the written questions sent to them by the Pension Bureau, and it had been twelve years, so he wrote directly to New Jersey native Van Cleve, who still had family just a few miles from Campbell's office in Trenton. If he obtained a short statement from Van Cleve, Campbell would feel he had helped his client immeasurably.

It was not difficult to track down Horatio Van Cleve, who had been living in Minnesota since the war, and was still active in state government, where he was the state's adjutant general.[34] Throughout his life, Willie McGee, a poor Irish drummer boy famous this last decade for being a disappointment, had interaction with some of America's most powerful military and political icons, and Horatio Van Cleve was another in a long line of such men. Van Cleve was a native of Princeton, born in 1809 and educated at West Point. His distinguished national career spanned almost half a century and included service as a soldier, engineer, philanthropist, and politician. Van Cleve began his Civil War stint as a colonel and ended it as a major general. He was seriously wounded at Stones River in 1863, and from December of that year to the end of the war was commanding officer of all forces at Murfreesboro, which corresponds with the sixteen months of McGee's tenure at the same fort.[35]

Following the war General Van Cleve settled in Minnesota, where he was elected the state's adjutant general twice, the first time from 1866 to 1870, during which time Willie was a prisoner in the Stillwater Prison.[36] Timing being everything, when Willie's friend Warden Webber was fired from the prison in November 1870, Governor Horace Austin first asked Van Cleve to become the new warden, which the former adjutant general rejected completely, saying he would never live in the river town.[37] Even in the Wild West of 1870, it was a small world. Eight years later, on May 13, 1878, while in his second term as Minnesota adjutant general, Horatio Van Cleve responded to the very innocent request of New Jersey attorney E.L. Campbell, who was attempting to help a down and out veteran Medal of Honor recipient. Campbell was shocked when Van Cleve responded quickly with the news that Willie McGee, Jersey hero, was a possible fraud:

General Headquarters
State of Minnesota
Adjutant General's Office
Saint Paul, May 13, 1878

E. L. Campbell

Sir

    While stationed at Murfreesboro, Tenn in 1865,— William Magee, of a Jersey
Regiment, was detached from a convalescent camp and that post — as one of my
orderlies.

    He knows well that he was never wounded while acting as an orderly for me,
and he also knows that the story circulated some years ago of his capturing a
rebel battery while he was acting under my orders — he knows is a sheer fabrica-
tion of his brain. How he ever obtained a medal for distinguished service, I
know not. Certainly not from any assistance of mine.

                         H.P. Van Cleve
                         Late Maj. General[38]

    In late 1865, Congressman Lovell Rousseau, in three sentences, enabled
William McGee — under the name Magee — to become one of the youngest
soldiers in United States history to gain the newly created Medal of Honor.
Thirteen years later, Horatio Van Cleve, Minnesota adjutant general, wrote
a terse three-sentence condemnation of his former orderly.

    E. L. Campbell's reaction must have been one of total surprise — if not
outright shock. As a former veteran himself, he was well aware of the Willie
Magee story of heroism in Tennessee. He had read the John Y. Foster book,
and probably owned a copy. Campbell was intimately associated with Marcus Ward, and indeed had known Willie in Trenton as the boy hero was being
tutored in 1866–67. In more than a decade, nobody — not even the Bramans — had questioned Willie's place in history. An honest man, Campbell
was compelled no doubt to contact the Pension Bureau, but first he contacted
McGee and confronted him with the new information. When E.L. Campbell was done, after a month or more of his own research, he added a postscript on the back of Van Cleve's letter, and forwarded all his work to the
Pension Bureau: "This looks much as though the boy was a fraud which I
consider confirmed by my correspondence with him. I respectfully withdraw
from the case as attorney. The boy was taken charge of by the Gov. of N.J.
(Gov Ward) — sent to school for sometime, and then a commission awarded
him in the army (U.S.). He appears to have gotten out of the Regular Army
in some not very honorable way. E. L. Campbell."[39]

    The paperwork was appropriately filed within some weeks and eventu-
ally signed off in the Fall of 1878 by the Commissioner of the Pension Bureau
and Campbell, as the attorney for the claimant, William Magee. Horatio Van
Cleve, like Willie a New Jersey native son, had solved the mystery of the Battle of the Cedars, and the subsequent Medal of Honor. The Pension request
was stamped ABANDONED.[40] Regina Magee, at home in Northumberland,
Pennsylvania, understood the word well.

CHAPTER FOURTEEN

"A Moral Wreck"

Heaven is all around us, and men do not see it.
— Jesus, The Gospel of Thomas

In the summer of 1878, Willie McGee abandoned his request for an invalid Civil War pension, costing him a possible $8–12 per month; though the original request would have provided Willie with some minimum economic gain, the decision to abandon meant much, much more, and, in fact, was a terrible life blow to the now twenty-nine-year-old ex–drummer boy.[1]

For over a decade Willie was, through self promotion, able to gain advantage and escape peril, no matter how ignominious, largely due to his fraudulent heroism as a young teenager on a December day in 1864 in Tennessee, which fraud resulted in his being awarded a Congressional Medal of Honor.[2] McGee became almost overnight a New Jersey hero, written into the history books[3]; he was protected, mentored, and educated by powerful New Jersey patricians eager to celebrate in the poor "mere" Irish lad something of the noble savage[4]; proof that even those of the lowest class can occasionally be elevated to a higher level of civilized society, all was possible because of McGee's Medal of Honor.

Willie was given a commission at eighteen by these very elitists and sent into the real world of the United States Regular Army, where he was greeted with skepticism due to his youthful age and his even younger looking Irish visage, which made appear to all the world just a boy, which of course he was. Amazingly, no one, even Willie's biggest critics, ever challenged his supposed valor in battle. It was written, so therefore it must be true.

Everything in McGee's life after the war began and ended with the Medal of Honor. Willie did not ask for it, and didn't even know what it was, but without question he embraced his great fortune, only to have the recognition it had brought become an albatross around his neck. No matter how poorly life twisted and turned on Willie McGee, and it did indeed become very twisted, Willie was always able to fall back upon the honor, the courage, and the youthful patriotism that earned for him the highest honor in American military life.

But a single mention on his pension application of his commanding officer, Major General Horatio Van Cleve, led to Willie's exposure as a flawed hero, if not a downright fraud, and a disgrace to the men and women who have been recipients of the Medal of Honor.[5] McGee's Trenton, New Jersey, attorney, a dear friend of Marcus Ward and himself a highly honored veteran of the war, no doubt informed Ward, Willie's mentor and protector, as well as notifying the U.S. Pension Bureau in Washington.[6]

McGee's reputation in New Jersey, already damaged due to his imprisonment and alcohol abuse, was dealt a fatal blow with Van Cleve's letter to attorney E.L. Campbell. Word of Willie's fall from grace first surfaced with discussion of his sticky private life in publication of the *History of Newark*, in 1878. Though much of Willie's career as a soldier had not yet surfaced and was grossly exaggerated — even more so than the version printed in *New Jersey in the Rebellion* in 1867, his personal life since the shooting of Dr. Braman was revealed in print to all, though mistaken in the details, for the first, and only, time.[7]

"Upon the close of the war Magee returned to Newark and resumed his old vocation, that of an eating-house waiter. But there were those who deemed him deserving of a better position. Means were furnished to him wherewith to obtain the rudiments of a liberal education," wrote author George Atkinson. "Within a year's time, through the efforts mainly of Governor Marcus L. Ward, of New Jersey, and Geary, of Pennsylvania, Magee was commissioned by President Johnson a Second Lieutenant of Infantry in the regular army. He was unable, however, to pass the examination. Governor Ward especially interested himself in the case, and by the time the next ordeal came Magee passed it successfully, and he was assigned to a regiment stationed at Tallahassee, Florida."[8]

Though Atkinson had the geography and some names wrong, the basic tenet of McGee's past was printed for all to read, and it was ugly:

> Most deeply is it to be deplored that the after-career of the Newark drummer-boy is sadly out of tune with the romantic opening outlined. The sapling, of most graceful and beautiful form grew, alas! into a decayed, decrepit, and

unsightly tree. While at Tallahassee [Baton Rouge], Lieutenant Magee had a personal difficulty with Surgeon Bainbridge [Braman], of the same command. Bainbridge charged Magee with the larceny of a watch. It was a base slander, subsequently so proven, but Bainbridge refused to so acknowledge it. Stung to the quick by the slander, Magee finally entered Bainbridge's quarters one day and demanded that he should retract. He refused, and then Magee drew a whip from his person and proceeded to flagellate his slanderer. The doctor — as Magee stated — ran as if to get a pistol. Then Magee drew one and shot Bainbridge so that he died. Magee was tried by the civil authorities and acquitted. Afterwards, upon being tried by court-martial, he was found guilty of having shot to death his superior officer.[9]

Brevet General Horatio Van Cleve, Commander of Fortress Rosecrans, Murfreesboro, Tennessee, 1864–65. Van Cleve's letter in 1878 to New Jersey lawyer E.L. Campbell would expose Willie McGee's legendary heroism during the war. A native of New Jersey, Van Cleve would lead a long and respected public life before passing away in 1891 in Minneapolis, Minnesota (Minnesota Historical Society).

Though Atkinson struggled with the specifics of the case, he had the gist of the story, and a good working knowledge of Willie McGee, the man:

He [Magee] was sentenced to serve five years in the State Prison, and of course, to be cashiered — a mild sentence, viewed from a military standpoint. Through the efforts of Governor Ward — who still stood by the unfortunate youth — Magee was pardoned, after serving a year or so. It is charity to draw a veil over his afterlife. The iron of shame and disgrace entered his spirit, and the proud hero of Murfreesboro became a moral wreck. It is said by his old comrades that he was meanly treated by some of his brother officers, graduates of West Point, because of his humble extraction. This, it is further said, goaded him into recklessness, which resulted in the blasting of a career full of the most brilliant promise.[10]

As degrading as this portrayal must have been to Will McGee, he still had his military career repeated in publication and was considered a certified war hero, until Horatio Van Cleve, a Jerseyan by birth, stepped into the picture right after the publication of the *History of Newark*. Beyond Van Cleve's assertion was the postscript of Willie's own lawyer, E.L. Campbell, that McGee's involvement at Murfreesboro was a figment of Willie's imagination. "This looks much as though the boy was a fraud," wrote Campbell, "which I consider confirmed by my correspondence with him."[11] Following the statements by Van Cleve and Campbell, the story of Willie McGee at the Battle of the Cedars was repeated in print only once more.[12]

McGee had more than abandoned his pension claim — he had been accused of fraud and admitted as much, thereby misrepresenting the historical record he himself created, which had cast him as a New Jersey legend. The unraveling of his personal life appeared in print and he faced the possible scandal over his Medal of Honor. Such scandal never came, and the United States War Department never got involved in McGee's Medal of Honor mistake. Perhaps they didn't know, but until 2005, Willie's Medal of Honor file, listed under the name Megee, and his pension application were both misplaced for more than one hundred years, which even a senior National Archive researcher felt was unusual.[13] In New Jersey, it was as if Willie Magee never existed, a Civil War Medal of Honor recipient ignored in print for more than a century. For a decade, drummer Willie Magee was compared in one book to Phil Kearny, and in another to the top echelon of soldiers "who are worthy to rank with the noblest and best of her patriots."[14]

Thirty-five years would pass before the last mention of Willie McGee, the legendary hero of Murfreesboro, would appear in print. In a 1913 three-volume *History of Newark, New Jersey,* there appeared a virtual reprint of the Atkinson version, but only of Willie's magnificently fictionalized war exploit. In a chapter heading, "Drummer Boy Magee's Brilliant Exploit," there is no mention of the disparaging revelations of McGee's postwar behavior, only concluding, "But alas, his bright star soon set. He became involved in a controversy with another officer and shot the latter so that he died. He was sent to prison, but afterward, through the efforts of Governor Ward, was pardoned out. He never recovered from the disgrace of his crime."[15]

How Willie, with a weakness for alcohol, a gallimaufry of nondescript employment, and relationships with two women in two states — both of whom he had married — how Willie balanced his life must have taken prodigious effort. His undeniably charismatic personality propelled him forward, but at what point did this tragically flawed first generation Irish-American, still not thirty years old, come to grips with reality? Or did he fall forward deeper into the abyss of alcoholic dementia? Yet, despite what many would consider a death blow to his reputation, McGee's scheming spirit was impossible to suppress. After Jane Van Brunt's pathetic attempts to solicit money from Marcus Ward and Willie's scammed pension application both failed, Willie successfully sought out Illinois Senator John Logan.

General John "Black Jack" Logan, military and political icon of Illinois, became one of many respected supporters of Willie McGee. Logan, a legend in southern Illinois, was unsuccessful in restoring Willie to the Army in 1880, and McGee soon after fled Illinois (U.S. Army Military History Institute).

Willie finally hit the jackpot with John A. Logan, a fellow veteran of the war and an Illinois senator for thirteen years. Logan, whose dark brows and visage earned him the sobriquet "Black Jack" from his beloved troops, was one of the most highly regarded civilian officers to serve in the war. "Black Jack" became a favorite of U.S. Grant, served, like McGee, in the Western Theater, and ended the war as a major general who had fought in eight full campaigns.[16]

Immediately after the surrender, John Logan, a lifelong Illinoisan, jumped into public service and held elective offices until he died at sixty in Washington, D.C., in 1886. If Marcus Ward was the "soldier's friend," "Black Jack" Logan, like McGee a first generation Irish-

American, was the soldier's champion from the moment of his first foray into public life as an Illinois congressman in 1867. If Willie McGee had sought out a place to run from troubles and find assistance for his financial woes, he could not have chosen a better advocate than Senator John Logan of Illinois. A true hero of the American Midwest, Logan worked ceaselessly for the benefits, well-being, and pensions of old soldiers his entire postwar career.[17]

In military life, Logan was a passionate general, but he was even more forceful in the political world, which eventually would lead to his nomination for vice president in 1884 on the unsuccessful ticket with James G. Blaine.[18] Willie McGee must have made overtures soon after the failed pension application, early in 1879, and it may have taken some months to persuade "Black Jack" and his staff of the ex-lieutenant's case for reinstatement to the army. There can be no doubt that Willie was up to the challenge and not intimidated by a United States senator — he had, after all, already mixed professionally with a president, generals, and governors, among others. Adding a senator to his dance card of life would be easy. Logan would also have been impressed with Willie's Medal of Honor status; he had been awarded many medals himself for bravery and leadership, and would in the future become known as the father of Memorial Day.[19] After ten years of failed jobs, failed schemes, a failed marriage, and a year fighting Indians as a private under an assumed identity, Willie McGee waited as Senator John Logan stepped into the breach and provided Willie with a major impetus of spirit for the future when he proposed on the Senate floor Bill #1039 during the second session of the 46th Congress. The bill, read twice on the floor of the senate, said simply, "To authorize the restoration of William McGee to the rank of 2nd Lieutenant in the Army."[20] It was a ray of hope for Willie McGee, the tenacious Irishman from Newark, who had been beaten up badly by his own terrible decisions, and now placed all of his new hopes on John Logan, much as he did on Marcus Ward exactly ten years before.

Senate Bill 1039 was duly referred to the Committee on Military Affairs, and for three months McGee waited for the United States Army to once again process his case. When Willie had initially approached Logan, he had to convince the senator he was victimized by a vengeful army, that his court-martial conviction was a case of double jeopardy, and therefore illegal. Only a man of prodigious personal charm, who had been a resident of Illinois for less than two years, could convince an Illinois legend of the purity of this case. All Willie could do at this point was wait.

As the winter of 1880 passed in Washington, D.C., McGee's bill inexorably worked its way through the military labyrinth. Eventually, on March 4,

E.D. Townsend, the adjutant general, wrote the following memo to Judge Advocate General W.M. Dunn:

> A.G.O.
> March 4, 1880
>   Respectfully referred to the Judge Advocate General. The within named officer (McGee) was dismissed by sentence of General Court martial. Copies of G.C.M. orders No. 20 and 24 of 1869 and 40 of 1870, are enclosed herewith. The restoration of Lieut. McGee "*with his original rank and date of commission*" [emphasis Townsend's], would not only place him at the head of the 2nd Lieutenants of Infantry, but would make him the senior 2nd Lieutenant in the entire Army on the active list.
>
>   E.D. Townsend
>   Adjutant General[21]

The judge advocate general, after receiving Townsend's memo, moved it along on March 6, and added copies of three reports comprising all the materials the army could muster in the life of William H. McGee.[22] Armed with every scrap of McGee's history, Judge Dunn sent the final army recommendation to the secretary of war on March 10, from whence it was submitted to the Committee on Military Affairs. At the end of March the following report was printed and submitted to the Senate regarding bill 1039. It would not please ex–Lieutenant McGee:

> The Committee on Military Affairs, to whom was referred the bill (S.1039) to authorize the restoration of William McGee to the rank of second lieutenant in the Army, having had the same under consideration, beg leave to submit the following report:
>   After careful examination of the case, your committee cannot recommend any interference by the Senate in the action of the court-martial which sentenced Lieutenant McGee to dismissal. He seems to have been convicted of all the charges and specifications preferred against him with the exception of the third and fourth specifications of the last charge which was that of drunkenness. The other charges and specifications included the killing of a brother officer, making false statements, and associating with noisy and boisterous citizens. There are, of course, some palliating circumstances attending the shooting, but they were not sufficiently so to warrant the committee in a recommendation for favorable action upon this bill.
>   Your committee, therefore, report the bill back adversely, ask to be discharged from its further consideration, and recommend its indefinite postponement.[23]

After months of convincing John Logan to believe in and support him, and three months of waiting for the decision, eternal optimist and con man Willie McGee was informed of the decision handed down by the Committee on Military Affairs, in early April 1880. Predictably, McGee handled the news of yet another major disappointment badly. A news report from the *Decatur* (Illinois) *Daily Republican* of April 12, 1880, tells a strange story:

46TH CONGRESS, 2d Session.	SENATE.	REPORT No. 459.

IN THE SENATE OF THE UNITED STATES.

APRIL 13, 1880.—Ordered to be printed.

Mr. BURNSIDE, from the Committee on Military Affairs, submitted the following

REPORT:

[To accompany bill S. 1039.]

The Committee on Military Affairs, to whom was referred the bill (S. 1039) to authorize the restoration of William McGee to the rank of second lieutenant in the Army, having had the same under consideration, beg leave to submit the following report:

After careful examination of the case, your committee cannot recommend any interference by the Senate in the action of the court-martial which sentenced Lieutenant McGee to dismissal. He seems to have been convicted of all the charges and specifications preferred against him with the exception of the third and fourth specifications of the last charge which was that of drunkenness. The other charges and specifications included the killing of a brother officer, making false statements, and associating with noisy and boisterous citizens. There are, of course, some palliating circumstances attending the shooting, but they were not sufficiently so to warrant the committee in a recommendation for favorable action upon this bill.

Your committee, therefore, report the bill back adversely, ask to be discharged from its further consideration, and recommend its indefinite postponement.

o

The Committee on Military Affairs report recommending the Logan bill for McGee's restoration is rejected by indefinite postponement April 13, 1880 (Library of Congress Archives).

Ewing's Rig Discovered

Saturday, about noon, Mr. C.A. Ewing received a telegram from Philo about 45 miles east of Decatur, conveying the gratifying intelligence that a farmer residing near that town yesterday morning had found a mare attached to a buggy answering the description of a rig stolen from Mr. Ewing on Saturday last, hitched to a fence on his farm, which it appeared had been abandoned by the thief whose identity is yet a mystery. Mr. Ewing, accompanied by a servant, left for Philo on a freight train early this morning to see if the abandoned rig is his. On Friday evening an ex-member of the regular army, named Billy McGee, who had been court-martialed and dismissed from the service for killing an army surgeon, was in this city, soliciting aid from old soldiers, claiming he lived at Sidney, 4 miles east of Philo, and that he wanted money to buy a ticket to St. Louis. Those who conversed with him thought him half-witted. From his description it is thought that he is the man who appropriated the mare and buggy, in order to get home. He was in this city Saturday forenoon about 9 o'clock, when he called on R.A. Newell, the overseer of the poor, and endeavored to persuade him an order for a railroad ticket. He got very angry when Mr. Newell refused to comply with his request. He could not be found in town after the disappearance of the rig. He may not be guilty of the theft, but the circumstances appear to implicate him.[24]

Less than two months later, on June 1, 1880, seventy-four-year-old Mary Van Brunt and her daughter, Jane, remortgaged fifty acres of their 176 acre farm for $500, a loan that was to be paid back within two years.[25] Did the Van Brunt women borrow the money to aid Willie? It was the first and last time any of the large Van Brunt family had ever remortgaged any of their land in more than thirty years of living in Sidney.[26] Dudley McLain, a justice of the peace, married (adding to the mysterious timing), three weeks to the day of the fifty-acre transaction, June 22, the thirty-one-year-old William H. McGee and Jane E. Van Brunt in Urbana, Illinois.[27]

Jane testified in the marriage register that this was her first marriage, and all records support this, but husband Willie, or Billy, as he was known in Illinois, was not as honest. McGee, a man who never let the truth get in his way, gave his correct birth date of May 13, 1849, but stated this was his first marriage as well.[28] As deformed as Willie's life had been for a decade, he always had a plan: the reputed attempt to escape jail in Stillwater; trying to gain a pension illegally in a battle in which he never participated; the attempt to be restored to the army twelve years after being cashiered; and joining the cavalry under an assumed identity to escape one marriage, among other incidents. Now McGee added to these failures by becoming a horse thief, and worse, a bigamist, marrying the thirty-eight-year-old spinster Jane for reasons we can only guess. Whatever the arcane Will McGee had in mind for Jane, the farm, or himself, one would expect it had to include money. Within months, life in Illinois would be over for Willie McGee.[29] As was customary with Willie, there were several possibilities. Did Jane just "figure out" McGee, or with peasant cunning discover the existence of Regina Magee? Did Jane's brothers, Charles and Henry, discover the con in Willie? Or did McGee just bail out and head back East? If so, Jane was luckier than Regina. The farm in Sidney foreclosed in 1882, none of the $500 being repaid. The bank waited until 1884 out of kindness before foreclosing on Jane Magee and her mother, Mary. Willie was not legally responsible since it was just prior to his marriage.[30] The two women relocated soon after, no doubt out of shame, to Nebraska, where some other Van Brunts had gone years before.[31]

They left so quickly they did not tell local residents that Willie had left them high and dry. In a local history published in 1988, *From Salt Fork to Chickamauga, Champaign County in the Civil War*, author Robert Behrens counts Willie as one of the county's renowned soldiers, telling a small, very small, version of Willie's heroics in Tennessee, and of course mentioning the Medal of Honor. He adds, "He was discharged from the army on July 17, 1865, but reenlisted and was commissioned second lieutenant in the 20th United States Infantry, being discharged from that regiment on April 9, 1868.... Prior to 1885, Magee moved west, possibly to Nebraska." Willie was long gone by 1885, but it was not to the West. It should come as no surprise that despite his very short tenure in Illinois, Willie impressed many with his "legend," and it was remembered for more than a hundred years.[32] Jane remarried in 1886 at age forty-four to Nels Nelson, a Swedish immigrant, and as Jane Nelson, far away from Willie McGee, would live a long life, dying childless at age eighty-nine in York County, Nebraska, in 1930.[33] Drummer boy Willie McGee was on the run again, headed for a new beginning in a new state, but following old tracks.

Approaching his thirty-first birthday, the Irish drummer boy of Newark, harried as usual by financial, family, and/or legal concerns, packed up and returned east late in 1880 or early 1881, leaving Jane McGee to her own devices. Four years after abandoning Regina, Willie McGee returned to Northumberland, and he must have used every ounce of magnetism and charisma to explain away his walkabout absence. Regina, with whatever reservations, accepted her husband back into her life, and as usual with McGee there were always caveats. Within months of his return to Pennsylvania, Willie soon convinced his wife that the family would be better served if he took a job at the Springfield, Massachusetts, Federal Armory. For the next five years, though Regina and the children lived in Northumberland, McGee roomed in Springfield, working at various jobs, including several stints for the U.S. Arsenal, where he also accepted mail for more than three years.[34]

Springfield was a perfect fit for Willie. The largest armory in the country was always looking for experienced weapons experts, and Willie McGee surely knew how to handle firearms. In addition, the large employment at the weapons factory guaranteed an eager number of ready-made McGee fans eager to hear his amazing tale of courage in Tennessee and the subsequent Medal of Honor story. The western Massachusetts town was also just a short forty-five miles directly north of McGee's brother John, the only sibling with whom he stayed close — one of the very brothers Willie told both Secretary of War Edwin Stanton and President Johnson in 1867 "had sacrificed themselves on the altar of the country" during the Civil War.[35]

Born in Newark on July 8, 1847, John McGee was only two years older than his little brother, William.[36] When the McGee family disintegrated after the death or disappearance of their father, James, Willie and John were sent to live with an aunt, where they stayed until the war.[37] After Willie's enlistment at fourteen, sixteen-year-old John found his way to New Haven, Connecticut, like Newark a very strong Irish enclave, where extended McGees had put down roots years before. By the time Willie McGee was a hero and officer in Louisiana, John had married a local New Haven girl, Elisabeth Bagshaw, and moved his young but growing family to nearby Meriden, Connecticut.[38]

What marital arrangements Regina and McGee worked out is unknown, but it had to be a strain on Regina. Raising two young daughters for three years plus, as a single mother on Water Street, the poorest neighborhood in tiny Northumberland, Regina welcomed her errant husband back, only to see him return on an occasional basis. There is no doubt Regina tried mightily to rein in her roaming husband, and in 1882 she traveled to Meriden, pregnant, and temporarily moved in with John and Elisa. Willie McGee made the trip down to his brother's home, but it would not be a happy journey. William Magee, Jr., as Regina spelled the family name, was born in Meriden in June only to die four days later. The baby, Willie and Regina's first son, died of a malfunction of the intestines, according to Meriden doctor E.M. Child.[39] Willie, whose address was listed as Springfield, and Regina, of Northumberland, would bury their son temporarily in Connecticut before each returned to their respective homes — Regina to the girls and McGee to pursue his newest notoriety in Springfield.[40] While a Massachusetts resident, Willie was employed as a piece-worker at the armory, working on Browning components, where he put the "blueing" on guns, a technique used to stop rust on the barrels.[41] When not working at the Armory, McGee would return to Northumberland and visit Regina, but a note from Marcus Ward revealed Willie had another place of residence.

A present-day view of Water Street, Northumberland, Pennsylvania, before it crosses the Susquehanna River. This area was the home of Regina and Willie McGee from 1874 to 1886. Regina, a native of the town, would spend the whole of her short life in Northumberland, but it was only an occasional residence for Willie (author collection).

Though Willie was unaware, his old-time friend was still showing interest in his welfare. Correspondence between McGee and Ward had ceased with Willie's run west when he abandoned Regina and joined the Seventh Cavalry for a short stint in 1876. Now an ill seventy, Ward wondered what had happened to his lost drummer boy. On October 19, 1882, Marcus sent a request to Surgeon General Charles Crane asking for a background check on the whereabouts of one William H. McGee.[42] Crane's response from the War Department on October 24 had to be disquieting to the old New Jersey governor. Crane wrote to his Republican friend, "I enclose the information you have asked for in your note. It has required some little time to make an accurate search in this case, because Magie had been an inmate in several hospitals."[43] The surgeon general's enclosed attachment, presumably listing dates, places and times of Willie's hospital stays, is missing from the Ward collection, perhaps an indication Marcus recognized the sensitivity of the note and destroyed it. The fact that Willie had been listed as an "inmate," and not a "patient" by Crane surely suggests he was undergoing alcoholic related treatment, if not worse. Since Ward was looking for information about Willie from 1877 suggests Crane's information dealt with the McGee years in Illinois and in Springfield. Not only does it help explain the past behavior of the Medal of Honor drummer, it will foreshadow future actions and personality disorders shown by the Irishman from the Brick City.

No further correspondence exists between Ward and the surgeon general, as Crane died of a hemorrhage at the early age of fifty-two, almost a year to the day of his letter regarding Willie McGee. Ward himself passed away in early 1884 at seventy-two in his beloved New Jersey.[44] In a sizable list of condolences on the news of the departure of the "soldier's friend," telegraphs, letters, even postcards flooded into the family from people in all walks of life, including many from men who served in the war. All were saved by the estate of the ex-governor, and deposited in the New Jersey Historical Society. Not one was from William McGee, who still had extended family in Newark and had much he might have said regarding the man to whom he once wrote, "I have no one to look to for counsel and sympathy, save you, who have seemed like a father to me."[45]

Despite the death of his son and frequent hospital stays, the McGee smile and hypnotic personality was still evident once again in Massachusetts, just as it was in Newark, Baton Rouge, Stillwater, Northumberland, and Sidney, Illinois. Beyond his effervescent amiability, Willie's greatest skill was his ability to court politicians and public officials, despite his problems. The McGee efforts at friendship in Springfield only offered further proof the aging drummer, whether he called himself Willie or Bill, could fool more than pretty girls in Pennsylvania, or illiterate Illinois spinsters.

By 1882, McGee had met, befriended and convinced one of the Bay State's most famous and popular politicos, George D. Robinson, that he was a victim of government persecution and malfeasance. This version of the Louisiana shooting of Dr. Braman was not new for Willie, who had practiced it three years before with Senator John Logan of Illinois. Robinson was simply the latest in a long line of McGee believers who succumbed to the wiles of Willie McGee. Robinson was classically educated at both the Lexington Academy and the Hopkins Classical School in Cambridge, before graduating from Harvard in 1856 at age twenty-two. Following Harvard, Robinson became principal of a high school in Chicopee, Massachusetts, before being admitted to the bar at thirty-two in Boston.

George Dexter Robinson wasted little time before jumping into the political arena, where he met with nothing but success. For thirteen years, from 1874 to 1887, Robinson served as a state senator, congressman, and then governor from 1884 to 1887. Despite such a stellar record, Robinson is best remembered for his post-political job successfully defending Lizzie Borden, for whom he earned an acquittal in America's most famous murder trial of the nineteenth century.[46] McGee always had good taste in choosing his influential friends, and he had Robinson in his corner, just as he did Andrew Johnson, Marcus Ward, Horace Austin, and so many others. In April of 1883, McGee continued to follow a proven formula and wrote to the judge advocate general in Washington, D.G. Swain:

> Springfield, Mass.
> April 14, 1883
> To the Judge Advocate General, U.S.A.
> Washington, D.C.
> Sir, I have the honor of addressing you, and would most respectfully request of you the favor of letting me know if it is in your power to furnish me with a certified copy of the full proceedings of the court-martial of Wm McGee, late 2nd Liet, 20th Inft. USA, which occurred at Baton Rouge La in 1868, for the shooting of Dr. Braman. Also I would like to have all the documents that are on file in your office connected with the trial, and if there are any papers showing that I was tried by the civil court for the same offense, I would like a copy of them.
> I wish to place them in the hands of Hon. Geo D Robinson, M.C., I order that he may have the necessary papers in readiness to lay before congress for their investigation as to the legality of the second trial. If it is not in your power to furnish me with the desired papers, I would be under lasting obligation if you would advise me what steps I will have to take in order to obtain them, and for any expense attached please let me know. And now I most anxiously await your earliest convenience in the acknowledgement of the receipt of this letter.
> > Very respectfully
> > Your obedient Servant
> > Wm McGee
> > Late 2nd Liet 20th Inft USA
>
> Address U.S. Army
> Springfield, Mass[47]

It did not take Willie long to work his magic on George Robinson. Writing for his infamous "papers" once more, McGee convinced Robinson of his plight, and it is fair to add that the letter was crafted by Robinson or a staffer, and then copied by McGee, another proof the congressman had bought into Willie's appeal. (In addition to the good grammar and structure, this letter is the only record we have that McGee ever spelled the name Braman correctly.) There can be little doubt McGee was repeating in Springfield his heroic history, perhaps leaving out a detail or two.

The Bureau of Military Justice, which by now had a full dossier on Willie, both his history and appeals for fifteen years, nonetheless followed the chain of command and within two weeks of receipt of McGee's letter, agreed to his request, at least that part they possessed, which were the court-martial papers.[48] Willie had asked for and received three previous times this paperwork, but the Bureau sent it to McGee in care of the Springfield Armory, this time charging Willie twelve cents per 100 words for the cost of reproducing, at a total of $22.53, or half a month's pay at the armory.[49] But the voluminous paperwork did not satisfy McGee or Robinson, and Willie sent another letter on June 24, 1883, once again to the judge advocate general:

> Springfield, Mass
> June 24, 1883
>
> D.G.Swain
> Judge Advocate General
> Dear Sir,
> I have the honor to again address you, and would respectfully ask if there are any papers on file in your office given in as evidence before the Military court-martial, showing that I had previously turned over by the Military authorities to the civil courts of Baton Rouge, La and was tried and honorable acquitted by that court. I was again taken up by the Military authority and tried a second time for the same offence and was sentenced to dismissal from the service, and to 5 years of imprisonment by the Military Court-Martial.
> My attorney in forms me that he was not furnished with any copy of the civil suit by the Bureau of Military Justice. The reason of the importance of these papers, the *civil court papers*, to me is to show that I have been tried twice for the same offence, and it is in order to test the legal right of the Military court, to trial, that ... the Hon G.D. Robinson, M.C. should have these civil suit papers, as he has a bill before congress for my relief. Now General, what I would like to know is whether these papers of the civil court are on file in your office or if they were ever introduced as evidence showing that I had been previously tried. For this desired information I would be under lasting obligation to you.
> Yours truly
> Wm McGee
> P.S. You no doubt will remember me as I wrot you some time ago in regard to my case, which was for the shooting of Dr. Braman, which occurred at Baton Roug, La on or about Aug 15, 1868, which is on file in your office.
> Wm McGee
> Late Liet 20th Inft USA
> Address
> U.S. Armory   Springfield   Mass[50]

This letter is more a McGee original, with spelling errors and less lawyerly phrasing, but the point is still clear. The judge advocate general sent all that was in Willie's file, but the record of the first trial — the civil case (not civil suit)—was never in any government file, and without it Congressman Robinson would have great difficulty proving double jeopardy, had it even been true. Fifteen years had passed, but Willie appeared to only now learn how to spell Chandler Braman's surname correctly, and the arrogance of the older drummer boy is evident. McGee is still sending and receiving mail at the armory and it would shock no one who knew Willie if Congressman Robinson had arranged a no-show job for the "victimized" boy wonder of the New Jersey 33rd Infantry.

There is no question George Robinson was sold on the McGee version of Baton Rouge, as was Illinois Senator Logan, and was not simply humoring the Irish dervish and Medal of Honor recipient. On December 10, 1883, H.R. 758 was introduced in the House of Representatives at the 48th Congress. It was read twice, and referred to the Committee on Military Affairs, and ordered to be printed. It reads as follows:

A BILL

To authorize the restoration of William Magee to the Army

Be it enacted by the Senate and the House of Representatives of the United States of America in Congress assembled, that the President be, and he is hereby, authorized to nominate and, by and with the advice and consent of the Senate, appoint William Magee, late a second lieutenant in the Twentieth Regiment of the United States Infantry, a second lieutenant of infantry in the Army of the United States, with his original rank and date of commission: and that he shall be assigned to the first vacancy of the service; and that he shall receive pay for the period he was out of the service.[51]

For the second time in four years, the bill died in committee, and William H. McGee was neither rewarded with a commission nor given a penny of the back pay he eagerly sought, and almost a year's work by both McGee and Robinson went nowhere. The proposed bill speaks volumes, however, about the continued powerful and magnetic presence of Willie McGee, who always had a tendency to manipulate the truth. Should Robinson have been as successful with McGee as he was later with Lizzie Borden, Willie would have received fifteen years back pay, almost $10,000 dollars, and a commission at age thirty-five.[52] McGee watchers could be forgiven for thinking the Newark drummer would accept the back pay and then resign the commission. Willie McGee had failed twice in his campaign against the United States military establishment. Senator Long and Congressman Robinson had accepted the righteousness of his cause, but the army was convinced McGee was a reprobate, not an engaging victim of injustice.[53]

As McGee's second run at the U.S. Army was played out, Regina gave birth to her fourth and last child, a son named John, in 1884. Named after

Riverview Cemetery, Northumberland, Pennsylvania. Regina and three of her children are buried in unmarked graves in the left background, just in front of the pine trees, in this bucolic hillside cemetery overlooking the Susquehanna River (author collection).

the only sibling known to have any contact with Willie, baby John, like his brother, William, died in infancy of dysentery at two years of age on September 10, 1886. In what had to have been a painful year in a most painful marriage, Willie and Regina brought back baby William's remains and buried both boys in a Northumberland cemetery.[54] The McGee years in Northumberland would only get worse, and the fragile Willie was scarred further when the loving Regina died of consumption at an old thirty-seven on July 12, and her firstborn, Julia Ward Magee, followed months later at fifteen of the same disease. Of the four Magee children, only Mary Alene would live to adulthood, her mother and three siblings buried in unmarked graves at the Riverview Cemetery overlooking the beautiful Susquehanna River.[55] The year 1886 closed with a note from an unknown official at the War Department writing a memo on McGee's file: "I have received a letter from William McGee from Northumberland, Pa. — He is a hard case!"[56]

Willie McGee, the dynamic war hero who never stayed anywhere long, a man who never felt comfortable in Northumberland, would leave the Pennsylvania river town for at least the third time after the burial of his firstborn, placing Mary Alene with her Aunt Sallie Faust.[57] The legend of New Jersey disappeared, no doubt soon to appear in a new locale, destined to spread his own version of American history to as many willing students as he could find, or whoever would buy him a pint.

CHAPTER FIFTEEN

The Lost Years

It's been a long jig, my boy, and I am only now
beginning to see the pathos in it.
— Dion Boucicault,
on his deathbed

The once promising career of William H. McGee had by 1889 become an American tragedy. Awakened one unsuspecting morning at sixteen in Michigan, Willie had been informed he was awarded a Medal of Honor, and in the whirlwind two years which followed had risen to dizzying heights of fame, only to have every dream disintegrate for twenty consecutive years. The glorious life of Will McGee had evaporated into a morass of lies, insecurity, and rotten bad luck.

Despite this two decade string of misfortune, mostly caused by McGee's long held attachment to liquor, which he pursued zealously, the hero of New Jersey was possibly crushed even further with the early demise of three young children and his loyal, loving Regina.[1] At each life turn, however, no matter how demoralizing, William McGee continually bounced back, somehow ignoring all salient details of his current predicaments, and removed himself to a new location where he always found friends, at least temporarily. After his second failed battle against the army, even the indefatigable McGee realized it would be fruitless to pursue such future action, and all correspondence, proposed lawsuits, and appeals to politicians ceased. Willie retreated temporarily to Northumberland, though he was never at ease in the cramped quarters of the small river village.

His reputation sullied in Springfield with the defeat of the recent Senate bill, and no full-time work available at the U.S. Armory; no future in New Jersey with mentor Marcus Ward, dead since 1884, nor attorney E.L. Campbell, aware of his fraudulent past during the war. Willie was still unwelcome in Illinois, both for the wife he married illegally and then abandoned and for his drunken behavior. Minnesota was out of the question, and in a unique twist, Holmes Pattison had abandoned McGee, relocating to Florida and adopting a different son.

The Civil War had now been over for twenty-five years, and it is possible Willie McGee felt his heroic tales were losing interest among listeners. Soldiers, as they always do, grew older, and in the coming decade electricity, telephones, and automobiles would capture the American imagination more than an aging drummer's story of a captured gun in Tennessee. If Willie headed south — an area he had previously avoided — the story of Union courage would never generate the same enthusiasm as in Illinois and New Jersey. Should McGee have given serious thought to his next move, he might have recognized the need to settle down and grow old in a community he could, for once in his life, call home.

In 1890 it appeared Willie had settled on New York as his next port of call.[2] On the first Monday of that June, work began nationwide on the Eleventh Census, the sole purpose of which was the counting of all Union war veterans and their widows. The unique census, created by a special order of the U.S. Congress, was an awesome task, and in preparation, the Census Bureau secured as much information as possible prior to the June 1890 count. A preliminary record of almost 500,000 surviving vets was compiled; letters and inquiries were published in over 500 newspapers to elicit responses from any veterans overlooked. The total study took a year to prepare, another month to conduct, and a second year to verify.[3] A still young forty-one-year-old, ex–drummer boy would surely be easy to find. The nationwide census showed that only two William McGees, by any spelling, had ever served in the Union Army as musicians. William A. Magee, from Ohio, had removed to California immediately after the war, never leaving there until he died in 1953 at 106, the last surviving vet in California.[4] The second musician was the Newark, New Jersey, drummer, Will McGee.[5]

"William McGee, drummer boy," was duly registered in Manhattan, living at 645 Washington Avenue on the West Side, a major Irish enclave.[6] Until he died in 1892, this McGee was almost a perfect double for the enigmatic and troubled war hero from Newark. The New York McGee worked as a bartender, had a serious alcoholic past, including at least two arrests for public drunkenness, and possessed a spirited personality. Though this New York

Willie passed himself off on the West Side as our Medal of Honor soldier — in a scam the real McGee would surely have appreciated — he was not the veteran of the New Jersey 33rd Infantry. Born the same year, 1849, to a similarly dysfunctional Irish immigrant family, New York McGee was the youngest son of Bernard and Susan McGee in Manhattan, and his middle name was John, not Henry.[7]

This McGee would marry Kate Egan, another Irish newcomer, in 1876, and raise five children. Kate McGee, like Regina, would spell her family name Magee, and kept the family together as a full time dressmaker and mother, in spite of her husband's serious alcoholism. These McGees would never leave tenement Manhattan, until the children and Kate moved to the Bronx after New York Willie died at the early age of forty-two.[8] He worked intermittently until his death, his family unaware of his fraudulent claim as a war hero and believing he was the owner of a saloon as well as a New York alderman, none of which was true, but notably similar to the real Willie McGee.[9] How many years New York

An undated photograph of William J. McGee, the New York City bartender who passed himself off as the famous drummer boy of the 33rd New Jersey Infantry. William J. was eerily similar to the real Willie McGee, but never served in the army at all and would die in Manhattan in 1892 at age forty-one (author collection).

McGee passed himself off as the New Jersey drummer boy is not known, but it confirms that the story and legend of the hero of the Battle of the Cedars was still impressing people in the nation's largest city during the 1880s.

But if New York McGee was simply a good imitation of a great fraud, where was the drummer of the 33rd New Jersey? Was it possible the peripatetic Willie would miss the opportunity to register for the 1890 census, anxious as he was to be the center of attention?

On July 22, 1891, William Henry McGee, a salesman living in Galveston, Texas, married a seventeen-year-old local girl, Louise Saunders.[10] McGee, who claimed to be thirty-six and born in Kentucky, would spend the last years of the century "traveling out of Houston and Galveston." Texas William McGee said his parents were both born in Ireland, that he was the youngest son of a widowed mother, and, according to authorities, "had arrived in Texas in 1890, and was well known by Officer Higgins" of Galveston. Higgins added that McGee "was a trumpeter for the seventh cavalry and a fine soldier."[11] Willie McGee, the drummer of Newark, had simply gone to Texas and reverted to his one year identity as "Indian fighter" William H. McGee of Ludlow, Kentucky. Willie, calling himself Bill, a name he had used in Illinois a decade earlier, relinquished his Civil War identity, either afraid of being exposed or of just starting over, his Medal of Honor useless, pawned or lost years ago. Texas for decades — especially Galveston — had been attractive to adventurers, dreamers, and visionaries, though toughness was the most necessary quality, a component McGee never lacked.

For the next seven years, Bill McGee, his young wife and two infant sons, Lee and Albert, resided in various rooming houses in Galveston, while the Irishman from the Brick City in New Jersey plied his trade as a drummer, only now it was as a cigar and whiskey drummer throughout southeast Texas. But family harmony and relative obscurity were never enough for McGee, who had already been where he was going. Bill wandered away for longer stretches, selling up and down the Mississippi as far north as Saint Louis and often abandoning Louise and the two boys.[12] McGee needed the limelight, and in November 1898, now claiming to be a resident of St. Louis, McGee found a willing listener, a reporter for the *Waukesha* (Wisconsin) *Republican-Freeman*. The resulting article is a story of heroism under fire, much like the story told about a cold December day in Tennessee years before:

> He Fought Under Miles
> And Is Loud in His Praise of Bravery
> And Daring of His Chief

> William H. McGee, of St. Louis, who fought under Gen. Miles with him in 1877, the Nez Perce Indians under Chief Joseph who were subdued, speaks highly of the courage on that occasion of the commanding general of the army.

> Five days, he says, we had had been marching at night, going into camp about 4 o'clock each morning. About 8 o'clock on the morning of Sept. 30 we went into camp. This time we had made fires and in the morning reveille was sounded.

> After we had gone about four miles on the march that day we came in sight of the Nez Perce camp. They must have known we were coming, because they were fully prepared for us. We could not see them, but as we saw the camp we formed the line of battle. The Second Cavalry, under Maj. Brisbane, taking the left flank and Companies D,K, and A of the Seventh Cavalry, in command of Capt Owen Hale, taking the right.

> There were fully 800 of the painted savages, and all told our companies did not number over 120 men. We were in a bad place and the captains of Companies D and A ultimately gave their men the signal to retreat. Capt Hale, who

was a dashing and brave officer, at the same time commanded: "Left wheel and prepare to attack on foot."

We seemed to be in an open spot in the foothills and we were plainly in a bad palce. There was Company K with only 38 and attacking the entire Nez Perce band.

I will never forget that Sgt Wilde ran out a few feet in front of his horse, Corporal Delaney was next to him and I next to Delaney. We were in the extreme front. The Indians had dropped down out of sight and were springing up here and there to draw our fire. They were making straight for us.

In a moment Wilde was shot through the breast, Delaney wounded in the head and I shot in the right knee and side. Capt Hale was killed and the rest of the company driven back and the Indians followed, passing right over our rear, stopping to strip the dead and wounded of their arms and ammunition.... For a time I was in a desperate situation. I could hear the bullets whistling on all sides.

Gen Miles came up to my company and pointing to a spot where the Indian shots were coming from, said, "Boys, I don't believe there are a dozen of them there. Attack at once." We were so close that the Indians heard the order and answered back jeeringly, "Charge 'em." This was a disastrous charge, and one of the few soldiers who leaped forward dropped in an instant, and the remainder were repelled to fall back in a hurry.

Gen Miles, telling the boys to remain where they were, said he would send us reinforcements. It was at this point that I saw him exhibit bravery and daring which have been seldom witnessed. He could have gone around the hills with perfect safety, but it would have required a little more time. Disdaining the secure move, he put his horse into a canter and moved across the open, the only real exposed place on the field. There were, at least, as I said, 800 Nez Perce within a short distance, and they opened fire on him at once. There must have been 2,000 shots fired at him as he rode across.

It seemed certain death, actually courting it, but he dashed along regardless of the rain of lead around him. It was a spectacle I shall never forget. When I hear Gen Miles called a parlor or a dress parade soldier, I think of that ride and the scene he presented, and I feel like fighting myself.

The Indians were finally forced to surrender and Gen Miles was raised to a brigadeship.[13]

Like so much of McGee's stories, this had historical basis, but not much historical truth. Miles never dashed across any field, or faced 2000 bullets from 800 Indians. There were only a dozen or so warriors left, and both the cavalry and the Nez Perce were dug in behind dense cover.[14] But Bill McGee was present, it was indeed very tough duty, and he did suffer a minor gunshot wound.[15] The story was twenty-one years old, and, though it may have generated some local renown for the traveling salesman, it did not catch on in any of the wire services and disappeared from the public scene quickly. The irrepressible McGee had, of course, seen a similar but fraudulent tale lead to national prominence, but this story of the Battle of Bear Paw Mountain in

1877 led nowhere. It would however, become the precursor to the next tale of courage told by William H. McGee of New Jersey and points beyond.

McGee had been gone from Galveston more than he was home until he left for good — without the family — in 1900.[16] Bill was found in a rooming house in the 600 block of the Bowery in New York, working as a salesman for *Harper's Weekly*.[17] This time the well traveled salesman said he was born in New York, and repeated his correct birth year and the truth about his parents Irish heritage. Though he didn't specify what kind, McGee would later admit he "got out of Texas because of trouble." When asked to explain, Bill replied, "I ain't saying! Whatever I done in Texas I done on the level [self-defense]."[18]

Louise might have been missing a husband, but it could have been worse. On June 1, 1900, the great Galveston Flood ripped through the "Jewel of Texas," killing more than 8,000 of the 38,000 residents in just hours. Another 6,000 were injured, 2,600 homes destroyed, and 10,000 people left homeless. The unnamed hurricane that caused this damage is the deadliest natural disaster in United States history.[19] Single parent Louise McGee and her two sons were all natives of Galveston, and undoubtedly suffered the loss of friends, relatives, and memories. If Bill McGee was anguished about the safety of his family, it remained a long-distance concern, for he never returned to Texas.[20]

By his own later account, even when pressed, McGee was vague about the years 1890 to 1901, but was feverish to talk about some of his past in 1902.[21] Canvassing the Great Lake's District in June for *Harper's Weekly*, Bill McGee forgot about Texas, and perhaps the Civil War as well, and gave another remarkable interview to a reporter from the *Bismarck Daily Tribune*, while passing time at the Hotel Allen in Minneapolis.[22] It is a tour de force mixture of truth, historical falsehoods, and outright fantasy, reminiscent in its scope of a tale told decades earlier by a younger William H. McGee. This interview, once printed in the Bismarck paper, would take on a life of its own, just as the tale told by McGee about Murfreesboro had in 1865:

HE WAS WITH CUSTER

Custer's last fight, one of the great tragedies in the winning of the west, was graphically described at the Hotel Allen in Minneapolis the other morning by W. McGee of St. Louis, who claims to be the only survivor of the Seventh Cavalry, the gallant troop massacred in the valley of the Little Big Horn River, June 25, 1876.

History records that not a man escaped from that ill-starred pursuit of Sitting Bull's braves but Mr. McGee, "Orderly McGee," as he was then known, is a living refutation of that report.

Mr. McGee was born in Ludlow, Ky. in 1857. He and his widowed mother left Cincinnati and moved to the Texas frontier. In 1871, he joined the regulars at Quincy, Ill. and went soon after to St. Louis whence he joined his regiment in the south and two years later was detached as orderly with the Seventh.

"Before Custer and Reno parted company the day of the fight," said Mr. McGee, "they decided to attempt a flank movement on the hostiles, whose position was well known to all of us. The two officers compared watches and set them alike. I did not overhear their conversation at the time but afterwards learned that the agreement or understanding was to make the onslaught at a certain prearranged time.

"As orderly I was keeping close to General Custer. Before we had gone a mile he found that he would be unable to make the point agreed upon at the time, and calling to me, he said 'Orderly, go back to General Reno and tell him to wait twenty minutes longer.'

"He asked me if I thought I could find the way. I replied that I could as the trail was very plain. He called the trumpeter, a German named Wagner and gave him the same order. He then made us both repeat our orders. We did so and as we started off he pointed out what he thought was a short cut and suggested that we go that way instead of following the regular trail.

"Wagner decided to take the short cut because the general told him to, but I was afraid of falling in with Indians off the beaten path and so I stuck to the old trail. The short cut lay through the woods along the river. I had not gone more than 300 yards when the Indians commenced their on-slaught on the Seventh. Wagner was in their path. It seemed as if all the imps of hell had broken loose.

"To my dying day I will never forget the wild chorus of discordant blood-curdling yells which broke upon my ears, mingled with the crack of carbines. I knew it was up with Wagner. He was riddled. If you ever read in history about the man of Custer's command found three-quarters of a mile away you may be sure it was Wagner, the poor good natured trumpeter.

"Fearing that a like fate awaited me I hurried along the trail and was in sight of Reno's troops, when my horse was shot under me. As the horse fell, my carbine, which was in the sling at my side, was discharged, the bullet striking me in the left leg near the knee. Although shot through the lungs, my horse regained his feet and kept on at a slow pace. By this time several Indians who had opened fire on me were within plain view.

"They kept blazing away at me. I let go with my carbine at a buck who had just tried to wing me. I'm not sure whether I hit him or not, but he dropped, and soon another appeared in his place. It may have been the same fellow, but I am a good shot and in those days wouldn't miss a man fifty yards away one time in a thousand.

"I managed to stick it out until I got in the lines, and the answering fire of Reno's men sent the reds flying over the prairie. I shouted my orders at him as soon as I came within hailing distance. He replied: 'It's too late, orderly, take care of yourself.'

"By that time, although I hardly knew it, I was shot in the right and left legs and sides. It was all over with Custer and his command. I was the last man he spoke to, or rather, the last living man he said anything to on that fatal afternoon.

"Custer was a brave man, but he was too foolhardy. These popular pictures of the fight are mostly misleading. The soldiers didn't wear sabers, nor did we have any wagons within a hundred miles of us. I fought under General Miles in subsequent Indian campaigns. He was the man for Indian fighting. He knew the treacherous Indian nature, and fought them on the theory that the only good Indian is a dead one."[23]

With this outrageous tale, Bill McGee stepped into the national spotlight once again.[24] Over the course of the next two years, the McGee rendition of the Little Big Horn was repeated in newspapers, big and small, throughout the country. McGee was, by his own account, toasted in villages, towns, and cities as he traveled from Minnesota to New York. Since the fall of Custer that fateful June 1876, the legend of the Little Big Horn has captured the American mind, as much or more than any single day in American history. One of the most discussed and studied aspects of the battle between General George Armstrong Custer and two thousand Northern Plains Indians is exactly who lived and who died that hot day in Montana.[25]

Since 1926, which marked the fiftieth anniversary of the battle, historians have unanimously agreed there were no survivors of the Little Big Horn except for one horse, Captain Myles Keogh's "Commanche." Whether Americans of the nineteenth century could not accept that "wild savages" could kill an entire command of magnificent white soldiers, or simply loved a great story, dozens of men between 1876 and 1920 would lay claim to being the lone dauntless survivor or last messenger of one of the darkest days in American military history.[26]

Each of the accounts has been rejected as fraudulent by experts, but in the last quarter of the nineteenth century many were believed, at least for a while, depending on the ability of the "survivor" to tell his story. Some of these men, according to Michael Nunnally, the author of *I Survived Custer's Last Stand,* "were casual liars, small town yarn spinners, and some with serious mental conditions." Others, said Nunnally, "were quite creative, and had books written about them, and one was featured in a movie."[27]

Bill — or Willie, as he was called by Custer historians Brian Dippie and Nunnally — McGee's tale was one of the most creative, though short-lived, of them all.[28] McGee was helped by nature of serving in the Seventh Cavalry just three months after the fight, no doubt garnering accurate information from men who actually fought that day for Major Reno or Benteen.[29] Nunnally has shown that even the better survivor stories changed with each telling, and McGee was no exception. In Bill McGee's narrative, it is a story full of information, most of it false. There was no McGee orderly — or Wagner — in any of the three commands in the confused action that day, but there were few alive in 1902 to challenge Bill McGee's retelling.[30]

Historically, of course, Custer sent no messenger to Reno, had no musicians with him, and Reno never heard from Custer, but those are just the tips of the iceberg in this sham of a tale.[31] Like much of the other Custer tales, McGee mixed truth with fiction regarding his own life. McGee told the naive reporter he was living at St. Louis in 1902, and that would fit the traveling salesman, though McGee was living in New York City in 1900, and he would move back there in 1904, with disastrous results.[32] Both Bill McGee, and Willie McGee, drummer boy, said they were raised by widowed mothers (neither ever mentioned their fathers), and Bill told the Bismarck paper he moved to Texas in the 1860s.[33] Texas newspapers reported later that McGee "arrived in 1891."[34] Though Bill McGee did indeed join the cavalry for one year at Quincy, Illinois, it was in 1876, not 1871.[35] Like a younger Willie McGee, Bill claimed to have been attached as an orderly to Custer, as Willie was indeed General Van Cleve's messenger at Murfreesboro.[36] McGee did serve under General Miles, where he was wounded, but certainly not at the Little Big Horn, a place he may only have visited or heard about months after the battle.[37]

By June 1902, Bill McGee, hero of the Little Big Horn or not, had been gone from Texas and his family for at least two years, but his third wife, Louise, would not be as forgiving as Regina or Jane. McGee's behavior toward the women and children in his life had been a matter of speculation for over two decades. Louise, after more than two years of abandonment, went to Sheriff Henry Thomas of Galveston County just weeks after the "Custer" interview when her missing husband appeared in print.[38]

Louise charged Bill with "unkind, cruel, outrageous and tyrannical conduct," and asked for a divorce.[39] A legal notice was filed in newspapers throughout Texas for a month requiring any law enforcement agent to arrest and hold William H. McGee to face charges in Galveston.[40] McGee, who always had his ear to the ground, denied all charges in a note sent to his court appointed attorney, Edward May, but refused to appear, and court records reveal "McGee put himself upon the country."[41] Nonetheless, the Texas proceedings continued, and in October 1902, Louise testified in open court that her husband, William Henry McGee, had since 1893 continually and violently beat her with his hands and fists, coming home intoxicated and drugged. In a December hearing, the Texas Mrs. McGee added that her husband had several times threatened to kill her and the children, telling the judge, "He has drawn his revolver many times and said he wanted to kill us."[42]

"He [McGee] was almost always drunk," said Louise, "and also drugged by opium which he has used regularly." The young Mrs. McGee, now only 28, completed her testimony with an ominous, "My husband is a very desperate man of violent temper and through drinking and opium habit he has degenerated so much as to be fully capable to commit crimes of the highest degree."[43] Not even Bill McGee's most severe critics would ever imagine this last statement by Louise to a Galveston judge would prove so accurate. Bill McGee, the self-proclaimed sole survivor of Custer's Last Stand, and a very real Medal of Honor recipient, would once again have his life inexorably altered in another act of temperamental violence, in a scene extremely reminiscent of an equally senseless act thirty-four years before in Baton Rouge, Louisiana.

Louise McGee was granted the divorce just before Christmas 1902, though Bill McGee had been long gone, spending the rest of 1902 and all 1903 in the Midwest, much of it in Indiana and Ohio, before returning to New York in August 1904. McGee, no stranger to Manhattan, ran into Frank Mitchell, a fellow salesman he had befriended and traveled with for six weeks in Shelbyville and Indianapolis, Indiana, the previous year. "Mitch" and "Mac" met purely by accident in the offices of Richard K. Fox, the publisher of the *Police Gazette*, where they had both gone to look for further employment. Mitchell invited McGee for dinner at his apartment on the third floor at 300 East 41st Street. After several months of dining and visiting with Frank and Mabel Mitchell, Bill McGee took a room on the floor above, moving in with Mrs. Martha Geraghty.[44]

On the night of December 8, 1904, one day after the fortieth anniversary of the Battle of the Cedars, the Mitchells, Bill McGee, and Mrs. Blondell, the owner of the rooming house, went to Proctor's Fifth Avenue Theatre, where there was a continuous performance of vaudeville running. Exiting about eleven P.M., the four stopped at a deli for cold cuts and beer before returning to the Mitchell apartment. Later, statements would differ on what had occurred, as they always do in murder cases, but the *New York Sun* alerted the city with a vivid chronicle, including a bizarre confession by Bill McGee:

ONE OF CUSTER'S MEN

William McGee Kills a Man in Kidney Stew Quarrel

Tells a Picturesque Story

Sole White Survivor of the Battle of the Little Big Horn —

Had Been Sent by Custer with a Message to Reno —

Wounded, but Reached the Troops —

Prepared to Meet any Fate Calmly

A stabbing affray between two men, which had its grotesque cause in a quarrel on the cooking of a kidney stew, has brought into public view again that quiet, unassuming hero, William McGee, the sole white survivor of the Custer massacre. McGee is charged with stabbing and mortally wounding Frank Mitchell, who later died of his injuries.

McGee has certainly had a checkered past, and there are some gaps in his history which he nonchalantly dismisses with a wave of his hand. He followed the border for forty years, he has three holes in his body and a clip over the scalp from Indian bullets and knives. He lay wounded one whole hot day in the trenches with Reno, standing off the rushes from Sitting Bull's braves. He's been in many a border scrap and now he has ended up by getting jailed for a stabbing affray that started over his ability to make kidney stew. That fact, as much as anything else, rankles in the bosom of Bill McGee.

"Had Trouble"

McGee, who is pretty well educated and has been a printer in his time, left Texas suddenly. "Had trouble," he says. He put back all the way to New York, and went to canvassing for *Harper's Weekly*. He roomed at 300 East Forty-first Street, and in the flat below lived Mitchell and his wife. Bill told Mitchell his troubles, and they got to be chums.

Thursday night they all went to the theatre. At home again the men folks said they were hungry and Mrs. Mitchell said she'd go to bed and they could warm over some beef stew. Here is what happened next, in the words of Bill McGee.

"We got to be kidding. No trouble, only fun. He joshed me about a kidney stew I'd made for him once."

"Go on," says I, just kidding. "I've cooked a lot for good people in my time."

"The hell you have," says he.

"You're right, I have," says I. "More'n that, where you can spend $2 I could spend $17 in my day."

Would Not Stand for the Lie

"He got mad and passed the lie. If there's anything I won't stand for it's that."

"Look out for me when you say that," says I.

"There's where Mitchell played the damn fool. There were a lot of kitchen knives on the sink that had been washed and not wiped. He grabbed one quick as a wink and I got another. He rushed, I ducked to one knee the way I learned from the Injuns. His first lick ripped my scalp but I got inside and gave him two in the body.."

"I didn't think I'd hurt him very bad. He kept to his feet. I shoved him back and say, 'Frank, you don't want me to kill you, do you?' His wife ran in. She carried on so bad I got out. At the door I met a copper and told him that a man had been stabbed inside."

Something of a Financier

Bill McGee had only 20 cents at the time. With that he bought a drink and borrowed 50 cents of the bartender. Then he made his way to a Bowery saloon, and passed the night on the table.

"And in the morning I moseyed back to the house to see how Frank stacked up," he said.

Mrs. Blondell the landlady met him at the door. "For heaven's sake, Mr. McGee, go away," she said. "Frank is dying and all the police in New York are looking for you."

I left and came to your office to set you right. "I'm Bill McGee, the man you're after, for stabbing Frank Mitchell, and you've got me wrong and I want to put you right. Say, you needn't edge away like that. I ain't going to hurt you."

This reporter conferred rapidly with Willie, the office boy. Willie tore for the police. McGee was arrested while he was telling his story. He took it with good-humored calm.

"All right, partner. I'm your man," he said.

His Part in Custer Fight

While waiting for his hearing before Magistrate Pool in the Yorkville police court, McGee told the story of his part in the Custer fight. It has been told before in the West of the doomed three hundred who were in that fatal and glorious charge only one man came out alive. That was Curley, a scout, who disguised himself in a war bonnet and sneaked away. This man McGee was of the detachment but not in the charge. He had been sent back not ten minutes before to carry a message to Major Reno.

"I was only a kid then, but strong. I enlisted as a civilian packer for the Little Big Horn expedition, and before we got up to the buttes I was kind of an orderly for Custer — scurrying 'round carrying messages — because I was light and rode fast."

"Custer had set his watch with Reno's and they were to charge from opposite sides of the village at the same time. They agreed to that when they split forces. But Custer couldn't make it as fast as he wanted. He was afraid that Reno would charge before his own detachment got up. He called me and Wagner, his trumpeter. He said, 'Get over to Major Reno and tell him to hold in for twenty minutes.' He said the same to Wagner. He sent two of us to make sure the message would get there, I guess."

Fatal Error of his Companion

"And keep out of sight," he said.

"Now, I knew Injuns and how to keep out of sight, but Wagner was a hard-headed swell-headed Dutchman. He wanted to cut straight across the buttes so's to get there quick.

"The Injuns'll see you you blame fool," says I. I knew there was plenty of time to go back and make it by following up the trail. I bet he argued half a mile, and at last he said he'd go anyhow. I let him go. He lived about three minutes. There were fourteen bullet holes in his body when they found it. I always believed that he gave Sitting Bull's band the first notice that Custer was coming — got 'em prepared to meet the charge they way they did.

"For in a minute there was shooting all along the Horn. I rode to the fork and took the trail for Reno's command. You know they caught Custer on a hillside and he made a running fight backward up the hill.

"When I came out on the summit, there they were — the troops blazing away in a bunch, and the valley filled with Indians as far as you could see, but it was my business to get down to him, so I spurred my horse and rode like hell."

Wounded, but Reached Reno

"I was half way down before the Indians saw me coming, all alone, and turned loose on me. I was thirty yards away from our rear when I felt my horse cave in and drop. He had got it through the flank. I jumped up to run for it — and I got it — square through the thigh. Somehow I made it into the line and up beside Reno. Of course, the message was too damn late.

"Well, it was simple hell, a whole day of it. We laid out, thirsty and done up, and the men fighting and everybody expecting Custer. I can't remember much. I was too sick. I just remember this — four hours before we were relieved, the boys see a bunch of men in blue army uniforms come riding down the river. They jumped out of the trenches and cheered and threw up their hats because they thought it was the relief. The men in blue uniforms turned and fired on us. They were the Sioux, dressed in the clothes they'd taken off Custer's men.

"You'll remember that it says in all the histories how Wagner's body was found three-quarters of a mile from the rest of Custer's men. They figure out that he'd tried to get away and the Indians had caught him on the run. That's rot, as I've told you. I always figured that Custer would have stood a heap better chance if that Dutchman hadn't got original.

"He got out of Texas because he'd been in trouble," said Mrs. Mitchell yesterday. "What was the trouble?" someone asked McGee.

"Now look here partner, I'm up against a hard game, and I aint sayin! I'll just say this. Whatever I done in Texas, I done on the level, just like the job last night.

"I never was afraid. I ain't afraid now. Mitch was a big man, and he came at me strong, but I could lick a roomful of him.

"They say a man can't fight except on his own ground. Why, hell! I can fight anywhere and there ain't a man alive, unless he's been educated in knife fighting, that I can't beat with a knife. He brought it all on himself—him and that gossipy little Irish woman that's going to try and swear me to the electric chair.

Prepared for any Fate

He mentioned the chair in an easy matter-of-fact way that brought comment from the police.

"Gentlemen," said McGee, "It ain't in the manner of life I've been leading to be afraid. When I rode to Reno I wasn't afraid. I wasn't afraid when I got into a damn sight tighter holes. I ain't afraid now if the jury was over in that box right now, and said to me, Bill McGee, you've got to die at 6 o'clock. I'd say: 'All right gentlemen. Suit yourselves. Howling won't help.'"

"That's sure the way I feel," concluded Bill McGee as Capt Shire's men led him away. He was held without bail to await the result of Mitchell's injuries. At 7 o'clock yesterday evening Mitchell died, and the charge was changed to homicide.

Mrs. Mitchell's story agrees roughly with McGee's, except that she says the ex-soldier picked the fight and stabbed first.[45]

Bill McGee, the man not afraid to fight or die, was a book salesman for several years, selling in the lobbies of hotels in the Midwest and East. Bill McGee, of the Seventh Cavalry, had one thing, and only one thing, right in his tale of the Little Big Horn: Custer fought on a hillside. Nobody checked, just as nobody checked in New Jersey in 1865 when a drummer boy told a similar outrageous story.

Newspapers around the country picked up the story, and within three days the murder of Frank Mitchell was on the front pages in more than fifteen states, including papers in Oakland, Atlanta, Washington, D.C., Montana and Kansas City, the majority with headlines like "Sole Custer Survivor Stabs Friend."[46] The Custer tale aside, the case of Frank Mitchell's death seemed fairly cut and dried. The *New York Times* on December 12, 1904, provided a glimpse of how papers throughout the country portrayed the upcoming trial:

Beef Stew Causes Tragedy

Sole Custer Survivor Stabs Friend in Quarrel

As a result of a quarrel over the proper method for the preparation of a beef stew, Frank Mitchell, a salesman of 300 East Forty-first Street, is dead and William Magee of the same address, a book agent who claims to be the sole survivor of Custer's last fight, is held for his murder.

Mitchell and Magee were great friends. They went to the theatre together Thursday evening and on their return about midnight Mitchell proposed they make a stew in his kitchen. Shortly after they went into the flat Magee came out, went to his room and then left the house. On the way out he exchanged greetings with Policeman Kochbender of the East Thirty-fifth Street Station.

He had hardly got out of sight when Albert Fulton, a tenant, told Kochbender, that a man had been stabbed in the Mitchell apartments. When the policeman entered the flat he found Mitchell with a knife wound in his left shoulder and the other in his abdomen. At first Mitchell refused to say who had stabbed him, and forbade his wife to speak, but after the husband was removed to Belleville Hospital, Mrs. Mitchell found her tongue and said that a quarrel had arisen about the best way to cook a stew, and that Magee had assailed her husband with a carving knife. The knife was found in Magee's room, under his pillow.[47]

As the case against Bill McGee approached trial in late February, newspapers again brought a small measure of fame back to the McGee name. Readers in California, Indiana, Texas, and Missouri, as well as the entire eastern seaboard, were alerted that McGee's trial had begun.[48] Attorneys Mann and Bell had little to work with, especially after their client's penchant for personal publicity produced a virtual confession.[49] The prosecution called a parade of witnesses, but it would eventually be Mabel Mitchell versus Bill McGee. On February 23, Mrs. Mitchell was sworn in and questioned by District Attorney James Ely.[50]

Mabel testified before Judge Kenefick that following a second pint of beer by all present, Mrs. Blondell began setting her clock, and asked Frank Mitchell, "What time will I call you in the morning?" After the soon to be dead man said seven o'clock, McGee added, "Call me at the same time." In jest, Mitchell replied, "Mrs. Blondell, don't let Mac cook the breakfast. That kidney slop or slush that he cooked this morning made me sick. I vomited on the street."[51]

Mabel Mitchell swore that both Blondell and Mitchell laughed at the joke, and as the landlord exited, she answered, "I will cook eggs for breakfast myself." Mabel said she began to rise and get ready for bed herself, when Bill McGee turned and said to his friend Mitch, "You never had better stew in your life."

Mitchell, according to his wife, said "Yes, Mac, but you know I have lived at some of the best hotels in this country, and ate where chefs were certainly better than you."[52]

McGee, said the new widow, never saw the humor, snapped and angrily responded, "You are a God damn liar." At that, Bill McGee grabbed the carving knife, which had been on the table, leaned across, and stabbed Frank Mitchell, who was trying to rise from his chair, which was pinned between the kitchen table and the wall. After stabbing his friend in the abdomen, McGee continued slashing, cutting Mitchell in the right shoulder. Both thrusts wounded Frank in the back, as he attempted to get up from his chair in tight quarters. But McGee, said Mabel, wasn't finished. As he tried to cut the wounded man a third time, Mabel reached across the table and deflected the knife, and was slashed herself in the left hand. At prosecutor Ely's request, Mabel Mitchell showed the wound to the jury, and testified that neither she nor her husband had any weapons, the carving knife being the only visible weapon in the room, a statement confirmed by the testimony of Mrs. Blondell. When asked what happened next, Mabel said she begged McGee, "For God's sake, give me the knife," but Bill yelled, "Stand back or I'll give you what he got and more, too." Mortally wounded, Frank Mitchell, leaning on his wife, made his way to Mrs. Blondell's room.[53]

William McGee, facing a possible death sentence, gave testimony in direct opposition to the wounded Mabel Mitchell. He swore that Mabel was not even in the room, that Frank Mitchell attacked him first with a second knife, after first verbally abusing the sole survivor of Custer's Last Stand. "Who in the hell ever told you you could cook," McGee testified his friend yelled at him. Bill said Mitchell continued, "That damn stuff made me sick this morning." McGee at the urging of his attorney, Hal Bell, said he kept answering Mitchell's badgering with restraint. "It did?" At that point, said the accused, Frank Mitchell yelled again, "Who told you how to make that shit?"[54]

McGee swore on the stand that he still held his temper, and softly answered, "Frank, I have made that for some of the best people, either one way or the other." Mitchell, said Bill, would have none of his restraint. "To hell you have." As McGee's testimony continued, his recollection of the argument strained credulity. After Mitchell's so-called harangue, McGee still replied quietly, "Yes, I have, Frank. Of course, I am not a chef or anything of that kind, but if you let me make you a breakfast you bet I will make you up a breakfast that you could eat all right."[55]

When Judge Kenefick told the accused to speak louder, McGee replied that Frank Mitchell rose quickly up from his chair in a threatening manner, and again yelled, "You are a God damn liar." Only then, Bill told the jury, did he jump away and raise his arms defensively as Mitchell hit him twice with a knife. "As I went down, I swung wildly, any place, just to get away," said McGee, who never mentioned during his description of the fatal argument how or when he had a knife in his own hand, or Mabel Mitchell's wounded hand.[56]

William McGee told the courtroom he was then struck from behind by Mrs. Mitchell, who had re-entered the room. He was bloodied in the head, and as he backed away from both Mitchells, Frank picked up a chair to strike him again, and at that point Custer's orderly said to the fatally wounded man, "Mitch, you don't want me to kill you, do you? You come at me with that chair and I will kill you." McGee added, "Go with your wife, don't you see you are bleeding?" As his long testimony neared conclusion, Bill McGee admitted he went upstairs with the carving knife to the room he shared with Mrs. Geraghty, who helped him clean up. McGee put the knife under his pillow and left the house, where he conversed for several minutes with a police officer before walking downtown and spending the night in a saloon on Chatham Square.[57]

In the morning, McGee went back to Mrs. Blondell's apartment and was told that Frank Mitchell was in the hospital. Concerned for his friend, Bill went back downtown to the same saloon, before eventually making his way to *Harper's Weekly*, where his employer at *Harper's* advised him to give himself up. Returning uptown, McGee saw an account of the incident in a morning paper, which he felt was "grossly incorrect." Bill went directly to the paper's offices to have his version heard, gave the interview, and was arrested as he left the building.[58]

Frank Mitchell died, according to testimony, at 7:30 P.M. from hemorrhage and shock. The fatal wound had penetrated seven inches, passing through his stomach and cutting into his liver.[59] The trial was over in two days, and the jurors were faced with a singular decision. Did they believe Mabel Mitchell, or William McGee? Did Mabel's husband die from a wild unprovoked attack, with no weapon to defend himself, as he helplessly tried to rise from his chair, much like a doctor in Baton Rouge thirty-six years before? Or was Bill McGee, Indian fighter and former Medal of Honor recipient, simply defending himself with great restraint, from a friend who had lost his mind, a man with no record of violence in his life?

Following closing arguments from defense attorney Bell and District Attorney Ely, the jury retired at 3:15 for three hours. They then asked Judge Kenefick the difference between murder and manslaughter. They retired again for fifteen minutes before they returned with a verdict of guilty on the charge of manslaughter in the first degree.[60]

McGee was removed to the Tombs until sentencing and there is no record if the man who had survived the Civil War and Indian conflicts was surprised to be convicted, or relieved he avoided the death penalty, but William H. McGee was always a man of hopeless hope. Judge Kenefick surprised everybody by sentencing Bill to only seven years and ten months — giving him two months credit for time served — out of a possible twenty-year term.[61] Like the minor five-year sentence young Willie McGee received in Louisiana in 1868, curtailed because of his Medal of Honor "and good conduct in the field during the war," Bill McGee was the beneficiary of leniency from the court. "There are some mitigating circumstances in your case," said the judge. "I cannot overlook the fact that you have been a brave soldier and suffered wounds in defense of your country. But soldiers and civilians stand equal before the law."[62]

The public and notorious life, or lives, of broken hero William McGee lasted one more week. Newspapers across the land announced the conviction of McGee with headlines like "Custer Survivor to Jail, May be Brave but He Broke the Law"; "Man with Custer Convicted"; in Galveston, "McGee in

Aerial view of the "Big House," Sing Sing Prison in Ossining, New York, early in the twentieth century. The main cell block is in the left foreground, close to the Hudson River (Ossining Historical Society).

Prison: Sole Survivor of Little Big Horn Massacre — Former Texan"; and "Survivor of Noted Massacre Guilty of Killing Roommate — Last White Man Living Who Was with Custer at Slaughter Convicted of Manslaughter — Claimed Self-Defense."[63]

By noon on Tuesday, March 3, 1905, William McGee was registered as inmate #55477 at the notorious Sing Sing Prison in Ossining, New York, thirty miles upriver from New York City. When asked to list the names of relatives or friends, the only person the well traveled and infamous McGee mentioned was his New York attorney, Morgan Mann. He stated his home address as 300 East Forty-first Street, where he had resided for less than three weeks, and the place where he killed his friend, Frank Mitchell.[64]

Even as he entered Sing Sing, Willie McGee's reputation was recognized, false though it was. At the top of the inmate register, a rare notation was included, suggesting a special personage was about to enter the famed "Big House." "He fought with Custer and was the sole survivor of the Little Big Horn."[65] It would be the last public notice of the Irishman from Newark. By April 1905, the real, or imagined, worlds of drummer boy William Henry McGee, the once promising hero of New Jersey, were silenced by the damp, cold, world of Sing Sing, the most notorious prison in the country. He was never heard of again.

Epilogue

We Irish are always being accused of
looking backward too much. Sometimes,
however, we don't look backward far enough —
or carefully enough, or honestly enough.
— Dervla Murphy

Right to the end, Willie McGee followed old tracks. In the winter of 1909, almost halfway through his sentence, the sixty-year-old convicted murderer applied to New York governor Charles Evans Hughes for clemency. But Hughes was not Marcus Ward, and the appeal was denied.[1] McGee was scheduled for release from Sing Sing in January 1913, when he would be 63.[2] While no federal prison was meant to be comfortable, "The Big House" was truly horrific and brutal, and Willie would long for the days in Stillwater. Prior to reforms that began in 1914 under Warden Lewis Lawes, the Ossining penitentiary was the ugly scene of corruption, violent deaths, inadequate sanitation, overcrowding, torture, and widespread sexual coercion.[3]

"Torture, disease, injury, insanity, and death: These were the daily realities of Sing Sing life," wrote Timothy J. Gilfoyle in his expert *A Pickpocket's Tale: The Life of Nineteenth Century New York*. "Sing Sing had more in common with a Soviet gulag than with any reformatory. Some convicts considered Sing Sing worse than war."[4]

There is no record of McGee after his appeal for clemency failed in 1910. There remains a possibility that one of America's greatest fakers died before release, but Sing Sing wardens prior to Lawes were generally an incompetent bunch. Willie saw five wardens in his eight years, not one a professional

Cell block in Sing Sing. Willie McGee would spend eight years here for the murder of his friend Frank Mitchell (Ossining Historical Society).

phrenologist, or even an adequate record keeper. One warden was a horse-man, another a transfer tax appraiser, and a third a Yonkers steamfitter.[5]

Prison deaths sometimes even went unrecorded. Although there was a prison cemetery on the grounds, all bodies were removed by 1940 and parceled out to cemeteries as far away as New York City.[6] Some convicts who died, insists at least one historian, vanished after being deposited in the Hudson.[7] With the exception of his inmate register, there is only a single notation show-ing McGee was present inside the walls. The Federal Census counted all the prisoners at Sing Sing in May of 1910, and Willie McGee was still a member of the general populace. In typical McGee fashion, he told the truth about most of his personal life, but said this time that he was born in Massachu-setts.[8] Willie claimed at least five states as his birthplace, either a sign of dementia or fear of being discovered.[9] If Will McGee passed away before his release, there is no record, and a check of six local cemeteries show no com-parable William McGees.[10] In the greatest irony of a strange, mysterious, and convoluted life, William McGee, the Irish waif from New Jersey, probably walked out of Sing Sing in early 1913 solitary and anonymous.

The young boy drummer who "defeated" General Nathan Bedford For-rest and murdered a doctor in cold blood; the young man who became a New Jersey legend and bigamist; the Medal of Honor recipient who lied to the pres-ident of the United States and was rewarded; the mature adult who fought the Nez Perce and became a great American liar; and the middle-aged psy-chotic drug addict who killed his best friend over a beef stew remained, to the end, alone and friendless.

The origins of the McGees in America are as shadowy as the life of Willie himself. McGee, by any spelling, is an Ulster name, just as often written Magee, which in Irish translates as the "son of Hugh."[11] Often the search for Irish surnames gives clear clues as to nationality and religion — the easily identifiable O'Connors and Sullivans being examples of Gaelic septs, and the Shaws and Mitchells examples of common Anglo-Norman surnames, though still very Irish. In a story of constant puzzles, however, even the McGee sur-name provides no help. There are two distinct Irish McGees, one of Scottish extraction that settled in the northern counties of Antrim and Down. There are also Gaelic McGees, who settled mostly in Tyrone and Donegal, only adding to the riddle.[12]

Though there had been unrecognized yet substantial Irish migration prior to 1845 for over 150 years throughout the United States, James, Mar-garet, and baby Michael McGee were among the early famine émigrés arriv-ing in Newark about 1845.[13] The Irish were settled in the swampy and unhealthy East Side, and James McGee was never prosperous or interested enough to be included in the free Newark city directories, a sure sign of poverty.[14] In 1850, James McGee was working in a factory as a tinsmith.[15] Though many Irish Catholics, especially those from Ulster, never registered births in nineteenth century America, James and Margaret baptized three children at St. John's, the first Roman Catholic Church in New Jersey. Mary Ann was born in November 1845, followed by brothers John in 1847 and William on May 13, 1849.[16]

In a family hidden behind falsehoods and poverty, James McGee disappeared or died by 1858, and possibly much earlier.[17] There is no record of James' death in New York, New Jersey, Massachusetts, or Connecticut, and it is very possible he abandoned the family — much like his son Willie would do two decades later.[18] Willie McGee never publicly mentioned — ever — the very existence of his father, much less his name, except on one marriage record in Illinois. Years later, James' youngest son would mirror such an abandonment three times over, and this behavior would not be limited to just Willie. The three McGee boys would become the fathers of twelve male children, and only Michael would name a son James, rare among Irish families of the nineteenth century.[19] By 1860, all four McGee children were living with relatives, John and Will with their Aunt Maria McDaniel and her husband, Tom, a blacksmith.[20]

Despite the promotions, honors, arrests, and newspaper articles throughout the life of Willie McGee, there survive no definitive photographs of the drummer boy. The physical description of Willie remained consistent however, from enlistment to Sing Sing. In July of 1863, when he was thirteen, Willie was 5' 2" with grey eyes, light brown hair, and a light complexion.[21] When he entered Stillwater prison just short of his twentieth birthday, the jailors listed the exact same characteristics, except for a natural growth spurt to five feet eight inches.[22] On the Sing Sing inmate register, Willie was now, at fifty-six years of age, listed as 5'7" with grey eyes, light complexion, and brown and gray hair, and at no time does any record show Willie weighed more than 146 pounds.[23]

Growing up, Willie, like so many new to the country, had a nonexistent family life. His older brother, Michael McGee, would marry at seventeen and raise a family, first in Jersey City and then Providence, Rhode Island. There is no record Michael ever corresponded with his famous little brother once in his adult life, even when in serious trouble, and Willie never mentioned Michael's name in print.[24] History swallowed up his sister, Mary Ann, and though John's family made Meriden, Connecticut, their home and hearth for almost a century, there were years when Willie was a phantom even to John. There were extended McGees, both in New Jersey and New Haven, including marriages up through 1895, but they would be lost or dismissed by the travels and antics of the drummer from Newark.[25] Willie, the youngest, survived both brothers, who died before they were 55, John in 1904, and Mike in 1894 in Providence.[26] The Texas McGees gave up on Willie completely. Following her divorce, Louise married Richard Adlof, an Austrian immigrant and stenographer, just months before the Mitchell shooting, and they raised their own family in Galveston. Willie's sons, Lee and Albert, whom he threatened to kill, went their own ways as "McKees."

The only known direct ancestors of Willie McGee are the seven great-grandchildren of Mary Alene Magee. These Magees, all residents of central Pennsylvania, are as remarkable for their solid faith and family ties as Willie was for his own idiorythmic disharmony. The lies, whether they were about age, name, or religion, never left Willie. Diane, McGee's Pennsylvania link, was surprised to even think he was Irish Catholic and not rock solid Scots Presbyterian, while the New England McGees would be shocked to think Willie was anything but a dyed in the wool Irish Gaelic rebel.[27] The Van Brunts of Nebraska would not have cared what age or religion the drummer claimed — they would have just wanted to lynch him. Roman Catholic by birth, Willie married three times, at least twice in Protestant denominations, and developed useful if not suspicious relationships with Protestant chaplains, yet claimed he was a Roman Catholic when imprisoned at Stillwater and Sing Sing.[28]

Willie McGee, exceptional for all the wrong reasons, was not alone in his inability to fit into mainstream America. Tens of thousands of dislocated Irish became rooted and successful Americans in their hearts before both feet touched United States soil, but the great majority sacrificed their own futures for the generations that followed. The toll taken on James and Margaret will never be truly known or calculated, though in some obscure cases it was recorded, remembered, and revered. In most others, like that of their son, William McGee, their story has been forgotten or framed in selective memory. Many of today's Irish descendants "learned not to know what happened to them."[29]

Alcohol, of course, was the driving force behind McGee's unsuccessful and unrewarding life, a problem so severe it contributed twice to murdering innocent and unarmed men, in addition to ruining his own life. Whether Willie's weakness was driven by genetics, environment, or personal failure is for others to consider, though there is little doubt the mood of nineteenth century America regarding alcohol abuse was not helpful, especially during the Civil War. Hundreds of boys drank throughout the war, and, once dismissed from service, many found it hard to stop and became addicted.[30] As

The Kulps of Pennsylvania. The seven great-grandchildren of William H. and Regina McGee from a 1970s photograph. Diane, third from the left, has searched for the mysterious Willie for decades (Diane Bretz Collection).

in Willie McGee's case, "Alcoholism created undue strain on marriages and personal lives, and made it difficult to stay employed," wrote William Keesee in his standard work on boy soldiers of the Civil War, *Too Young to Die*. "After the war, veterans organizations fueled the problem by offering an outlet where men could sit around the campfire and exchange drinks," and at GAR encampments liquor and prostitutes were often freely available.[31]

It did not help that McGee was Irish. The stereotype of the drunken Paddy was so all-pervasive in America during the late 1800s that when the *New York Times* reported one hundred thousand Irish (Irish-Americans) had taken the pledge at a temperance meeting in 1890, the reporter noted "few looked Irish; all looked like substantial American citizens."[32] Though the stage Irish of Willie's era often portrayed alcoholics — Irish alcoholics — as intrinsically humorous, harmless creatures, most Americans know it has, as

Maureen Dezell pointed out, "turned many men and women monstrous, and chewed up and swallowed many lives."[33] The women in McGee's life — Regina, Jane, Louise, Mabel Mitchell, and Cecilia Braman — would all be witnesses to Willie's abuse.

In the end, McGee had become, according to his last wife, Louise, addicted as well to opium. By the 1880s, and for decades afterward, there were scores of overcrowded opium joints in New York, especially in the Bowery, where McGee would live for a while in 1900. But in truth, every city in the country had opium dens, most often winked at by law enforcement. Opium, alcohol, and prostitution were often linked in the same establishments, and with Willie spending several years as a traveling whiskey salesman, it should surprise no one that the weak McGee would succumb.

In the end, William Henry McGee, the Jersey drummer boy, was living proof of what the great American historian Dennis Clark of Philadelphia once observed. "Almost anything you can say about Irish-Americans is both true and false."[34] He wasn't Magee; he wasn't from Kentucky; he never fought with Custer; he surely was not a hero; and, most importantly, McGee was not a good father or husband. He was Willie McGee, another precocious boy who went to war too soon in a world where no one cared how old you were; a displaced spirit who wove a life behind the cloak of lies and a brilliant, hypnotic personality; a son of New Jersey never able to fondly embrace life; and a forgotten, broken man who fought demons and lost.

Appendices

1. The Bonfoey Case

The reconstructed South was rough and tumble, and Willie McGee was not the only suspected murderer and thief in the officer ranks of the U.S. 20th Infantry. In August 1867, a year before McGee shot Chandler Braman, Mrs. Emma Bonfoey of Marshall, Texas, was beaten to death in her home, and while we cannot count Willie among the direct players in that drama, the story does connect with some of his friends and fellow officers, leading to all kinds of questions.[1]

Marshall, Texas, in Harrison County, is just over the Louisiana border, forty miles west of Shreveport; the regular U.S. Army garrisoned both towns in 1867. Second Lieutenant McGee had been assigned to the 20th since May of '67 in Louisiana, primarily working out of Shreveport, while others in the Willie McGee story were nearby.[2] Lieutenant Charles Clark, whose stolen watch precipitated the shooting of Dr. Braman, also worked out of Shreveport and Marshall, eventually marrying a local girl in Marshall itself.[3] Captain William Fletcher, who would retire after thirty plus years, in 1888, was often stationed at Shreveport, Marshall, and Baton Rouge. Lieutenant Tom Latchford, Fletcher's partner on the Baton Rouge barracks porch who tried to calm Willie down just before he shot Braman, was also there, acting as the commander of both Marshall and Shreveport in 1867.[4]

Davis Brainerd Bonfoey was "a Union man by birth and conviction," but had been a resident of Marshall for almost twenty years. The Bonfoeys, whose ancestors had been New England staples for over two centuries, were beloved residents of the town. Emma had established and run the first school for girls in the area, for more than fifteen years, and Davis Bonfoey was universally described as "temperate, intelligent, energetic, and diligent," by neighbors and business acquaintances alike. Davis and Emma were the parents of four boys. The elder two, George and Clarence, were away in New England at school, preparing for Yale and West Point, respectively; the younger two boys, Beverly, age twelve, and Edwin, just a baby, were at home.[5]

At the end of the war in 1865, Davis Bonfoey was appointed, and then reappointed several times, as the Internal Revenue collector for the Fourth District of Texas, with his headquarters at home on West Burleson Street. With the postwar cotton industry incredibly lucrative, Bonfoey's job, and those of his three assistants, centered mainly on the collecting and accounting of the cotton tax. Sometime during the summer of '67 Davis had reason to suspect one of his deputies, W.H. Fowler, of fraud. When Bonfoey traveled the twenty miles to Fowler's home in Jefferson, Texas, he confronted the assistant with his suspicions that more than $18,000 was withheld from the government. Fowler not only refused to cover the payment or admit wrongdoing, but took out his pistol, placed it on his desk, and demanded that Bonfoey sign a receipt that Fowler owed nothing and was free and clear of any crime.[6]

Davis Bonfoey may have been New England born and bred, but he had been in Texas long enough to handle himself when threatened. Refusing to sign the paper, Bonfoey pulled his own "peacemaker" and shot Fowler to death before Fowler could get his shot off. The tax collector immediately turned himself in to the Jefferson sheriff, and awaited a bail hearing. Later testimony showed that Fowler indeed had withheld $29,000, almost three million in today's economy.[7]

When the news reached Emma Bonfoey in Marshall, the caring mother of four became concerned about the large amount of money at her home. There was a safe with the family savings of $13,000, as well as tax collections of over $34,000 belonging to the federal government, and another large sum was known to be in Bonfoey's other safe downtown. Mrs. Bonfoey, fearing for her safety as well as her boys, sought out Lieutenant William Hawley at the small Marshall garrison, and asked him to provide security until her husband's return. Hawley complied after checking with Lieutenant Tom Latchford, his superior at Shreveport. Two soldiers were sent to guard the entrances to the house, and to sleep on the premises, one at each end of the veranda. Both men were undoubtedly aware of the presence of the money.[8]

On the night of August 28, 1867, Emma and her two youngest sons retired for the night, with the soldiers on the porch, one outside Mrs. Bonfoey's bedroom, the other at the front of the house. Future testimony showed there were no outcries or disturbances, but sometime during the night twelve-year-old Beverly was awakened by his mother's groans, and called for help from the two soldiers. Both were gone, and when help arrived for Emma, she was still unconscious, her head having been battered in by an ax or hammer. The safe with the money was untouched, and Emma Bonfoey died the next day. There was little, if any, doubt that the murder was orchestrated by the two soldiers, one of whom was named "Jack." Their footprints were traced by Deputy Sheriff J.D. McGranaghan to a brothel, and some wine and cake Emma Bonfoey had prepared to take to her husband were found there as well; testimony given by some of the professional women said the food was brought by the two men. They were arrested and charged with murder by Sheriff Perry and placed in jail. In addition, a knife given to one of the men the night before was traced to the crime.[9]

In the morning after the fatal attack, Lieutenant Hawley informed his superior in Shreveport, Lt. Latchford, of the murder and the unsafe condition of the money still in the Bonfoey home. Latchford ordered Hawley to take possession until a revenue agent could be sent to take care of the problem. Hawley, with six soldiers armed with bayonets and rifles, took the books, papers, and money back to his own quarters. The next day Emma Bonfoey was laid to rest, and Hawley, armed with a military order from somewhere, had both soldiers released from Perry's custody, and they were placed on a train to Shreveport and points unknown. They were never seen in Marshall again, their identities never revealed.[10]

Charges have never been brought in the murder of Emma Powers Bonfoey, but the story of Marshall was not over. According to a score of witnesses, Davis Bonfoey was granted bail upon news of his wife's death, and arriving back home just after the funeral stopped at the fresh grave of his wife. Bonfoey fell unconscious, was removed to his West Burleson Street home, and died in less than twelve hours, without any previous sickness. When the dust of East Texas had settled, Lieutenant William Hawley and friends were in the possession of almost $140,000. Hawley and his successor at Marshall, Captain Kirby Smith, deposited $68,000 with the government, but never turned in the safe from the Bonfoey house. The large deposit handed over apparently satisfied the government, but nobody missed the almost $83,000 from the safe in Hawley's quarters. All later reports, most more than two decades later, confirmed the above numbers. None of the money controlled by at least three officers — Hawley, Latchford, and Smith — was ever recovered, and nobody was even questioned about the murder of Emma Bonfoey.[11]

There was ample testimony through the years that Hawley "drank deeply and gambled heavily," and also that "he loaned large sums from the Bonfoey safe," and another that "he spent the money in a careless and extravagant manner, loaning money to friends, especially when intoxicated." A decade or more after the fact, a former commissioned officer of the 20th Infantry, Adam Malloy, testified that "the safe was taken directly to Hawley's quarters and was there for several months." Malloy further added that Hawley said the safe contained more than $50,000.[12] Perhaps this would also explain how Lt. Tom Latchford was able to afford his own servant in Baton Rouge the next year — Chelsea Walker — who would be the key eyewitness in the McGee shooting of Chandler Braman.

During the course of time, citizens of Marshall sought redress for themselves, the reputations of the departed Emma and Davis Bonfoey, and the return of the $13,000 to the four Bonfoey boys, who were raised by local residents of Marshall. In 1892, twenty years on and after Senate hearings on the matter, the United States government agreed to return the $13,000, but refused to pay either the interest, which was considerable, nor the $6,000 in Davis Bonfoey's account after his affairs was settled.[13]

Lieutenant Hawley died young at thirty-three, in January 1873, as did his boss at the time, Lieutenant Latchford, who passed away at age forty-eight in Maryland that same year in July.[14] While the Bonfoey case appears to have no direct link to the saga of Willie McGee, there can be little doubt that both the murder and the theft were common knowledge among the officers' corps of the 20th Infantry, if for no other reason than drunken stupidity. McGee, who arrived in Louisiana in May 1867, was stationed with Latchford, Charles Clark, and Fletcher in Shreveport before, during, and after the events described. Three years after the Bonfoeys' deaths, and two years after Chandler Braman's demise, Lieut. Charles Benton Clark resigned from the army under mysterious circumstances at Fort Snelling, Minnesota, just around the bend from Willie McGee's Stillwater Prison.[15] Before his resignation was confirmed, Clark went on the run without permission and was sought in his home area of Syracuse, as well as in Chicago and Tennessee before being found and arrested in, of all places,

Marshall, Texas. Held briefly, Clark was just as mysteriously released, his resignation accepted with no explanation for either the arrest or the release. Charles Clark settled for a few years in town with his wife, and became a deputy sheriff.[16] The 20th United States Infantry during Reconstruction in Louisiana and Texas obviously had more mysteries, alcoholics, displaced officers, and murderers than just 2nd Lieutenant William H. McGee.

2. McGee Timeline

1813 — Birth of James McGee, father of Willie, in Ireland, very likely Ulster Province.

1823 — Birth of Margaret Doyle, later Willie's mother, in Ireland. Birth of Andrew S. Herron, grandson of Irish immigrants, in Tennessee.

1827 — Birth of Holmes Pattison, Willie's adoptive father, in Elk County, Pa.

1841 — Birth of Chandler Balch Braman in Brighton, Massachusetts.

1842 — Birth of Michael McGee, Willie's older brother, in Ireland, to James McGee and Margaret Doyle.

1844 — Probable immigration of James McGee to America with family, settling in New Jersey.

1845 — Arrival in Philadelphia of Margaret and Michael McGee, February 12. Birth of James and Margaret McGee's first child in the United States. Mary Ann is born in Newark, New Jersey, July 13.

1847 — Birth of John McGee to James and Margaret, in Newark, July 8.

1849 — Birth of William J. McGee (New York Willie) in Manhattan to Bernard and Susan McGee. Birth of William Henry McGee to James and Margaret McGee on May 13, in Newark, New Jersey. Willie, like his sister, Mary, and brother John, are baptized by Father Moran at St. John's Roman Catholic Church in Newark, the oldest Catholic Church in Newark, N.J.

1850 — Bernard McGee, forty-five, New York Willie's father, is in jail in New York City for grand larceny, and is out of touch with his family for some years.

1855 — Approximate date of death or disappearance of James McGee, Willie's father, at age forty-two.

1860 — Willie's family has been split for several years. Mary Ann, fifteen, working as a domestic in New Brunswick, New Jersey; Michael, seventeen, working in Jersey City; and John, twelve, and Willie, ten, living with their aunt, Maria (Doyle) McDaniel, and her husband, Tom McDaniel, a blacksmith, in Newark. Mother Margaret McGee, thirty-eight, said to be living and working as a domestic around Beaver Street in Newark.

1863 — Willie leaves job as waiter at thirteen and enlists in the New Jersey 33rd Infantry as a drummer boy, Company C, on August 29. Less than two months later, his uncle, Michael McGee, of New Haven, Ct., would die of typhoid in New Orleans while serving with the 9th Connecticut Infantry, known as "The Irish Regiment." Seven thousand of the 12,000 Union dead buried there would lie in unmarked mass graves, and Mike would be one of them.

1864 — Willie contracts typhoid in January and is sent to Fortress Rosecrans, Murfreesboro, Tennessee, to regain his health. By November, he is healthy and acting as an orderly for General Horatio Van Cleve, the administrative commander of the fort. On December 7, Willie participates — so it is claimed — in the Battle of the Cedars, a small action outside Murfreesboro. Chandler B. Braman graduates from Harvard University as a doctor.

1865 — Willie rejoins the 33rd in April in Virginia and is mustered out on July 17 in Washington with the rest of his regiment when the war ends. He returns briefly to Newark before going to Muskegon, Michigan, to live with Holmes Pattison, his adoptive father.

1866 — Willie, still only sixteen, receives the Medal of Honor in February in Michigan. His brother, John McGee, aged nineteen, marries Elizabeth Bagshaw in New Haven, Connecticut.

1867 — Willie returns to New Jersey in April at the request of Governor Marcus Ward when a book by John Y. Foster portrays McGee as a hero. Ward recommends Willie for an army commission, but Willie fails the test in Louisville, Kentucky. After meeting with President Andrew Johnson, McGee is given a three-month reprieve. He passes the second test after strenuous tutoring in New Jersey and is commissioned and sent to Louisiana.

1868 — Chandler Braman accepts commission as an assistant surgeon on March 13 and is sent to Louisiana. Willie shoots and kills the doctor in Baton Rouge on August 15. He is tried in civil court and acquitted by a jury, then court-martialed and sentenced to five years imprisonment and sent to Stillwater Federal Prison in Minnesota. Charles B. Clark, whose stolen watch and money were the impetus of the whole case, marries Della Rowe, of Marshall, Texas, in October, just a month before the trial.

1869 — Willie arrives at Stillwater, Minnesota, prison in April.

1870 — In July Willie is granted a presidential pardon based on a campaign led by ex-gov. Marcus Ward of New Jersey. He has spent one and a half years in prison. Willie tells Governor Ward his mother had died, but never mentioned where or when. Margaret was forty-seven.

1871 — In December, Willie leaves Minnesota and heads to Pennsylvania, eventually settling in Northumberland Township, Northumberland County.

1873 — Willie marries a local twenty-one-year-old named Regina Faust, a native of Northumberland. John McGee, already a father of three children, including one boy named William after his famous brother, writes a letter to the United States Army looking for Willie, on December 23. The army cannot be of assistance. Michael McGee is raising a family in Jersey City, then Providence, Rhode Island. Mary is lost to history. Lt. Tom Latchford dies in Maryland July 31 of consumption, aged thirty-three. Lt. Hawley dies at age forty-eight on January 15. Septimus Carncross dies November 4, age sixty-one. John White Geary, ex-general and governor of Pennsylvania, dies at age fifty-four.

1874 — Willie and Regina are parents to a young daughter born in Northumberland they name Julia Ward Magee. Willie pawns his Medal of Honor, but Marcus Ward provides money for its return.

1875 — In July, Mary Alene Magee is born in Northumberland, Pa. She will be the only child of four that Willie and Regina have who reaches adulthood.

1876 — New York Willie McGee marries Kate Egan in Manhattan on Christmas Day. Michael McGee, Willie's older brother, now living and working in Providence, Rhode Island, with growing large family. Willie McGee enlists in the cavalry in Illinois in September, after abandoning Regina and their two daughters in Northumberland.

1877 — Willie suffers a minor wound at Battle of Bear Paw Mountain, and is discharged from the cavalry; he heads back East.

1878 — Willie is living and working on a farm in Sidney, Illinois, after being robbed, beaten, and thrown off a train. Willie applies for an invalid pension, claiming he was wounded twice in the December 7, 1864, battle known as the Cedars. Request denied after investigation reveals Willie's claim as a hero was false, and his wounds "imagined."

1880 — Willie marries Jane Van Brunt, the widow Van Brunt's thirty-eight-year-old spinster daughter, in June. In July, Senator John Logan proposes a bill in the U.S. Senate for relief of Willie, asking for his back pay for a year and the return of his commission. Willie more than likely a horse thief. General George Sykes dies at Fort Brown, Texas, February 8.

1881 — Willie takes off on his Illinois wife, Jane. Regina still living in Northumberland with two girls. Jane realizes Willie was after the farm and goes to Nebraska with some family members. Willie ends up in Springfield, Massachusetts, not far from brothers John and Michael.

1882 — Regina gives birth to son William McGee at the Meriden, Ct., home of John McGee, with Willie present. The baby dies after four days. Willie returns to Springfield, and Regina to Northumberland, Pa. Andrew S. Herron, "a household word in every parish in Louisiana," dies at sixty.

1883 — Willie working part time in Springfield, Mass., Armory, where he befriends a local congressman, George Robinson, and another bill is proposed in Washington to reinstate him with back pay for his "innocence" in the Braman murder. It goes nowhere, just like the first one in 1880.

1884 — Regina Magee gives birth to a boy named John A. Magee in Northumberland, Pa. New York Willie, a Tammany gopher, is working as a bartender on the West Side of Manhattan and is arrested for at least the second time for public drunkenness. Marcus Ward dies in Newark, aged seventy-two. Willie still in Springfield, Massachusetts.

1886 — John A. Magee, son of Willie and Regina, dies in Northumberland, Pennsylvania, at age two of consumption. Jane Van Brunt remarries in Nebraska to Swedish-born Nels Nelson. They have no children and Jane never leaves Nebraska. Willie's last known letter is written to an army official in Washington, D.C., from Northumberland.

1887 — New York Willie McGee still an occasional bartender, his wife, Kate, a dressmaker and the family breadwinner in the East Side of Manhattan.

1888 — Regina Magee dies in Northumberland at age thirty-seven of consumption.

1889 — Julia Ward Magee dies of consumption in Northumberland, age fifteen. She is buried with her mother and two brothers. Only Mary Alene Magee survives, living in Northumberland with her aunt and cousins, the Fausts.

1890 — New York Willie and family (four children) still in Manhattan, where he officially tries to steal Willie McGee's identity by signing the 1890 Veterans Census as "William J. McGee, drummer boy."

1891 — Willie marries for the third time to Louise Saunders in Galveston, Texas. They have two sons. Willie spends some years working as a whiskey and cigar salesman. Horatio Van Cleve, who exposed Willie McGee in 1878, dies in Minneapolis at age seventy-two.

1892 — New York Willie McGee dies of diarrhea and exhaustion at age forty-two in August in Manhattan. He is buried in Calvary Cemetery, New York.

1895 — Emma Magee, John's daughter and Willie's niece, marries a Newark, New Jersey, man in Meriden, Connecticut.

1900 — Mary Alene Magee living with aunt Sue Faust in Northumberland at age twenty-five. Willie living on the Bowery in New York City, working as a book salesman.

1902 — Louise divorces an "absent" Willie in Galveston. He abandoned her in 1898. McGee begins his new career as the sole survivor of Custer's Last Stand, a cottage industry of the late nineteenth century.

1903 — Mary Alene Magee marries the Rev. Charles Kulp in Northumberland. They will move to Phillipsburg, Pennsylvania, and have three children.

1904 — Willie murders his friend Frank Mitchell in December in New York City.

1905 — McGee is sentenced in March to seven years and ten months in Sing Sing prison for the murder of Mitchell.

1909 — Willie applies to New York's Governor Hughes for clemency.

1910 — Willie McGee's bid for clemency from Sing Sing is denied.

1914 — Captain William Fletcher dies February 22 in Washington, D.C., age eighty-three. Testified on Willie's behalf at the Braman trial in 1868. Probable perjurer.

1929 — Catherine "Kate" Magee, widow of New York Willie, dies in the Bronx, aged sixty-eight.

1930 — Jane Van Brunt dies in York County, Nebraska, at age eighty-five, the second of Willie's three wives.

1945 — The last Magee of Meriden, Connecticut, John Magee, Jr., dies at age sixty-six.

2006 — Willie has seven great-grandchildren living in Pennsylvania, the only known direct descendants of Willie McGee, drummer boy.

3. The McGee File *(Letters and Memos)*

N.A.	The National Archives, Washington, D.C.
Alexander	Rutgers University Library, New Brunswick, New Jersey
N.J.H.S.	New Jersey Historical Society, Newark, New Jersey
C.M.	McGee Court Martial File, N.A.
MOH	McGee Medal of Honor File, N.A.

1865
December 8 Holmes Pattison to Congressman Rousseau, N.A.
10 Response from Rousseau to the Secretary of War, N.A.

1866
February 5 War Department memo to Rousseau re: Magee MOH, N.A.

7 War Department to Rousseau, N.A.
9 E.D. Townsend, Asst. Adj. General to Willie McGee re: MOH, N.A.
10 Holmes Pattison to E.D. Townsend, N.A.

1867
April 26 Governor John W. Geary

(Pa.) to Edwin Stanton, Sec. of War, Court-martial file, N.A.

May 30 Governor Marcus Ward to Stanton, C.M. file, N.A.

May 16 McGee to Adjutant General, N.A.

18 Gen. George Thomas to Stanton, C.M. file, N.A.

18 McGee to Stanton, N.A.

18 Board of Examiners, Louisville, to Sec. of War Stanton, N.A.

June 20 McGee to President Andrew Johnson, N.A.

20 President Johnson response in memo to Sec. of War, N.A.

September 13 Ward to Thomas, Ward Collection, NJHS. Lovell Rousseau to Sec. of War, N.A.

20 McGee to Sec. of War, N.A.

21 Board of Examiners, Louisville, to Adjutant General, N.A.

October 4 McGee to General U.S. Grant, Acting Sec. of War, N.A.

15 McGee to Adjutant General, N.A.

22 Assistant Adj. General Kelton to Adj. General Townsend, N.A.

December 4 Pattison to Kelton, N.A.

1868

August 21 General George Sykes to Holmes Pattison, NJHS.

31 Sykes to Pattison, NJHS.

September 4 Sykes to Pattison, NJHS.

December 14 Court-martial Proceedings, Baton Rouge, La., N.A.

16 Isaac Braman to General Schofield, Sec. of War, N.A.

1869

January 22 Joseph Holt, Military Bureau of Justice, to Sec. of War, N.A.

April 9 Court-martial official sign-offs on appeal, N.A.

May 4 Chaplain Edward B. Wright to Holmes Pattison, Alexander.

September 14 Chaplain Robert Langley to Pattison, Alexander.

28 Langley to Pattison, Alexander.

October 19 Isaac Braman to Townsend, N.A.

November 1 Adjutant General to Judge Advocate General, N.A.

3 Joseph Holt to Adjutant General, N.A.

29 Ward to McGee, NJHS.

December 16 McGee to Ward, NJHS.

23 Langley to Ward, NJHS.

1870

March 21 Pattison to Ward, NJHS.

June 9 McGee to Ward, NJHS.

9 Dwight Sabin to Ward, Alexander.

16 Ward to William Belknap, Sec. of War, NJHS.

17 Ward to Robeson, Secretary of War, NJHS.

27 Governor Horace Austin (Mn.) to Ward, NJHS.

29 Joseph Holt to Sec. of War, NJHS.

July 3 Ward to Horace Austin, Alexander.

13 Belknap to Ward, NJHS.

14 McGee to Ward, NJHS.

21 Warden Webber to Ward, NJHS.

22 McGee to Ward, NJHS.

23 Dwight Sabin to Ward, Alexander.

27 Ward to McGee, NJHS.

28 Langley to Holmes Pattison, Alexander.

August 1 McGee to Ward, NJHS.

21 McGee to Ward, NJHS.

September 6 McGee to Ward, NJHS.

December 5 Judge Advocate General to McGee, NJHS.

10 Langley to Ward, Alexander, NJHS.

27 Ward to Pattison, NJHS.

1871

March 10 Langley to Ward, NJHS.

15 Sabin to Ward, NJHS.

December 27 Ward to Pattison, NJHS.

1873

December 18 John McGee to United States Army, Washington D.C., N.A.

1874

January 24 McGee to Ward, NJHS.

March	8	McGee to Ward, NJHS.
	31	McGee to Ward, NJHS.
	31	Rev. William Phoenix to Ward, Alexander.
April	8	Regina Magee to Willie McGee, NJHS.
	21	McGee to Ward, NJHS.
May	10	Regina Magee to Marcus Ward, NJHS.
December	21	McGee to Ward, NJHS.

1876
December	13	Willie McGee to J.D. Cameron (Sec. of War), N.A.

1878
March	10	Jane Van Brunt to Marcus Ward, NJHS.
	13	Jane Van Brunt to Ward, NJHS.
April	8	Civil War Pension Application sent to E.L. Campbell, N.A.
May	1	Campbell files pension with Pension Bureau in Washington, D.C.
	13	Van Cleve to E.L. Campbell, N.A.
July	3	Pension Bureau to Campbell re: wounds, N.A.
August	1	Campbell to Pension Bureau re: wounds, N.A.
October	10	McGee to Campbell re: doctors, etc., N.A.
November		Campbell to Pension Bureau, abandoning pension claim, N.A.

1879
December	11	Sec. of War to McGee, N.A., copy to McGee lawyer, Junius Simons, Washington, D.C.

1880
March	3	Adjutant General Townsend to A.E. Burnside, U.S. Senate, N.A.
	4	Adj. General Townsend to Judge Advocate Gen. Dunn, N.A.
	6	Dunn to Townsend, N.A.
	10	Townsend to U.S. Senate, N.A.

1882
October	24	Surgeon General Charles Crane to Marcus Ward, NJHS.

1883
April	14	McGee to Judge Adv. General, N.A.
	21	D.J. Swain to McGee (response), N.A.
	30	Secretary of War to McGee, N.A.
June	24	McGee to Swain, N.A.

1886
August	3	War Department memo regarding McGee, N.A.

1909
December	19	Robert Fuller, Secretary to Governor Charles Evans Hughes, to William Jerome Travers, NYC District Attorney. New York, Municipal Archives, NYC.

1910
June	5	Travers to Hughes regarding the clemency appeal, Municipal Archives, NYC.

4. 33rd New Jersey Infantry Regiment Musicians

Company A
None

Company B
Richard Halloway — enlisted 8/17/63; mustered out 7/17/65; died 1/7/1901, and is buried in Evergreen Cemetery, Hillside, New Jersey.

Terence Riley— enlisted 8/17/63; mustered out 7/17/65. Born in 1847 in New York, his father, Charles, was a hatter. He had no siblings and no mother in 1860. After the war he went gold mining in Virginia City, Nevada, where something catastrophic happened to him, and by 1880 he was living maimed and crippled, unable to read or write, at a National Military Home for Disabled Soldiers in Montgomery City, Ohio. He was dead before 1890.

Company C

James H. Harrison— enlisted 7/24/63; mustered out 7/17/65. Born in New York, 1846, one of seven children; mother, Elizabeth, became a widow. Most of his adult life following the war he lived in Waterbury, Ct., as a carpenter, with his wife and two sons, Irving and Elliot. Died before 1910.

Elsi B. Dawson— enlisted 8/18/63; mustered out 7/17/65. Native New Jerseyan born in 1845 in Bedminster, Somerset County. Following the war, he lived a prosperous and long life in Boonton Township, Morris County, with his wife, Marie, and three children. Elsi was a longtime postmaster and hardware and general store operator on Lincoln Street in Boonton. He died April 5, 1926, and is buried in Greenwood Cemetery, Boonton. Dawson Street, two blocks from the cemetery, is named after the fellow drummer of Willie McGee.

Company D

Alfred Dell— enlisted 8/17/63; mustered out 7/17/65; died 2/15/1905. Born in Succasunna (Roxbury), New Jersey, 1849. His father, Thomas, was a constable in 1860, aged 64. Following the war, Alfred married and opened a saloon in Butte City, Montana, but is buried in Woodlawn Cemetery, Newark, N.J.

William Preston— enlisted 8/20/63; mustered out 7/17/65. Born in England in 1844 and in 1870 was living in Belleville, N.J. Died just three weeks before New York Willie McGee on July 29, 1892, and is buried in Greenwood Cemetery, Brooklyn.

Company E

John Mailey— died as P.O.W. at Andersonville, Georgia, Prison Camp on June 24, 1864 at age 16. A native of Newark, N.J., whose father was an Irish immigrant tinsmith. The name Mailey was probably changed from O'Malley at enlistment.

George Shelton— enlisted 9/15/63; mustered out 7/17/65. Born in 1850 in Pennsylvania. Reported to have moved to Salt Lake City, Utah, with his entire family, where he married and raised his own family.

Thomas Whalen— enlisted 8/24/63; mustered out 7/17/65; died June 12, 1911, age 64. Born in New Jersey in 1847, lived in Newark both before and after the war. Had a mother and three siblings, all living together in 1870. Name was probably corrupted from Whelan. Tom is buried at Arlington Cemetery, Kearny.

Company F

Charles Petit— enlisted 8/3/63; mustered out June 12, Trenton, N.J. Born 1846 in New York. Most of his adult life Charles lived in Newark, first with his parents and siblings, then with his wife, Julia, and his five children. His father was a blacksmith, and Charles worked as a paint mixer, though for a while, he and Julia lived in Rockland County, New York, where he was an actor.

Company G

Robert G. Gardner— enlisted 8/24/63; mustered out 7/17/65. Born in New Jersey, 1846. His father was a widower and there were no other children. Following the war Gardner moved to Ogden, Kansas, where he became a farmer with his wife, Kate, who was born in New York. He died before 1900.

Allen Ramsey — enlisted 8/18/63; mustered out 7/17/65. Son of another blacksmith, Allen was born in 1848, and was raised in Pequannock, N.J. After the war, he stayed in Pequannock and raised a family of five children, working almost his whole life in a rubber mill. In 1910, he was living in Kearny, aged 62, at the Old Soldiers Home, and was not heard from again. Ramsey is buried in the Boonton Cemetery, Boonton, N.J.

Company H

William C. Hall — enlisted 8/28/63; mustered out 7/17/65. Deserted at Bridgeport, Alabama, on October 16, 1863. Never heard of again.

Company I

William R. Adams — enlisted 8/10/63; mustered out 7/17/65. The youngest musician in the regiment, born in 1851 in Pennsylvania. The oldest of three children, he became a dry goods clerk and esteemed city councilman, living in Newark until at least 1910, when he was 69. Died at age 74 in Irvington on January 21, 1924, and is buried in Clinton Cemetery, Irvington, New Jersey.

Mark Fohs — Unknown

John Megill — enlisted 8/15/63; mustered out 7/17/65. Born 1847 in New Jersey, his mother, Margaret, was a widow by 1860 with two other children. Megill, whose real name was McGill, first enlisted as a drummer at age 13 in October 1861, before deserting in Alexandria, Virginia, in September 1862. He then enlisted with the 33rd New Jersey a year later and completed his term. Following the war he joined the U.S. Regular Army and was serving as a private in Mohave City, Arizona, in 1880.

Chapter Notes

Introduction

1. Susan E. Hirsch, *Roots of the American Working Class: The Industrialization in Newark, 1800–1860* (Philadelphia: University of Pennsylvania Press, 1978), 2–3.

2. *Ibid.*, 3–4.

3. Joseph Atkinson, *History of Newark, Being a Narrative of Its Rise and Progress,* (Newark, NJ: William Guild Press, 1878), 23.

4. Patrick O'Sullivan, ed., *The Irish in the New Communities* (New York: St. Martin's Press, 1992).

5. K.H. Connell, *Irish Peasant Society* (Dublin: Irish Academic Press, 1996).

6. Stuart Galishoff, *Newark, the Nation's Unhealthiest City, 1832–35* (New Brunswick, NJ: Rutgers University Press, 1998), 51.

7. Atkinson, *The History of Newark,* 45.

8. *Ibid.*, 48.

9. *Newark Daily Advertiser,* July 3, 1863.

10. *Ibid.*, July 6, 1863.

11. *Ibid.*, July 7, 1863.

12. *Ibid.*, July 11, 1863.

13. James McCague, *The Second Rebellion: The New York City Draft Riots of 1863* (New York: Dial Press, 1968), 63.

14. *Newark Daily Mercury,* July 15, 1863.

15. *Ibid.*, July 16, 1863.

16. *Ibid.*, July 23, 1863.

17. John Zinn, *The Mutinous Regiment: The Thirty-third New Jersey in the Civil War* (Jefferson, NC: McFarland Press, 2005), 11.

18. *Ibid.*, 5.

19. *New Jersey 33rd Infantry,* Enlistment Papers, William Magee, July 23, 1863.

20. Zinn, *The Mutinous Regiment,* 11.

21. *Newark Daily Advertiser,* July 21, 1863.

22. Zinn, *The Mutinous Regiment,* 15–16.

23. *Newark Daily Advertiser,* September 9, 1863.

24. *Ibid.*

25. Zinn, *The Mutinous Regiment,* 228–230.

26. *Newark Daily Advertiser,* July 22, 1865.

27. MOH, George Mindil, Historical Data Systems American Civil War Research Database (HDSACWRD), http://www.civilwardata.com.

28. MOH, John Toffey, HDSACWD, http://www.civilwardata.com.

Chapter One

1. Regular Army Commissioned Officers Service Records, William McGee, 20th United States Infantry, 1867–1870, National Archives Record Administration, Washington, D.C.

2. E.D. Townsend, Assistant Adjutant General, to William Magee, February 9, 1866. Medal of Honor file, NARA.

3. John Y. Foster, *New Jersey in the Rebellion* (Newark, NJ: Dennis & Company, 1867), 856–859.

4. St. John's Catholic Church Birth and Baptismal Records, Newark, New Jersey, 1845–1885, FHL number 1398540. Church records show McGee was born on May 13, 1849, and baptized May 27 by Father Moran, with his father's name as James and his mother's as Margaret (Doyle) McGee. His godparents were James Holland and his aunt Maria Doyle, with whom he would later live before enlisting.

5. *General Court Martial, United States Army, Order No. 40, 1868,* Baton Rouge, Louisiana. Sgt. Jones and Private George Mayhew both testified that it was general knowledge of the troops at Baton Rouge. Theft of money by officers in the 20th Infantry was not unusual. See Appendix 1, *The Bonfoey Case,* NARA.

6. Charles Benton Clark, 122nd New York Infantry. *Historical Data Systems' American Civil War Database,* http://www.civilwardata.com.

7. C.B. Clark, 122nd Regiment History, Historical Data Systems American Civil War Research Database (HDSACWRD).

8. Clark Family Genealogy, Onondaga County Library, Syracuse, New York.

9. *State vs. McGee,* Fifth District Court, East Baton Rouge Parish, Louisiana, November 27, 1868, General George Sykes testimony, p. 5.

10. *State vs. McGee,* Sykes testimony, p. 5.

11. General Court Martial, Order No. 40, pp. 18–19. McHenry was referred to in testimony several times as an "unreliable resident." In addition, McHenry's claim to have been an agent for General Sherman never specified which General Sherman. There were three in the Union Army; Francis T. Sherman of Illinois, Thomas W. Sherman of Rhode Island, and the most famous — and likely — General William Tecumseh Sherman (NARA).

12. Chandler Balch Braman, 12th Massachusetts Infantry, HDSACWRD; Joseph Balch Braman, 3rd Massachusetts Cavalry, HDSACWRD.

13. *Secretary's Report No. 6,* Harvard College Class of 1864 Yearbook (Boston: Harvard Press, 1889), 30–31.

14. Galusha Balch, *Balch Genealogy* (Salem, MA: 1897), 309.

15. *Ibid.,* 310.

16. *State vs. McGee,* Mayor Elam testimony, pp. 7–8.

17. *General Court Martial,* Jones and Mayhew testimony, pp. 14–15, NARA.

18. *General Court Martial,* Mayhew testimony, p. 15, NARA.

19. *General Court Martial,* Sykes testimony, p. 24, NARA.

20. *State vs. McGee,* Exhibit B, as introduced by Andrew Herron.

21. *General Court Martial,* Sykes testimony, p. 2, NARA.

22. *State vs. McGee,* Elam testimony, p. 9.

23. *Ibid.*

24. *State vs. McGee,* Sykes testimony, p. 6.

25. Ibid, 7.

26. *Ibid.*

27. Larry Tagg. *The Generals of Gettysburg* (New York: DaCapo Press, 2003), 81–82.

28. George Sykes, HDSACWRD; Tagg, *The Generals of Gettysburg,* 81–83.

29. *State vs. McGee,* Sykes, pp. 5–6.

30. *Ibid.,* 6.

31. *Ibid.*

32. *Ibid.*

33. *General Court Martial,* Sykes testimony, p. 25, NARA.

34. *General Court Martial,* Lieutenant Septimus Carncross testimony, p. 29, NARA.

35. *Boston Daily Evening Transcript,* August 18, 1868, p. 4.

36. *Ibid.,* August 24, 1868, p. 3. Lieutenant John Coe, who wrote several times to the Bramans, thought McGee may have been "seventeen or eighteen." Coe would go on to have a distinguished career with the regular army, serving with distinction for over thirty years, and would write a short history of the 20th Infantry, but he didn't include the Bonfoey or Braman affairs.

37. Willie may have weighed much less than 150 pounds; he was only 146 when he was 55 years old: July 23, 1863, enlistment paper; Stillwater Prison inmate register, 1869; and Sing Sing inmate register, 1905.

38. *General Court Martial.* Of the five charges lodged against McGee, two involved specific misuse of alcohol, and subsequent letters throughout his life substantiate these charges (NARA).

39. *General Court Martial,* Lieutenant Morris testimony, p. 42.

40. *Ibid.,* 42–43.

41. *State vs. McGee,* Sykes, p. 6.

42. *General Court Martial,* Sykes testimony, pp. 24–25.

43. *State vs. McGee,* Sykes, p. 6.

44. George Sykes, HDSACWRD.

45. *State vs. McGee,* Sykes, p. 6.

46. *General Court Martial,* Morris testimony, p. 43.

47. *Ibid.,* 44–45.

48. *General Court Martial,* Sgt. Jones testimony, pp. 12–14.

49. Medal of Honor file, William Magee, NARA; United States Army Commission, May 16, 1867, William McGee, NARA.

50. *State vs. McGee,* Private George Mayhew testimony, p. 2.

51. Ibid, 2.

52. *State vs. McGee,* Carncross, p. 8.

53. *Ibid.,* 8–9.

54. *State vs. McGee,* Chelsea Walker testimony, pp. 3–4.

55. *Ibid.,* 4.

56. *General Court Martial,* Chelsea Walker testimony; also the testimony of Doctor Louis Favrot, who performed the autopsy.

57. *State vs. McGee*, Carncross, p. 9.
58. *State vs. McGee*, Walker, p. 5.
59. *State vs. McGee*, Carncross, p. 9.
60. *Ibid.*
61. *State vs. McGee*, Carncross, pp. 9–10.
62. *Boston Daily Evening Transcript*, August 24, 1868, p. 3.

Chapter Two

1. John G. Zinn, *The Mutinous Regiment: The Thirty-third New Jersey in the Civil War* (Jefferson, NC: McFarland Press, 2005), 228–231.
2. *Ibid.*, 5–8.
3. *Ibid.*, 7.
4. *Ibid.*, 9.
5. William J. Jackson, *New Jerseyans in the Civil War: For Union and Liberty* (New Brunswick, New Jersey: Rutgers University Press, 2000), 44–45.
6. Zinn, *The Mutinous Regiment*, 11. Though the majority of the regiment was from Essex County, Sussex, Morris, and Passaic each had companies of their own.
7. Susan E. Hirsch, *Roots of the American Working Class: The Industrialization in Newark, 1800–1860* (Philadelphia: University of Penn Press, 1978), 27.
8. *Newark Daily Mercury*, August 20, 1863.
9. Zinn, *The Mutinous Regiment*, 11.
10. *Ibid.*, 15.
11. *Ibid.*
12. *Ibid.*, 16.
13. Zinn, *The Mutinous Regiment*, 18; *Newark Daily Mercury*, September 9, 1863.
14. Interview with Colonel Bob Jones, *33rd New Jersey Infantry*, reenactor, October 2005.
15. Zinn, *The Mutinous Regiment*, 27.
16. *Ibid.*, 36.
17. *Ibid.*, 26.
18. *Ibid.*, 57.
19. *Ibid.*, 231.
20. *Ibid.*, 49.
21. *Ibid.*, 66
22. Holmes Pattison in Michigan to Marcus Ward, Newark, March 23, 1870 (New Jersey Historical Society).
23. *33rd New Jersey Infantry*, Civil War Military Service Record, William Magee, 1863–1865, NARA.
24. Zinn, *The Mutinous Regiment*, 134.
25. Governor John W. Geary, governor of Pennsylvania, to Edwin Stanton, secretary of war, April 26, 1867, NARA.
26. Zinn, *The Mutinous Regiment*, 220–222.
27. *Ibid.*, 225.
28. *Ibid.*, 226–227.

29. Pattison to John Kelton, assistant adjutant general, December 4, 1867, NARA.
30. *Newark Daily Advertiser*, May 13, 1865.
31. Wiley Sword, *Embrace an Angry Wind: The Confederacy's Last Hurrah — Spring Hill, Franklin, and Nashville* (New York: Harper Collins, 1992), 263–269.
32. War Department to William Magee, Michigan, February 9, 1866, and May 13, 1867, United States Commission to William McGee (NARA).
33. *8th Census of the United States*, Colon, Michigan, Holmes A. Pattison, roll M653, p. 1, image 98.
34. Holmes Pattison, 11th Michigan Infantry, HDSACWRD, http://www.civilwardata.com.
35. 11th Michigan Infantry Regiment History, HDSACWRD.
36. Pattison in Michigan to Congressman Lovell Rousseau of Kentucky, December 8, 1865.
37. 33rd New Jersey Infantry muster rolls, William Magee, January, 1864; 33rd New Jersey Regiment history, HDSACWRD.
38. Dennis M. Keesee, *Too Young to Die: Boy Soldiers of the Union Army, 1861–65* (Huntington, WV: Blue Acorn Press, 2001), 7–20.
39. Holmes Pattison to Marcus Ward, March 21, 1870, New Jersey Historical Society.
40. Zinn, *The Mutinous Regiment*, 217.
41. E-mail interview with Jim Lewis, National Park Ranger, Murfreesboro, Tennessee, in the summer of 2005, regarding Union hospitals at Fortress Rosecrans during the war. Jim Lewis has given symposiums and written articles on the war in the Murfreesboro area of Tennessee for more than a decade.
42. Keesee, *Too Young to Die*, 130–131; Zinn, *The Mutinous Regiment*, 126–127.
43. Horatio Van Cleve, in Michigan, to E.L. Campbell, New Jersey, May, 1878; Pattison to Rousseau, December 8, 1865, NARA.
44. Pattison to Marcus Ward, New Jersey, March 21, 1870, NJHS.
45. 11th Michigan Infantry, Holmes Pattison, chaplain, HDSACWRD.
46. McGee letters to Marcus Ward, June and July 1870; Pattison to Ward, March 1870, Sykes to Pattison, August 1868, NJHS.
47. *10th United States Federal Census*, Holmes A. Pattison, Jacksonville, Duval County, p. 539, e.d. 34, image 0670.
48. Pattison to Rousseau, December 8, 1865, NARA
49. Rousseau to Secretary of War, Edwin Stanton, December 15, 1865, NARA
50. E.D. Townsend, assistant adjutant general, to Rousseau, February 7, 1866, NARA.

51. Pattison to Townsend, February 26, 1866, NARA.

52. William Magee Medal of Honor file, under the name "Megee," NARA.

53. Pattison to Rousseau, December 8, 1865, NARA.

54. 11th Michigan Infantry, Holmes Pattison, chaplain, HDSACWRD.

55. Zinn, *The Mutinous Regiment*, 178.

56. Sword, *Embrace an Angry Wind*, 448–451.

57. *Ibid.*, 263–269.

58. Pattison to Rousseau, December 8, 1865.

59. Keesee, *Too Young to Die*, 201.

Chapter Three

1. *Baton Rouge Tri-Weekly*, August 17, 1868.

2. *Ibid.*

3. Lieutenant John Coe, U.S. 20th Infantry, to Dr. Isaac Braman, Boston, August 16, 1868. Coe would remain a career officer and later write a brief history of the 20th Infantry, but he would not mention the Braman shooting.

4. General George Sykes, Baton Rouge, to Isaac Braman, August 1868, NARA.

5. Isaac Braman to General Schofield, War Department, Washington, D.C., December 16, 1868, NARA.

6. State of Louisiana, Parish of East Baton Rouge, Bail Hearing, September 26, 1868; Sykes to Pattison, September 4, 1868; Andrew Herron defense summary in *General Court Martial*, December 1868, Baton Rouge.

7. *State of Louisiana vs. William McGee*, Indictment Number 1028, 5th District Court, East Baton Rouge Parish, Louisiana, August 28, 1868.

8. Sykes to Braman, August 1868, NARA.

9. Sykes to Holmes Pattison, Michigan, August 21, 1868, NJHS.

10. *State vs. McGee*, William McGee written statement to Sheriff Buckner, August 27, 1868, pp. 4–5.

11. *State vs. McGee*, Indictment 1028.

12. *Boston Daily Evening Transcript*, August 24, 1868.

13. Sykes to Pattison, August 29, 1868.

14. *Ibid.*

15. *Ibid.*, September 4, 1868.

16. Jude Brand, "His Image Over a Column of Undying Marble," *Bienville Rifles* (March/April 1999): 5–6.

17. *Baton Rouge Daily Capitolian*, December 1, 1882.

18. *Ibid.*, December 5, 1882.

19. Brand, "His Image," 6.

20. *Ibid.*, 5–6.

21. Terry L. Jones, *Lee's Tigers: The Louisiana Infantry in the Army of Northern Virginia* (Baton Rouge, LA: LSU Press, 1987), 231.

22. *Ibid.*, 229–230.

23. *Ibid.*, 231.

24. *Baton Rouge Daily Capitolian*, December 1, 1882.

25. Brand, "His Image," 6.

26. *Fifth District Court Bail Hearing*, East Baton Rouge Parish, September 26, 1868, Andrew S. Herron for the defendant, William McGee.

27. Bail Hearing, September 26, 1868.

28. Written Declaration of William H. McGee to Sheriff George Buckner, August 27, 1868, Baton Rouge jail.

Chapter Four

1. Holmes Pattison to Lovell Rousseau, December 8, 1865; Joseph Atkinson, *The History of Newark, New Jersey* (Newark, NJ: William B. Guild Press, 1878), 284; and Pattison to John Kelton, assistant adjutant general, December 4, 1867, NARA.

2. Secretary of War Edwin Stanton to Pattison and Magee, February 12, 1866, NARA.

3. *Newark Daily Advertiser*, May 10, 1865.

4. *Ibid.*, May 13, 1865.

5. John Y. Foster, *New Jersey in the Rebellion* (New Jersey: 1867), 856–859.

6. *Ibid.*, 857.

7. *Ibid.*

8. *Ibid.*, 856–859.

9. Atkinson, *History of Newark*, 278–284.

10. *Ibid.*, 283–284.

11. *Ibid.*, 283–284.

12. *Ibid.*, 284.

Chapter Five

1. *Baton Rouge Tri-Weekly Advocate*, April 27, 1868; J.G. Randall and David Donald, *The Civil War and Reconstruction* (Boston: D.C. Heath, 1961), 691–692.

2. *Baton Rouge Tri-Weekly Advocate*, July 20, 1868.

3. Randall, *The Civil War and Reconstruction*, 691–693.

4. David Cohen, *The Atlantic Monthly* 165, no. 4 (April 1940, New Orleans): 67.

5. *Baton Rouge Tri-Weekly Advocate*, July 20, 1868.

6. *Ibid.*, August 19, 1868.

7. *Ibid.*, June 5, 1868.

8. *Baton Rouge Tri-Weekly Advocate*, May 27,

1868; *Eighth Federal U.S. Census,* Burnet Texas, 1860, R.T. Posey, p. 157, image 319.

9. *United States General Court Martial,* Special Order No. 40, December 1868, Baton Rouge, Louisiana; Captain Lewis Morris testimony, p. 4; Preliminary Statement of Lieutenant William H. McGee to Sheriff George Buckner, August 27, 1868 (NARA).

10. *State vs. McGee,* Lieutenant Thomas Latchford testimony, p. 1. Latchford would also be involved in the Bonfoey affair (Appendix 1).

11. *State vs. McGee,* Latchford testimony, p. 1.

12. *State vs. McGee,* Private George Mayhew testimony, pp. 2–3.

13. *Ibid.*

14. Alcece Fortier, *Comprising Sketches of Parishes, Towns, Events, Institutions, and Persons,* vol. 3 (New Orleans, LA: Century Historical Association, 1914), 374–75.

15. *General Court Martial,* Dr. Favrot testimony, pp. 37–39, NARA.

16. *Ibid.,* 39.

17. *Baton Rouge Tri-Weekly Advocate,* August 19, 1868.

18. *State vs. McGee,* Chelsea Walker testimony, pp. 3–4.

19. *Ibid.*

20. *Ibid.,* 4.

21. Preliminary Statement, William H. McGee to Sheriff Buckner, August 27, 1868, now referred to as Exhibit A.

22. Penciled note of Dr. Chandler Braman to McHenry, now labeled as Exhibit B.

23. General George Sykes to Holmes Pattison, September 4, 1868, NJHS.

24. *State vs. McGee,* Sykes testimony, p. 5.

25. *Ibid.,* 6.

26. *Ibid.*

27. *State vs. McGee,* Baton Rouge Mayor Elam testimony, pp. 7–8.

28. *State vs. McGee,* Sykes and Elam testimony, pp. 7–8.

29. Septimus Carncross, HDSACWRD, http://www.civilwardata.com.

30. *State vs. McGee,* Lieutenant Septimus Carncross testimony, pp. 8–9.

31. *State vs. McGee,* Carncross testimony, pp. 8–9.

32. *General Court Martial,* Carncross testimony, which was not mentioned in the civil trial, NARA.

33. *State vs. McGee,* Captain William Fletcher testimony, pp. 10–11. Fletcher would remain a captain until his retirement, in 1887, after forty years of service. Many of his future posts ran, quite interestingly, near those of McGee's. When Willie was sent to Minnesota, Fletcher was at nearby Fort Snelling. Later Fletcher would fight Indians in the Northwest and then in Texas. There is no record they ever reunited their friendship after the trial, but the times and places give pause.

34. *State vs. McGee,* Fletcher testimony, p. 10.

35. *Ibid.*

36. *Ibid.,* 11.

37. *State vs. McGee,* Sykes testimony, pp. 6–7.

38. *State vs. McGee,* Mayhew testimony, p. 3.

39. Sykes to Pattison, August 29, 1868, NJHS.

40. *State vs. McGee,* Jardot testimony, p. 10.

41. *State vs. McGee,* Lefebreve testimony, p. 10.

42. *State vs. McGee,* Dr. Thomas Buffington of Baton Rouge testimony, p. 11.

43. *General Court Martial* Defense Summation, Andrew S. Herron, December 1868, pp. 1–20, NARA.

44. *General Court Martial,* Defense Summation, Andrew Herron, p. 4.

45. *Ibid.,* 5.

46. *Ibid.,* 6–7.

47. *Ibid.*

48. *Ibid.,* 7.

49. *Ibid.,* 10.

50. *Ibid.,* 11.

51. *Ibid.,* 13–14.

52. *Ibid.,* 15.

53. *Baton Rouge Tri-Weekly,* December 4, 1868.

54. *State vs. McGee,* Judge R.T. Posey, charge to the jury, November 25, 1868, pp. 15–18.

55. *Ibid.,* 16–17.

56. *Ibid.,* p. 17.

57. *Baton Rouge Tri-Weekly,* November 27, 1868.

58. *Boston Daily Evening Transcript,* December 5, 1868.

59. Lieutenant John Coe, 20th U.S. Infantry, Baton Rouge, to Dr. Isaac Braman, Watertown, Massachusetts, December 1868.

60. *General Court Martial Defense Summation,* Andrew Herron; Andrew Herron to Judge Posey during McGee bail application; Sykes to Pattison, August 29, 1868 (NARA).

Chapter Six

1. *33rd New Jersey Infantry,* Muster Rolls, William Magee, drummer, Company C, 1863–65, NARA

2. Zinn, *The Mutinous Regiment,* 174.

3. James McPherson, *For Cause and Comrades: Why Men Fought in the Civil War* (New York: Oxford University Press, 1997), 30–32.

4. *Ibid.*, 31.

5. Mauriel Phillips Joslyn, ed., *A Meteor Shining Brightly: Essays on Major General Patrick R. Cleburne,* (Milledgeville, GA: Terrell House Press, 1999), 265–268.

6. Joslyn, *A Meteor Shining Brightly,* 291.

7. Sword, *Embrace an Angry Wind,* 2–5.

8. Joslyn, *A Meteor Shining Brightly,* 265–282; Sword, *Embrace an Angry Wind,* 261–271.

9. Sword, *Embrace an Angry Wind,* 269–70.

10. *Ibid.*, 268.

11. Zinn, *The Mutinous Regiment,* 174.

12. Sword, *Embrace an Angry Wind,* 293.

13. Lenard E. Brown, "Fortress Rosecrans: A Fortification built in Murfreesboro by the Union Army after the Battle of Stones River; A History, 1865–1990," *Tennessee Historical Quarterly* 50, no. 3 (1991): 135–141.

14. Carroll Van West, "Fortress Rosecrans," *Tennessee Encyclopedia of History and Culture,* Nashville, TN: Tennessee Historical Society: Rutledge Hill Press, 1998.

15. McGee to E.L. Campbell, May 1878; Sword, *Embrace an Angry Wind,* 293.

16. James Grant, John Fiske, and Stanley Klos, eds., *Appleton's Cyclopedia of American Biography,* 6 vols. (New York: Appleton & Company, 1887–89).

17. Sword, *Embrace an Angry Wind,* 293.

18. Van Cleve to E.L. Campbell, May 15, 1878, NARA.

19. James Lee McDonough, *Five Tragic Hours: The Battle of Franklin* (Knoxville: University of Tennessee Press, 1983), 30.

20. Sword, *Embrace an Angry Wind,* 293.

21. *Ibid.*

22. Herbert S. Norris and James R. Long, "The Long Road to Redemption," *Civil War Times* (August 1997): 35.

23. Edson Dean Washburn, *Memoirs of Edson Dean Washburn* (Monticello, MN: 1907), 7.

24. Norris, *The Road to Redemption,* 32; Sword, *Embrace an Angry Wind,* 263. Some estimates of shoeless Confederates at Nashville range up to 33 per cent.

25. Norris, *The Road to Redemption,* 33; Sword, *Embrace an Angry Wind,* 295.

26. Norris, *The Road to Redemption,* 33.

27. Sword, *Embrace an Angry Wind,* 296.

28. Foster, *New Jersey in the Rebellion,* 858.

29. Sword, *Embrace an Angry Wind,* 296.

30. Ed Bearss, *The History of Fortress Rosecrans* (Internal National Park Service Publication, 1960) (ch. 6, p. 6).

31. Foster, *New Jersey in the Rebellion,* 858.

32. Bearss, *History of Fortress Rosecrans* (ch. 6, p. 6).

33. Norris, *The Road to Redemption,* 32–33.

34. *Ibid.*, 32.

35. *Ibid.*, 35.

36. Sword, *Embrace an Angry Wind,* 296–297.

37. Norris, *The Road to Redemption,* 35.

38. Don Hillhouse, "The Colors Lost Twice," *Confederate Veteran* (September/October 1988): 19.

39. Bearss, *History of Fortress Rosecrans* (ch. 6, p. 14).

40. Sword, *Embrace an Angry Wind,* 297.

41. Norris, *The Road to Redemption,* 36.

42. Foster, *New Jersey in the Rebellion,* 858.

43. 8th Minnesota Infantry Regimental History, HDSACWRD; Washburn, *Memoirs,* 5–10.

44. Sword, *Embrace an Angry Wind,* 296.

45. Van Cleve to Campbell, May 15, 1878, NARA.

46. Bearss, *History of Fortress Rosecrans* (ch. 6, p. 19).

47. *Ibid.* The Florida brigade in Bate's division is listed as "Finley's Brigade," but Major G.A. Ball was listed as the commander, suggesting that Finley was elsewhere for whatever reason. In the Bearss narrative quoted above, the commander of the battle was listed as "Major Lash." In *Battles and Leaders,* Major Jacob A. Lash is listed as commander of the 4th Florida infantry, so perhaps Ball was also elsewhere on December 8.

48. Sword, *Embrace an Angry Wind,* 297.

49. *Ibid.*, 298.

50. Foster, *New Jersey in the Rebellion,* 858.

51. Bearss, *History of Fortress Rosecrans* (ch. 6, p. 19).

52. Sword, *Embrace an Angry Wind,* 298; Hillhouse, "Colors Lost Twice," 17; Norris, *The Road to Redemption,* 37.

53. Bearss, *History of Fortress Rosecrans* (ch. 6, p. 23).

54. Atkinson, *The History of Newark,* 283–284.

55. United States Government, *The War of the Rebellion: A Compilation of the Official Records of the Union and Confederate Armies,* 128 Volumes, Washington, D.C. (hereafter cited as *OR*, ser. I, vol. II, pt. 1; or *OR*, vol. XLV, pt. I), 618, report of Major General Robert Milroy.

56. Benjamin C.G. Reed, 174th Ohio Infantry, HDSACWRD; John J. Jones, *History of the 174th O.V.I.* Address delivered August 30, 1894, Marysville, Ohio.

57. Norris, *The Road to Redemption,* 56.

58. Zinn, *The Mutinous Regiment,* 178.

59. Hillhouse, "The Colors Twice Lost," 19–20.

60. Congressman Lovell Rousseau to Edwin Stanton, secretary of war, December, 1865, William Magee, MOH file, NARA.

61. Bearss, *The History of Fortress Rosecrans* (ch. 6, pp. 24–25).

62. Rousseau to Stanton, December 1865, NARA

63. *OR,* vol. XLV, part 1, p. 614.

64. Foster, *New Jersey in the Rebellion,* 858.

65. *OR,* vol. XLV, part 1, p. 613.

66. Jasper County, Indiana Public Library, home of the papers of General Robert Milroy. Reference librarian Jean Palmer, in separate e-mail and phone interviews, told the author there is no mention of a William Magee, McGee, Magie, or McGhee in any of the general's papers.

67. Bearss, *History of Fortress Rosecrans* (ch. 6, p. 19).

68. *OR,* vol. XLV, part 1, p. 623.

69. Kosciusko "Kos" Ellliot in Murfreesboro, to his sister Mary, December 14, 1864.

70. *OR,* vol. XLV, part 1, p. 627.

71. Washburn, *Memoirs,* 7.

72. *Ibid.,* 8.

73. *Ibid.*

74. *Ibid.*

75. *Regimental History,* 12th Indiana Infantry, HDSACWRD.

76. *OR,* vol. XLV, part 1, p. 627.

77. *Ibid.,* 612–628.

78. Norris, *The Road to Redemption,* 57.

79. John Bowers, "The Rock of Chickamauga," in *With My Face to the Enemy: Perspectives on the Civil War,* edited by Robert Cowley (New York: Berkley Books, 2001), 320–331.

80. John White Geary, HDSACWRD; Letters of George Thomas, John White Geary, and Lovell Rousseau, 1865–1867, recommending William Magee for an appointment to the officers corps of the regular army, and then again for a second chance at examination, NARA.

81. Between 1866 and 1883 there are more than 100 letters found either in the National Archives or the Marcus Ward collection at the New Jersey Historical Society or the Alexander Library at Rutgers University, to, from, or about William McGee. At no time is General Robert Milroy or one of the "other mere boys" mentioned. In that seventeen-year span, Horatio Van Cleve was mentioned only once, and McGee's single mistake was obvious and damning.

82. Rousseau to the secretary of war, December 1865, NARA.

Chapter Seven

1. *General Court Martial,* Special Order No. 40, Baton Rouge, Louisiana, December 14, 1868, NARA.

2. General George Sykes to Holmes Pattison, August 27, 1868, New Jersey Historical Society (NJHS).

3. Andrew S. Herron to Judge R.T. Posey, September 26, 1868.

4. Sykes to Pattison, September 4, 1868, NJHS.

5. *General Court Martial,* Andrew Herron Summation, December 1868, pp. 2–3, NARA.

6. Pattison to Congressman Lovell Rousseau, February 7, 1865, NARA.

7. *General Court Martial,* p. 10, NARA.

8. *Ibid.,* 3–10.

9. *Ibid.*

10. Will McGee to Marcus Ward, December 16, 1869, NJHS.

11. *General Court Martial,* Sgt. Jones testimony, p. 12, NARA.

12. *Ibid.,* 14–17.

13. *General Court Martial,* Judge Carncross question to General George Sykes, p. 17, NARA

14. *General Court Martial,* Sykes testimony, pp. 17–20, NARA.

15. *Ibid.,* 20–22.

16. *Ibid.,* 26.

17. *Ibid.,* 27–28.

18. *General Court Martial,* Chelsea Walker testimony, pp. 27–28, NARA.

19. *Ibid.,* 30–34.

20. *Ibid.,* 35.

21. *General Court Martial,* Defendant William McGee to Judge Septimus Carncross, p. 36, NARA.

22. *General Court Martial,* Dr. Reynaud testimony, p. 39, NARA.

23. *General Court Martial,* Lieutenant Louis Morris testimony, pp. 41–48, NARA.

24. *General Court Martial,* Lieutenant Thomas Latchford testimony, pp. 50–52, NARA.

25. *General Court Martial,* Private George Mayhew testimony, pp. 52–53, NARA.

26. *General Court Martial,* Dr. Thomas Buffington testimony, pp. 52–58, NARA.

27. *Ibid.*

28. *General Court Martial,* transcript, pp. 58–63, NARA.

29. *Ibid.,* 65.

30. *General Court Martial,* Septimus Carncross testimony, p. 66, NARA.

31. *General Court Martial,* Exhibits A, B, C, D, E, F (NARA).

32. *General Court Martial,* Andrew S. Herron Summary, pp. 1–20, NARA.

33. *General Court Martial,* transcript, p. 91, NARA.

34. *Ibid.*

35. *General Court Martial,* Headquarters of the Army, April 27, 1869, Washington, D.C., NARA.

36. William McGee to the secretary of war, April 14, 1883, NARA.

Chapter Eight

1. Edwin Stanton, secretary of war, to William Magee; Lovell Rousseau to Holmes Pattison, February 9, 1866, NARA.

2. McGee originally accepted his appointment as a second lieutenant three days after his eighteenth birthday, May 16, 1867, and obviously must have received the appointment earlier, possibly when he was still seventeen. He was formally appointed on September 21, 1867, when he was eighteen years and four months old, still incredibly young for a regular army commission in peacetime.

3. *Newark Daily Advertiser*, April 21, 1867.

4. Marcus Ward, General George Thomas, and John W. Geary each sent a letter to Edwin Stanton, the secretary of war, in April 1867 on behalf of the young McGee, NARA.

5. Geary to Stanton, April 26, 1867, NARA.

6. John White Geary History Marker Website, http://www.mtpleasantpa.com/geary.html.

7. *Ibid.*

8. *Ibid.*

9. *Ibid.*

10. Ward to Stanton, April 30, 1867, NARA.

11. Maxine N. Lurie and Marc Mappen, *Encyclopedia of New Jersey* (New Brunswick, New Jersey: Rutgers University Press, 2004), 846–847.

12. William Magee to Adjutant General, Washington, D.C., May 16, 1867, NARA.

13. McGee to Military Board of Examiners, Louisville, Kentucky, May 16, 1867, NARA.

14. McGee before the Board of Examiners, May 16, 1867, NARA.

15. Board of Military Examiners to the Adjutant General, Washington, D.C., May 18, 1867, NARA.

16. McGee to Edwin Stanton, secretary of war, May 18, 1867, NARA.

17. McGee to the Board of Examiners, Fall 1867, regarding the spelling of his name and date of birth, at Louisville, Kentucky, NARA.

18. McGee to President Andrew Johnson, Washington, D.C., June 20, 1867, NARA.

19. President Andrew Johnson memo to the secretary of war, June 20, 1867, NARA.

20. Marcus Ward to Military Board of Examiners, Louisville, Kentucky, September 13, 1867, NARA.

21. Ward to Examiners, September 13, 1867, NARA,

22. McGee to Brevet Brigadier General Cady, president, Board of Examiners, September 20, 1867, NARA.

23. Pattison to Assistant Adjutant General John Kelton, December 4, 1867, from Muskegon, Michigan, NARA.

24. McGee to General U.S. Grant, secretary of war, October 4, 1867, NARA.

25. McGee to adjutant general, October 15, 1867.

26. Muster Rolls, *33rd New Jersey Infantry*, drummer William Magee, July 1863 to July 1865, NARA.

27. Memorandum from the War Department, Washington, D.C., by John Kelton, assistant adjutant general, to the adjutant general, October 21, 1867, regarding the newly appointed "William McGee," NARA.

28. McGee testimony before the Board of Examiners, November 1867, Louisville, Kentucky, NARA.

29. Military Board of Examiners to the adjutant general, Fall 1867, NARA.

Chapter Nine

1. E.D. Townsend, assistant adjutant general, to the secretary of war, April 9, 1869, NARA.

2. Townsend to Magee, February 9, 1865, NARA.

3. *General Court Martial,* Order No. 40, Baton Rouge, Louisiana, NARA.

4. *General Court Martial,* Andrew S. Herron summary statement at Baton Rouge, December 1868, NARA.

5. Ezra Warner, *Generals in Blue: Lives of the Union Commanders* (Baton Rouge: Louisana State University Press, 1964), 232–233.

6. Joseph Holt, judge advocate general, to the secretary of war, January 22, 1869, pp. 1–20, NARA.

7. Judge Advocate General Report, January 22, 1869, p. 4, NARA.

8. Geoffrey Perret, *Ulysses S. Grant: Soldier & President* (New York: Random House, 1997), 101–102.

9. *Ibid.*, 41–42.

10. Warner, *Generals in Blue,* 48–49.

11. Judge Advocate General Report, Buchanan letter to the Bureau of Military Justice, January 22, 1869, p. 4, NARA

12. Ward to Belknap, June 16, 1870, NARA.

13. Judge Advocate General Report, pp. 4–5, NARA.

14. *Ibid.*, 17–18.

15. *Ibid.*

16. Stillwater Prison Register, 1869, Minnesota Historical Society.

17. Stillwater Prison Register, 1869. Though there are other possibilities, the most likely reason for the transfer was the movement of the 20th Infantry from Louisiana and Texas to the Northwest, in particular Fort Snelling, Minnesota.

18. Ted Genoways, *Hard Time: Voices from a State Prison, 1849–1914* (St. Paul, MN: Minnesota Historical Society, 2002), 9–13.

19. Genoways, *Hard Time*, 27.

20. *Ibid.*, 57.

21. W.C. Heilbron, *Convict Life at the Minnesota State Prison* (Stillwater, MN: Valley History Press, 1996), 112–115.

22. *Ibid.*, 50–51.

23. *Ibid.*, 117–118.

24. *9th U.S. Federal Census, 1870*, Stillwater, Minnesota, Edward Wright, p. 98, image 478, July 1870.

25. Chaplin Wright to Holmes Pattison, May 4, 1869, Alexander Library, Rutgers University.

26. *13th U.S. Federal Census*, Austin, Texas, Edward Wright, Ward 3, p. 3B, E.D. 70, image 112.

27. Wright to Pattison, May 4, 1869, NJHS.

28. McGee to Edwin Stanton, May 16, 1867, NARA.

29. The Reverend Robert Langley to Marcus Ward, September 14, 1869, Alexander Library, Rutgers University.

30. *Stillwater Messenger*, August 9, 1872.

31. Langley to Pattison, September 14, 1869, Alexander Library, Rutgers University.

32. *Ibid.*

33. Langley, HDSWACWRD.

34. Langley to Pattison, September 28, 1869, NJHS.

35. Dr. Isaac Braman to Assistant Adjutant General E.D. Townsend, October 19, 1869, NARA.

36. Ward to McGee, November 29, 1869, NJHS.

37. *Ibid.*

38. John McGee to the U.S. Army, Washington, D.C., December 18, 1873, searching for the whereabouts of his brother Willie, NARA.

39. Lurie & Mappen, *Encyclopedia of New Jersey*, 847.

40. Ward to McGee, November 29, 1869, NJHS.

41. McGee to Ward, December 16, 1869, NJHS.

42. Langley to Pattison, September 14, 1869, Alexander Library, Rutgers University.

43. Langley (McGee) to Ward, December 23, 1869, Alexander Library.

44. Langley correspondence, 1869–1871, NJHS and Alexander Library, Rutgers University.

45. Langley to Ward, December 23, 1869, Alexander Library, Rutgers University.

46. Langley to Pattison, February 28, 1870, NJHS.

47. Pattison to Ward, March 21, 1870, NJHS.

48. Ward to McGee, November 29, 1869, NJHS.

Chapter Ten

1. Holmes Pattison to Marcus Ward, March 21, 1870. This letter was sent in a package that also included all the correspondence of the McGee-Pattison relationship from 1867 to 1870, New Jersey Historical Society.

2. McGee to Ward, June 9, 1870, NJHS.

3. Ward to Minnesota governor Horace Austin, July 3, 1870. This letter reveals as well previous requests to have Austin visit McGee, which may have occurred, NJHS.

4. McGee to Ward, June 9, 1870, NJHS.

5. *Ibid.*

6. Ward to George Robeson, June 17, 1870. Robeson was the secretary of the navy and a highly placed Republican born and raised in Warren County, New Jersey, NJHS.

7. Austin to Ward, June 27, 1870, NJHS.

8. Ward to William Belknap, secretary of war, June 17, 1870, NJHS.

9. *Ibid.*

10. Joseph Holt, judge advocate general, to the secretary of war and the Bureau of Military Justice, June 29, 1870, NARA.

11. Holt to Bureau of Military Justice, June 29, 1870, NARA.

12. Michael W. Kauffman, *American Brutus* (New York: Random House, 2004), 367–370.

13. William Belknap to Marcus Ward, July 13, 1870, NJHS.

Chapter Eleven

1. Genoways, *Hard Time*, 9–10.

2. *Convict Registers, 1869–70, Stillwater Prison*, Minnesota Historical Society; *1870 United States Census*, Washington County, Stillwater Township, Minnesota, pp. 57–59, June 20, 1870.

3. Genoways, *Hard Time*, 9–11.

4. Marcus Ward to William Belknap, July 14, 1870, NJHS.

5. Joseph Holt to the War Department, Bureau of Military Justice, June 29, 1870, NARA.

6. *New York Times,* October 22, 1890.

7. Ward to Secretary of the Navy George Robeson, June 17, 1870, NJHS.

8. Warden Webber to Ward, July 21, 1870, NJHS.

9. Webber to Ward, July 21, 1870, NJHS.

10. McGee to Ward, July 22, 1870, NJHS.

11. St. John's Catholic Church, Newark, New Jersey, Baptismal and Birth records, May 13, 1849, Father John Moran compiler, New Jersey State Archives, Trenton, New Jersey.

12. McGee to Ward, July 22, 1870, NJHS.

13. *Ibid.*

14. McGee correspondence, genealogy records, census records, in New Jersey, Connecticut, Rhode Island, and Michigan.

15. McGee to Ward, July 22, 1870, NJHS.

16. *Ibid.*

17. Pattison to the War Department, December 4, 1867. McGee left New Jersey in September 1867 for his second examination in Louisville and never returned to reside in New Jersey, NARA.

18. McGee to Ward, July 22, 1870, NJHS.

19. *Ibid.*

20. McGee correspondence, genealogy, and census records.

21. Correspondence from the Reverend Robert Langley and Holmes Pattison to Marcus Ward and each other, June 1869 to June 1870, Alexander Library, Rutgers University and the NJHS.

22. McGee to Ward, July 22, 1870, NJHS.

23. *Ibid.*

24. *Ibid.*, July 27, 1870.

25. *Stillwater Republican,* August 14, 1870.

26. *Ibid.*

27. Genoways, *Hard Time,* 12.

28. *Ibid.*

29. McGee to Ward, August 21, 1870, NJHS.

30. *Ibid.*, September 6, 1870.

31. *Ibid.*

32. *Stillwater Republican,* October 8, 1870. There is no record however, that young Langley ever attended the Naval Academy, and he did not ever graduate from the academy, according to a spokesman for the U.S. Naval Academy Alumni Office.

33. Langley to Ward, December 10, 1870. Alexander Library, Rutgers University, New Brunswick, New Jersey.

34. Judge advocate general to William McGee, December 5, 1870, NARA.

35. Langley to Ward, March 10, 1871, Alexander Library.

36. Congressman Dwight Sabin to Ward, March 17, 1871, NJHS.

37. *Ibid.*

38. Pattison to Ward, December 22, 1871, NJHS.

39. *Ibid.*

40. Ward to Pattison, December 27, 1871, NJHS.

Chapter Twelve

1. McGee had left Newark three times since war's end, going back and forth to Michigan. He had left Stillwater for Pennsylvania, and had, of course, previously been removed forcibly from Louisiana. The pattern would continue.

2. Cole Younger, *The Story of Cole Younger & the Great Minnesota Northfield Raid — by Himself* (St. Paul, Minnesota: Valley History Press, 2000); Kenneth Hammer, *Men with Custer: Biographies of the 7th Cavalry, June 25, 1876* (Fort Collins, CO: Old Army Press, 1972).

3. Dwight Sabin to Marcus Ward, March 17, 1871, NJHS.

4. McGee to Ward, January 21, 1874, NJHS.

5. *1870 United States Federal Census,* Hudson County, Jersey City, New Jersey, Michael McGee, Ward 2, p. 1, image 289; New Haven, Connecticut, Ward 5, p. 476, image 308, John McGee.

6. *Northumberland Point Township, Pa. Bicentennial, 1772–1972* (Northumberland, PA: The Susquehanna Press, 1972), 28.

7. McGee to Marcus Ward, January 21, 1874, NJHS.

8. Edwin Burrows and Mike Wallace, *Gotham: A History of New York City to 1898* (New York: Oxford University Press, 1998), 1021.

9. *Ibid.*, 1021–1023.

10. Lally Weymouth, *America in 1876: The Way We Were* (New York: Random House, 1976), 144.

11. *Northumberland Point Township,* pp. 28–29.

12. *Ibid.*

13. Kevin Kenny, *Making Sense of the Molly Maguires* (New York: Oxford University Press, 1998), 128.

14. *Ibid.*, 152.

15. McGee to Ward, January 21, 1874, NJHS.

16. Laurie, "Marcus Ward," in *Encyclopedia of New Jersey,* 847.

17. *Ibid.*, 848.

18. McGee to Ward, February 25, 1874, NJHS.

19. Atkinson, *History of Newark,* 282.

20. Foster, *New Jersey in the Rebellion,* 856–859.

21. Weymouth, *America in 1876,* 144.

22. Ward Collection, New Jersey Historical Society; Alexander Library, Rutgers University.

23. Kenny, *Making Sense of the Molly Maguires,* 190.

24. McGee to Ward, March 8, 1874, NJHS.

25. *Ibid.,* March 31, 1874.

26. *Ibid.*

27. William E. Phoenix to Marcus Ward, March 31, 1874, NJHS.

28. Regina Magee to Willie McGee, April 8, 1874, NJHS.

29. McGee to Ward, April 21, 1874, NJHS.

30. Regina Magee to Ward, May 10, 1874, NJHS.

31. McGee to Ward, April 21, 1874, NJHS.

32. Author's thirty-year genealogy search of Irish and Irish-American families throughout the United States.

33. McGee to Ward, May 16, 1874, NJHS.

34. *Ibid.,* June 18, 1874.

35. *Ibid.,* December 21, 1874.

36. *Ibid.,* January 1874 to December 1874.

37. McGee correspondence, 1874, Marcus Ward Collection, New Jersey Historical Society, and Alexander Library, Rutgers University, New Brunswick, New Jersey.

38. Kenny, *Making Sense of the Molly Maguires,* 190.

39. *Ibid.,* 227.

40. 1900 *United States Federal Census,* Northumberland County, Pennsylvania, Mary Alene Magee, e.d. 171, p. 3B.

41. Author interviews with Diane Bretz, granddaughter of Mary Alene Magee, January to May 2006.

42. McGee to Ward, January 21, 1874, NJHS.

43. Author interview with Diane Bretz.

44. *Ibid.*

45. Riverview Cemetery records, 1848–1924, Northumberland, Pennsylvania. Magee oral tradition always knew Regina as "Alene," and while that may have been her legal name, she signed her letters as Regina, and is buried as well with that name.

46. Atkinson, *The History of Newark,* 284.

47. *Massachusetts Archives,* death records, City of Boston, pp. 181–182, Isaac G. Braman, July 31, 1876, Boston, Massachusetts.

Chapter Thirteen

1. Edwin Burrows and Mike Wallace, *Gotham: A History of New York City to 1898* (New York: Oxford University Press, 1999), 1023.

2. McGee to J.D. Cameron, secretary of war, December 13, 1876, NARA.

3. McGee to Ward, July 22, 1870, NJHS.

4. *Ibid.*

5. *7th Cavalry Regiment,* Fort Abraham Lincoln Post Returns, William H. McGee, September 26, 1876. McGee is classified as a recruit from the depot.

6. Bruce Hampton, *Children of Grace: The Nez Perce War of 1877* (New York: John Macrae Book, 1994), 64.

7. *Ibid.,* 65.

8. *7th Cavalry Regiment,* Fort Abraham Lincoln Post Returns, September 26, 1876.

9. Charles D. King, Local History Archivist, Kenton County, Kentucky. E-mail interview with the author, October 2006.

10. James A. Greene, *Nez Perce Summer 1877: The U.S. Army and the Nee-Me-Poo Crisis* (Helena: Montana Historical Society Press, 2000), Appendix A, 15: Bear's Paw; September 30–October 5, 1877, no. 25, William H. McGee.

11. *7th Cavalry Regiment,* Fort Abraham Lincoln Returns, William H. McGee.

12. Hampton, *Children of Grace,* 65.

13. Jane Van Brunt to Marcus Ward, March 10, 1878, NJHS.

14. *Ibid.*

15. *Ibid.*

16. United States Census, 1870 and 1880, Sidney, Champaign County, Illinois.

17. *10th Illinois Cavalry, 1861–64,* Henry Van Brunt, HDSWACWRD.

18. Robert Behrens, *From Salt Fork to Chickamauga: Champaign County in the Civil War* (Urbana: University of Illinois Press, 1988), 354–355.

19. *Ibid.,* 354.

20. Van Brunt to Ward, March 14, 1878, NJHS.

21. *Ibid.*

22. *Declaration for an Invalid Pension,* April 10, 1878, Champaign County, Illinois. William Magee, Number 252747, NARA.

23. *Ibid.*

24. *Ibid.*

25. *Ibid.*

26. E.L. Campbell to United States Bureau of Pension, Washington, D.C., May 1, 1878, NARA.

27. E.L. Campbell to United States Bureau of Pensions, May 1, 1878, regarding pension request no. 252747, William Magee, NARA.

28. Department of the Interior, Pension Office, to E.L. Campbell, September 30, 1878, NARA.

29. 33rd New Jersey Infantry, Muster Rolls, William Magee, July 1863 to July 1865, NARA.

30. *Ibid.*

31. William McGee to E.L. Campbell, October 10, 1878, NARA.

32. *Ibid.*

33. Campbell to Horatio Van Cleve, May 1878, NARA.

34. New Jersey Historical Society Rolls, 1865–1890, Newark, New Jersey, NJHS.

35. Horatio Van Cleve, HDSACWRD.

36. *Ibid.*

37. Genoways, *Hard Time,* 13.

38. Horatio Van Cleve to E.L. Campbell, May 13, 1878, NARA.

39. Campbell to Pension Bureau, 1878, NARA.

40. *Declaration for Pension,* No. 252747, 1878, William Magee, NARA.

Chapter Fourteen

1. *Invalid Pension Request,* no. 252747, William Magee, abandoned 1878, NARA.

2. *Medal of Honor Citation,* February 9, 1866. Medal of Honor file, under the name "Megee," NARA.

3. Foster, *New Jersey in the Rebellion,* 856–859.

4. Atkinson, *History of Newark,* 282–285.

5. Horatio Van Cleve to E.L. Campbell, May 13, 1878, NARA.

6. E.L. Campbell to U.S. Pension Bureau, undated, 1878, NARA.

7. Atkinson, *History of Newark,* 284–285.

8. *Ibid.*

9. *Ibid.,* 285.

10. *Ibid.*

11. E.L. Campbell to U.S. Pension Bureau, undated, 1878.

12. *History of Newark, New Jersey,* 3 vols. (Newark, NJ: Lewis Publishing company, 1913).

13. Author interview with several Old Army archivists, May and August 2005, Washington, D.C, NARA. When the author was able to locate the files, there was no visible record they had ever been called for or inspected since the original date of filing.

14. Foster, *New Jersey in the Rebellion,* 857.

15. *History of Newark,* 1913, "Drummer Boy Magee's Brilliant Exploit."

16. Carl D. Cottingham, *Life and Times of General John A. Logan* (Carbondale, IL: Kestrel Press, 1989), 11–17.

17. Cottingham, *Life and Times,* 20–22.

18. *Ibid.,* 24.

19. *Ibid.*

20. *United States Senate, 46th Congress, 2nd Session,* Senate Bill 1039, March 10, 1880.

21. E.D. Townsend, adjutant general, to Judge Advocate General W.M. Dunn, March 4, 1880, NARA.

22. E.D. Townsend to William McGee, March 4, 1880, March 6, 1880, and March 10, 1880, NARA.

23. *Committee on Military Affairs,* Report 459 on Senate Bill 1039, March 10, 1880, NARA.

24. *Decatur* (Illinois) *Daily Republican,* Illinois, April 12, 1880.

25. Champaign County Circuit Court Chancery Cases, September 1884, *Samuel T. Busey vs. Jane E. Magee and Mary Van Brunt,* Foreclosure Number 1570.

26. *Ibid.*

27. Champaign County, Illinois, Marriage Certificate, June 21, 1880, Number 0406188000860, Jane Van Brunt and William H. McGee.

28. *Ibid.* Though Willie himself never wrote the names of his mother and father in any of his known correspondence, James and Margaret are listed as his parents in this marriage certificate, the only public record after the birth and baptismal record of May 25, 1849, Newark, New Jersey. Typically McGee, he lists his mother's name as Margaret Paterson, giving some truth. A four state search for Margaret Paterson found no search person fitting what we know about Willie's mother.

29. McGee correspondence from Springfield, Massachusetts, 1881; Springfield, Massachusetts, City Directories, 1880–1881.

30. *Busey vs. Magee and Van Brunt,* September 1884.

31. Behrens, *From Salt Fork to Chickamauga,* 355.

32. *Ibid.* The date of publication is 1988, so Willie McGee has been remembered in Champaign County for a long time, especially interesting since he was there — on and off— for less than three years.

33. *Elgin Family Genealogy.* Jane Van Brunt (marriage number two) to Nels Nelson, who was born November 26, 1846, in Sweden. The wedding took place April 6, 1886, in Polk County, Nebraska; York County, Nebraska, death certificate, Jane Nelson, 1930.

34. McGee correspondence to several attorneys and government officials in Washington, D.C., 1880–1886, NARA; Springfield, Massachusetts, Directories, 1881–86.

35. McGee to Edwin Stanton, Secretary of War, May 18, 1867, NARA.

36. St. John's Catholic Church Baptismal and Birth Records, July, 1847, Newark, New Jersey, Father John Moran compiler.

37. *8th United States Federal Census,* Essex

County, Newark, New Jersey, William and John Magee, Ward 7, p. 322, image 422.

38. New Haven, Connecticut, Marriage Certificate; *10th United States Federal Census,* Meriden, Connecticut, John McGee, e.d. 52, p. 322, image 0004.

39. Meriden, Connecticut, Town Hall Records, June 1882, birth of William Magee.

40. Meriden Birth Records, June 1882, William Magee.

41. Springfield Armory, National Historic Site, Springfield, Massachusetts, September 10, 2005. Payroll records, March 1883, William Magee.

42. Ward to Surgeon General Crane, October 19, 1882, NJHS.

43. Crane to Ward, October 24, 1882, NJHS.

44. Lurie and Mappen, *Encyclopedia of New Jersey,* 846.

45. McGee to Ward, July 1870, NJHS.

46. State Library of Massachusetts, Reference Department. E-mail interview with Pamela Schofield, reference librarian, regarding George D. Robinson, February 28, 2006.

47. McGee to Judge Advocate General D.G. Swain, April 14, 1883, NARA.

48. Judge Advocate General Swain to McGee, April 21, 1883, NARA.

49. *Ibid.*

50. McGee to Swain, June 24, 1883, NARA.

51. *United States Senate, 48th Congress, 1st Session.* House of Representatives Bill #758, December 10, 1883. Proposed by George D. Robinson of Massachusetts, Congressional Record, Volume XV, Washington, D.C.

52. *Ibid.*

53. U.S. Army memo, August 3, 1886, refers to McGee as a "hard nut," NARA.

54. Riverview Cemetery Records, Northumberland County, Pennsylvania, 1848–1924, compiled by Henry Frisch.

55. *Ibid.*

56. *Ibid.*

57. *12th United States Federal Census,* Northumberland County, Northumberland, Pa., Mary A. Magee, p. 3B, e.d. 171.

Chapter Fifteen

1. Riverview Cemetery Records, Northumberland Township, Northumberland, Pennsylvania, 1848–1924.

2. *11th United States Federal Census,* Special Schedule of Surviving Civil War Veterans and Widows, Manhattan, New York, June 1890, supervisor's district 247, William J. McGee.

3. Rose Watkins, *"Introduction to 1890*

Census," Bucknell University, http://www.eg.bucknell.edu.

4. 12th Ohio Cavalry, William A. Magee, Company M, HDSACWRD.

5. *33rd New Jersey Infantry,* William H. Magee, HDSACWRD.

6. *11th U.S. Federal Census,* William J. McGee, p. 1, e.d. 247.

7. *7th United States Federal Census,* Bernard and Susan McGee, New York City, Ward 5, p. 237, image 477.

8. *9th U.S. Federal Census,* New York City, p. 438, image 370, William McGee; Genealogy of William J. McGee and Katherine (Egan) McGee; New York City Directories, 1877–1920; Calvary Cemetery Records, Woodside, Queen's, New York.

9. Author interview with William Saich, Sr., great grandson of William J. McGee, September 2005; New York Municipal Archives, business directories, tax rolls, and minutes of Manhattan city council meetings, 1884–1892. Municipal Archives, New York City.

10. State of Texas, District Court, Galveston, marriage certificate, William H. McGee and Louise Saunders, July 22, 1891, No. 270.

11. *Galveston Daily News,* Galveston, Texas, March 12, 1905, p. 5.

12. *Galveston Daily News;* Galveston City Directories, 1890–1898; *Bismarck Daily Tribune,* June 26, 1902.

13. Waukesha *Republican-Freeman,* Waukesha, Wisconsin, November 12, 1898.

14. Hampton, *Children of Grace,* 289–305.

15. *7th Cavalry Regimental Returns,* October 16, 1877. McGee was classified as sick.

16. Waukesha *Republican-Freeman,* November 12, 1898; *New York Sun,* December 10, 1904, p. 1; Galveston, Texas, divorce records, December 21, 1902, William H. McGee and Louise McGee, District Court, Galveston, Texas, No. 23394.

17. *12th United States Federal Census,* New York County, New York, William H. McGee, Roll T623, p. 3A, e.d. 304.

18. *New York Sun,* December 10, 1904, p. 1; District Court, Galveston, Texas, October Term 1902, No. 23394.

19. Erick Larson, *Isaac's Storm* (New York: Random House, 1999), 16.

20. Criminal Trial Term of the New York Supreme Court, Part 1, County of New York, *People vs. McGee,* February 24, 1905, testimony of William McGee as reported by District Attorney William J. Travers to New York governor Charles Evans Hughes in letter of June 5, 1910, Municipal Archives, NYC.

21. Travers to Hughes, June 5, 1910, pp. 1–3, Municipal Archives, NYC.

22. *Bismarck Daily Tribune,* June 26, 1902, p. 1.

23. *Ibid.*

24. Michael L. Nunnally, *I Survived Custer's Last Stand!* (Memphis, TN: Monnwolf Press, 2005), 4–5.

25. *Ibid.,* 7–35.

26. Brian W. Dippie, *Custer's Last Stand: The Anatomy of an American Myth* (Lincoln: University of Nebraska Press, 1976), 85.

27. Nunnally, *I Survived Custer's Last Stand!,* 4.

28. Author interview with Michael Nunnally, November and December 2006.

29. *McGee Service Record, 1876–77.* Willie enlisted in the 13th Illinois Cavalry in September 1876, just months after the Little Big Horn, and served all of 1877 with many members of Reno's and Benteen's forces, who would have had first hand knowledge of that June 26, 1876, affair: Fort Abraham Lincoln Post Returns.

30. Hammer, *Men with Custer.*

31. Dippie, *Custer's Last Stand,* 62–88.

32. *Twelfth United States Federal Census, 1900,* New York County, New York. William H. McGee, p. 3a, E.D. 134.

33. *Bismarck Daily Tribune,* June 26, 1902.

34. *Galveston Daily News,* March 12, 1905; McGee testimony, New York Supreme Court, Part 1, February 24, 1905, Municipal Archives, NYC.

35. National Archives Memo, October 17, 2006; William McGee testimony, February 24, 1905, New York Criminal Court, Part 1, *People vs. McGee,* pp. 1–2, Municipal Archives, NYC.

36. Horatio Van Cleve to E.L. Campbell May, 1878.

37. 7th Cavalry Muster Rolls, 1876–1878, William H. McGee. Two officers of the 7th, Myles Moylan, Company A, and Owen Hale, of McGee's Company K, as well as many privates were all privy to actions involving Custer and the Little Big Horn.

38. District Court, County of Galveston, State of Texas, August 12, 1902, Book K, No. 270, p. 135, *Louise Josephine McGee vs. William Henry McGee.*

39. District Court, County of Galveston, August 12, 1902, Book K, No. 270, p. 135.

40. District Court, County of Galveston, October Term 1902, Judge William H. Stewart, No. 23, 394. Sheriff Henry Thomas was ordered to place the ads throughout the state for one month.

41. Statement of Evidence, December 4, 1902, District Court, County of Galveston, Texas. Edward May, Willie McGee's attorney, read the quote into evidence before Judge Stewart.

42. District Court, County of Galveston, December Term 1902, No. 23, 394. *Louise Josephine McGee vs. William Henry McGee,* statement of evidence.

43. William J. Travers, district attorney for New York County, to Governor Charles Evans Hughes, June 5, 1910, pp. 1–3, Municipal Archives, NYC.

44. *Baton Rouge Tri-Weekly,* August 18, 1868, p. 1.

45. New York Criminal Court testimony of William McGee, February 24, 1905, *People vs. McGee,* New York Supreme Court, Part 1, Municipal Archives, NYC.

46. *New York Sun,* December 10, 1904, p. 1.

47. *New York World,* December 10, 1904; *Oakland Tribune,* December 10, 1904; *Washington Post,* December 22, 1904; *Atlanta Constitution,* December 11, 1904; *Kansas City Star,* December 12, 1904; *Anaconda Standard,* December 14, 1904.

48. *New York Times,* December 12, 1904, p. 2.

49. *Kansas City Star,* March 4, 1905; *Williamsport* (Pa.) *Daily Gazette,* February 17, 1905; *Galveston Daily News,* March 12, 1905; *Fort Wayne Sentinel,* February 24, 1905.

50. *New York Sun,* December 10, 1904, p. 1.

51. Criminal Trial Term, Part 1, New York Supreme Court, February 1905, testimony of Mabel Mitchell, pp. 5–9, Municipal Archives, NYC.

52. *People vs. McGee,* Mitchell testimony, p. 5.

53. *Ibid.,* 6.

54. *Ibid.,* 7.

55. Criminal Trial Term, Part 1, New York Supreme Court, February, 1905, William McGee testimony, pp. 9–13, Municipal Archives, NYC.

56. *People vs. McGee,* McGee testimony, p. 11.

57. District Attorney William J. Travers, New York County, New York, to Governor Charles Evans Hughes, June 5, 1910, pp. 13–14. Municipal Archives, NYC.

58. Travers to Hughes, p. 13.

59. *New York Sun,* December 10, 1904.

60. Travers to Hughes, p. 14.

61. *Ibid.*

62. *New York Sun,* March 4, 1905.

63. *Galveston Daily News,* March 12, 1905; *New York Sun,* March 4, 1905; *Kansas City Star,* March 4, 1905; *Wellsboro Gazette,* March 2, 1905; *Syracuse Post-Standard,* February 24, 1905.

64. Sing Sing Prison, Inmate Register, March 10, 1905, William H. McGee, No. 55477, New York State Archives, Albany, New York.

65. Inmate Register, William McGee, No. 55477.

Epilogue

1. Jack McPeters, Head Archivist, New York State Archives, Albany, New York.

2. Judge Kenefick of the New York Supreme Court, Part 1, sentenced McGee to seven years and ten months on March 2, 1905, making his release, if full term, January 2, 1913 — provided he was not allowed an early exit or remanded for a later release, Municipal Archives, NYC.

3. Timothy J. Gilfoyle, *A Pickpocket's Tale: The Life of Nineteenth Century New York* (New York: W.W. Norton, 2006).

4. Gilfoyle, *A Pickpocket's Tale, 172.*

5. *Wardens of Sing Sing, State of New York, Department of Correctional Services, Sing Sing Correctional Facility,* Ossining, New York. Compiled by Corrections Officer Arthur M. Wolpinsky, 2004, New York State Archives, Albany, New York.

6. Roberta Arminio, director, Ossining Historical Society, in an interview with the author, October 2006.

7. Roberta Arminio to the author, October 2006.

8. *13th United States Federal Census,* Ossining, New York, Sing Sing Prison, William McGee, e.d. 103, p. 12.

9. 1870 Minnesota Census: McGee said he was born in New Jersey; 1900 New York Census: Willie claimed New York as his birthplace; 1910 New York Census: McGee said it was Massachusetts; and in the December 10, 1904, *New York Sun* and other newspapers he said he was born in Kentucky.

10. Dale Cemetery, Ossining; St. Augustine Cemetery, Ossining; Ryder Cemetery, Ossining; Sing Sing Cemetery; Calvary Cemetery, Woodside, Queen's, New York.

11. Dubhaltach MacFirbhisigh, ed., *Leabhar Mor Na nGenealac: The Great Book of Irish Genealogies,* 5 vols. (Dublin: DeBurca Press, 2003).

12. *Ibid.,* vol. 3.

13. *7th U.S. Federal Census, 1850,* Newark, New Jersey, West Ward, Essex County, p. 326, image 43, James and Margaret McGee.

14. Newark City Directories, Newark Public Library, Newark, New Jersey, 1850–1900.

15. *7th U.S. Federal Census,* Newark, 1850, New Jersey, James McGee, p. 326.

16. St. John's Roman Catholic Church, Birth and Baptismal records, 1828–1878, New Jersey State Archives.

17. William McGee correspondence with Holmes Pattison and Marcus Ward, 1864–1875; 1860 U.S. Federal Census, Newark, New Jersey; enlistment record, William Magee, July 1863, 33rd New Jersey Infantry; Foster, *New Jersey in the Rebellion,* 1867.

18. William H. McGee genealogy, 1874–1904, including correspondence, divorce, and marriage records.

19. *9th U. S. Federal Census, 1880,* John McGee of Meriden, Connecticut, p. 371, e.d. 52; *13th U.S. Federal Census,* 1910, Michael McGee of Providence, Rhode Island, Ward 2, p. 9B, e.d. 160; *12th U.S. Federal Census, 1900,* Meriden, Connecticut, p. 8B, e.d.317.

20. *8th U.S. Federal Census, 1860,* Newark, New Jersey, William Magee, Ward 7, p. 322, image 428.

21. 33rd New Jersey Infantry, State of New Jersey, William Magee, July 23, 1863, NARA.

22. Minnesota Historical Society, Stillwater Prison, Inmate Registers, 1868–1872, William McGee.

23. Sing Sing Prison Inmate Register, William McGee, March 10, 1905, #55477.

24. McGee correspondence, 1867–1886, NARA; Ward Collection, 1850–1884, NJHS.

25. Genealogy records of John and Eliza McGee, Meriden, Connecticut, 1870–1930, census, birth, marriage, and death records from Meriden Town Hall and the Meriden Public Library.

26. *12th U.S. Federal Census,* Providence, Rhode Island, shows Della McGee as Mike's widow; 1905 Meriden, Connecticut, city directory lists Eliza McGee as John's widow.

27. Author interviews with Diane Bretz, Willie McGee's great granddaughter, 2005–2006.

28. Inmate registers at Stillwater prison and Sing Sing Prison, Minnesota Historical Society and New York State Archives.

29. Maureen Dezell, *Irish America Coming into Clover: The Evolution of a People and Culture* (New York: Doubleday, 2000), 220.

30. Keesee, *Too Young to Die,* 101–102.

31. *Ibid.,* 102.

32. *New York Times,* May 4, 1890.

33. Dezell, *Irish America,* 139.

34. Ronald H. Bayor and Timothy Meagher, *The New York Irish* (Baltimore: Johns Hopkins University Press, 1996), 553.

Appendix 1

1. Howard T. Dimick, "The Bonfoey Case at Marshall," *Southwestern Historical Quarterly* 48, no. 4 (April 1945): 6.

2. Regular Army Reports, 20th United States Infantry, 1866–1868; Lt.William McGee, Lt. Charles B. Clark, Lt. Thomas Latchford, NARA.

3. *The Texas Republican,* Marshall, Texas, October 16, 1868. Lt. Charles B. Clark, 28, married Miss Della Rowe, 18, of Marshall on October 14, in a ceremony conducted by Rev. J. H. Johnson.

4. *United States Senate, 52nd Congress, 1st Session,* Report No. 800, to accompany S. 238, p. 12. June 13, 1892.

5. Dimick, *The Bonfoey Case at Marshall,*3.

6. *Ibid.,* 3–5.

7. *Senate Report 800,* pp. 2–3.

8. Dimick, *The Bonfoey Case at Marshall,* 5–7.

9. *Senate Report 800,* pp. 3–6.

10. Dimick, *The Bonfoey Case at Marshall,* 9–10.

11. *Ibid.,* 10.

12. *Senate Report 800,* pp. 11–13.

13. "Bonfoey Killer Never Punished," *Marshall News-Messenger,* November 10, 1963.

14. Thomas Latchford and William Hawley, HDSWACWRD, http://www.civilwardata.com.

15. Regular Army Reports, 20th U.S. Infantry, Lt. Charles B. Clark, 1866–70, NARA.

16. Randolph Campbell, *A Southern Community in Crisis: Harrison County, Texas, 1850–1880* (Austin: Texas State Historical Association, 1983).

Bibliography

Newspapers

Anaconda *Standard*
Atlanta *Constitution*
Baton Rouge *Capitolian-Advocate*
Baton Rouge *Tri-Weekly Advocate*
Bismarck *Daily Tribune*
Boston *Daily Evening Transcript*
Boston *Globe*
Brooklyn *Eagle*
Chicago *Daily Tribune*
Decatur *Daily Republican*
Elizabeth (NJ) *Daily Journal*
Fort Wayne *Sentinel*
Galveston *Daily News*
Irish *World*
Kansas City *Star*
Marshall (TX) *News Messenger*
New Jersey *Herald*
New York *Sun*
New York Times
New York *Tribune*
New York *World*
Newark (NJ) *Advertiser*
Newark (NJ) *Daily Advertiser*
Newark (NJ) *Daily Mercury*
Newark (Ohio) *Advocate*
Oakland *Tribune*
St. Paul *Pioneer*
State College (PA) *Centre Daily Times*
Stillwater (MN) *Messenger*
Stillwater (MN) *Republican*
Sussex (NJ) *Register*
Syracuse *Post-Standard*
Texas *Republican*
Washington *Post*

Waukesha *Republican-Freeman*
Wellsboro (PA) *Gazette*
Williamsport (PA) *Daily Gazette*

Books

Ackerman, Kenneth D. *Boss Tweed: The Rise and Fall of the Corrupt Pol Who Conceived the Soul of Modern New York.* New York: Carroll & Graf Press, 2005.

Akenson, Donald H. *Small Differences: Irish Catholics and Irish Protestants, 1815–1922.* Dublin: Gill and Macmillan, 1991.

Allen, Oliver. *The Tiger: The Rise and Fall of Tammany Hall.* Reading, MA: Addison-Wesley Publishers, 1993.

Anbinder, Tyler. *Five Points: The 19th Century New York Neighborhood That Invented Tap Dance, Stole Elections, and Became the World's Most Notorious Slum.* New York: Plume Books, 2002.

Atkinson, Joseph. *History of Newark, Being a Narrative of Its Rise and Progress.* Newark, NJ: William B. Guild, 1878.

Atlas to Accompany the Official Records of the Union and Confederate Armies. Washington, D.C., 1891–1895.

Balch, Galusha B. *Genealogy of the Balch Family.* Salem, MA: 1897.

Bardon, Jonathon. *A History of Ulster.* Belfast: Blackstaff Press, 1992.

Barrett, Tom. *The Mollies Were Men.* New York: Vantage Press, 1969.

Bayor, Ronald & Timothy Meagher, eds. *The New York Irish.* Baltimore: Johns Hopkins University Press, 1996.

Behrens, Robert. *From Salt Fork to Chickamauga: Champaign County Soldiers of the Civil War.* Champaign, IL: Urbana Free Library, 1988.

Bell, Herbert, ed. *History of Northumberland County, Pennsylvania.* Chicago: 1891.

Bernstein, Iver. *The New York City Draft Riots.* New York: Oxford University Press, 1990.

Beyer, W.F., and O.F. Keydal. *Deeds of Valor: How America's Civil War Heroes Won the Medal of Honor.* Detroit: Perrian-Keydal Company, 1903.

Bilby, Joseph G., and William C. Goble. *"Remember You Are Jerseymen!": A Military History of New Jersey's Troops in the Civil War.* Hightstown, NJ: Longstreet House, 1998.

Bimba, Anthony. *The Molly Maguires.* New York: International Publishers, 1932.

Birkner, Michael, and Paul A. Stellhorn, eds. *The Governors of New Jersey, 1664–1974.* Trenton, NJ: New Jersey Historical Society, 1982.

Booth, Andrew B. *Records of Louisiana Confederate Soldiers and Louisiana Confederate Commanders.* Vol. 1. New Orleans, LA: 1920.

Bradford, Ned, ed. *Battles and Leaders of the Civil War.* New York: Appleton, Century, Croft, 1956.

Brands, H.W. *The Reckless Decade: America in the 1890s.* Chicago: University of Chicago Press, 1995.

Broehl, Wayne. *The Molly Maguires.* Cambridge, MA: Harvard University Press, 1964.

Buck, Irving. *Cleburne and His Command.* Jackson, TN: McCourt-Mercer Press, 1959.

Burrows, Edwin, and Mike Wallace. *Gotham: A History of New York City to 1898.* New York: Oxford University Press, 1999.

Campbell, Randolph. *A Southern Community in Crisis: Harrison County, Texas, 1850–1880.* Austin, Texas: Texas State Historical Association, 1983.

Civil War Society. *Encyclopedia of the Civil War.* New York: Portland House, 1997.

Clark, Dennis. *Hibernia America: The Irish and Regional Cultures.* New York: Greenwood Press, 1986.

Connell, K.H. *Irish Peasant Society.* Dublin: Irish Academic Press, 1996.

Coogan, Tim Pat. *Wherever Green Is Worn: The Story of the Irish Diaspora.* New York: Palgrave Publishers, 2000.

Cowley, Robert, ed. *With My Face to the Enemy: Perspectives on the Civil War.* New York: Berkley Books, 2001.

Daniel, Larry. *Days of Glory: The Army of the Cumberland, 1861–1865.* Baton Rouge: Louisiana State University Press, 2004.

Davis, Major George B. *The Official Military Atlas of the Civil War.* New York: Barnes & Noble Books, 2003.

Dezell, Maureen. *Irish America, Coming into Clover: The Evolution of a People and a Culture.* New York: Doubleday, 2000.

Dippie, Brian. *Custer's Last Stand: The Anatomy of an American Myth.* Lincoln: University of Nebraska Press, 1976.

Ellis, Edward Robb. *The Epic of New York City: A Narrative History.* New York: Kondasha International, 1966.

English, T.J. *Paddy Whacked: The Untold Story of the Irish-American Gangster.* New York: Regan Books, 2005.

Falley, Margaret. *Irish and Scotch-Irish Ancestral Research.* Chicago: Shenandoah Publishing House. 1962.

Farmer, Thomas P. *Fighting to Be Heard: New Jersey in History.* West Creek, NJ: Down the Shore Publishers, 1996.

Flanagan, Thomas. *The Tenants of Time.* New York: E.P. Dutton, 1988.

Foner, Eric. *Reconstruction: America's Unfinished Revolution, 1863–1877.* New York: Harper & Row, 1988.

Fortier, Alcee, ed. *Comprising Sketches of Parishes, Towns, Events, Institutions, and Persons.* Vol. 3. New Orleans, LA: Century Historical Association, 1914.

Foster, John Y. *New Jersey in the Rebellion.* NJ: Dennis & Company, 1867.

Galishoff, Stuart. *Newark, the Nation's Unhealthiest City, 1832–1895.* New Brunswick, NJ: Rutgers University Press, 1988.

Gannon, James. *Irish Rebels — Confederate Tigers — The 6th Louisiana Volunteers, 1861–1865.* Campbell, CA: Savas Publishing, 1998.

Gillette, William. *Jersey Blue: Civil War Politics in New Jersey, 1854–1865.* New Brunswick, NJ: Rutgers University Press, 1994.

Genoways, Ted. *Hard Time: Voices from a State Prison, 1849–1914.* St. Paul: Minnesota Historical Society Press, 2002.

Gleeson, Edward. *Rebel Sons of Erin.* Indianapolis, IN: Guild Press, 1993.

Gordon, Michael. *The Orange Riots: Irish Political Violence in New York City, 1870 and 1871.* New York: Cornell University Press, 1993.

Greene, James. *Nez Perce Summer of 1877: The U.S. Army and the Nee-Me-Poo-Crisis.* Helena: Montana Historical Society Press, 2000.

Hammer, Kenneth. *Men With Custer: Biographies of the 7th Cavalry, June 25, 1876.* Fort Collins, CO: Old Army Press, 1972.

Hampton, Bruce. *Children of Grace: The Nez Perce War of 1877.* New York: John Macrae Books, 1994.

Heilbron, W.C. *Convict Life at the Minnesota*

State Prison. Stillwater, MN: Valley History Press, 1996.

Heitman, Francis. *Historical Register and Dictionary of the United States Army, from its Organization, September 29, 1789 to March 2, 1903.* Baltimore, MD: Genealogical Publishing Company, 1994.

Hernon, Joseph. *Celts, Catholics, & Copperheads: Ireland Views the American Civil War.* Columbus, OH: Ohio University Press, 1968.

Hirsch, Susan E. *Roots of the American Working Class: The Industrialization in Newark, 1800–1860.* Philadelphia: University of Pennsylvania Press. 1978.

History of Newark, New Jersey. Newark: Lewis Publishing Company, 1913.

Homberger, Eric. *Historical Atlas of New York City.* New York: Henry Holt & Company, 1994.

Ignatiev, Noel. *How the Irish Became White.* New York: Routledge Press, 1995.

Jackson, William. *New Jerseyans in the Civil War: For Union or Liberty.* New Brunswick, NJ: Rutgers University Press, 2000.

Jewett, Frederick. *History and Genealogy of the Jewets in America.* New York: 1908.

Jones, Terry. *Lee's Tigers: The Louisiana Infantry in the Army of Northern Virginia.* Baton Rouge: Louisiana State University Press, 1987.

Joslyn, Mauriel, ed. *A Meteor Shining Brightly — Essays on Major General Patrick Cleburne.* Milledgeville, GA: Terrell House Press, 1998.

Keesee, Dennis. *Too Young to Die: Boy Soldiers in the Union Army, 1861–1865.* Huntington, WV: Blue Acorn Press, 2001.

Kenny, Kevin. *Making Sense of the Molly Maguires.* New York: Oxford University Press, 1998.

Knobel, Dale T. *Paddy and the Republic: Ethnicity and Nationality in Antebellum America.* Middletown, CT: Wesleyan University Press, 1986.

Lawes, Lewis. *Invisible Stripes.* New York: Farrar, Straus & Rinehart, 1938.

_____. *20,000 Years in Sing Sing.* New York: Ray Long & R Smith, 1932.

Lewis, Arthur. *Lament for the Molly Maguires.* New York: Harcourt, Brace & World, 1964.

Leyburn, James G. *The Scotch-Irish: A Social History.* Chapel Hill: University of North Carolina Press, 1962.

Livermore, Thomas. *Numbers and Losses in the Civil War in America, 1861–1865.* Carlisle, PA: John Kallman Publishers, 1996.

Lurie, Maxine, and Marc Mappen, eds. *Encyclopedia of New Jersey.* New Brunswick, NJ: Rutgers University Press, 2004.

MacDonald, John. *Great Battles of the Civil War.* Edison, NJ: Chartwell Books, 2003.

MacLysaght, Edward. *Irish Families, Their Names, Arms, and Origins.* New York: Crown Publishers, 1972.

Marten, James. *The Children's Civil War.* Chapel Hill: University of North Carolina Press, 1998.

McCague, James. *The Second Rebellion: The New York Draft Riots of 1863.* New York: Dial Press, 1968.

McDonough, James Lee. *Chattanooga: A Death Grip on the Confederacy.* Knoxville: University of Tennessee Press, 1984.

_____. *Five Tragic Hours: The Battle of Franklin.* Knoxville: University of Tennessee Press, 1983.

McPherson, James. *For Cause and Freedom: Why Men Fought in the Civil War.* New York: Oxford University Press, 1997.

Miers, Earl Schenck. *New Jersey and the Civil War.* Princeton, NJ: Van Nostrand Books, 1964.

Miller, Kerby. *Emigrants and Exiles: Ireland and the Irish Exodus to North America.* New York: Oxford University Press, 1985.

Moulton, Candy. *Chief Joseph: Guardian of the People.* New York: Tom Doherty Books, 2005.

Niehaus, Earl. *The Irish in New Orleans, 1800–1860.* Baton Rouge: Louisiana State University Press, 1965.

Northumberland Point Township, Pennsylvania Bicentennial, 1772–1972. Northumberland, PA: The Susquehanna Press, 1972.

Nunnally, Michael L. *I Survived Custer's Last Stand!* Memphis, TN: Moonwolf Publishing, 2005.

O'Shea, Richard. *Battle Maps of the Civil War.* New York: American Heritage, 2002.

O'Sullivan, Patrick, ed. *The Irish in the New Communities.* New York: St. Martin's Press, 1992.

O'Tuathaigh, Gearoid. *Ireland Before the Famine, 1798–1848.* Dublin: Gill & MacMillan, 1972.

Parry, Owen. *Bold Sons of Erin.* New York: William Morrow, 2003.

_____. *Faded Coat of Blue.* New York: Avon Books, 1999.

Perley, M.V.B. *History and Genealogy of the Perley Family.* Salem, MA: 1906.

Perret, Geoffrey. *Ulysses S. Grant: Soldier & President.* New York: Random House, 1997.

Quinn, Dermot. *The Irish in New Jersey: Four Centuries of American Life.* New Brunswick, NJ: Rutgers University Press, 2004.

Quinn, Peter. *Banished Children of Eve — A Novel of the Civil War.* New York: Viking Press, 1994.

Randall, J.G., and David Donald. *The Civil War and Reconstruction*. Boston: D.C. Heath, 1961.

Sante, Luc. *Low Life: Lures and Snares of Old New York*. New York: Farrar Strauss Giroux, 1991.

Schecter, Barnet. *The Devil's Own Work: The Civil War Draft Riots and the Fight to Reconstruct America*. New York: Walker & Company, 2005.

Siegel, Allan. *Beneath the Starry Flag — New Jersey's Civil War Experience*. New Brunswick, NJ: Rutgers University Press, 2001.

Skemer, Don, and Robert Morris, eds. *Guide to the Manuscript Collections of the New Jersey Historical Society*. Newark: New Jersey Historical Society, 1979.

Sklenar, Larry. *To Hell with Honor: Custer and the Little Big Horn*. Norman: University of Oklahoma Press, 2000.

Stellhorn, Paul A., and Michael Birkner, eds. *The Governors of New Jersey, 1664–1974*. Trenton: New Jersey Historical Commission, 1982.

Sword, Wiley. *Embrace an Angry Wind: The Confederacy's Last Hurrah*. New York: Harper Collins, 1992.

Van West, Carroll. *The Tennessee Encyclopedia of History and Culture*. Nashville, TN: Tennessee Historical Society: Rutledge Hill Press, 1998.

War of the Rebellion. A Compilation of the Official Records of the Union and Confederate Armies. Washington: 1882–1900.

Warner, Ezra. *Generals in Blue: Lives of the Union Commanders*. Baton Rouge: Louisiana State University Press, 1964.

Weymouth, Lally, ed. *America in 1876: The Way We Were*. Random House, New York, 1976.

Wilson, John Grant, ed. *Appleton's Cyclopedia of American Biography*. New York: D. Appleton & Co., 1887–1889. (Reprinted in 1990).

Wittke, Carl. *The Irish in America*. Baton Rouge: Louisiana State University Press, 1956.

Wyeth, John Alan. *The Life of Nathan Bedford Forrest*. New York: Barnes & Noble, 2006.

Younger, Cole. *The Story of Cole Younger — by Himself*. St. Paul: Minnesota Historical Press, 2000.

Zinn, John G. *The Mutinous Regiment: The Thirty-third New Jersey in the Civil War*. Jefferson, NC: McFarland & Company, 2005.

Articles and Manuscripts

American Civil War Database, http://www.civilwardata.com.

Ancestry.com. Census records, 1840–1930. http://www.ancestry.com.

Bearss, Edward. *The History of Fortress Rosecrans*. Internal National Park Service Paper: 1960.

Brand, Jude. "His Image Over a Column of Undying Marble." *The Bienville Rifle*. Louisiana (March/April, 1999).

Brennan, Pat. "The Battle of Nashville." *North and South Magazine* 8, no. 3 (May 2005): 19–45.

Brown, Leonard E. "Fortress Rosecrans : A History, 1865–1990." *Tennessee Quarterly* no. 4 (1988).

Chancery Court Document No. 1570, Champaign County, Illinois. Foreclosure, *Samuel T. Busey vs. Jane E. Magee and Mary Van Brunt*, September Term, 1884.

Clark, Charles B. Letters received by the Commission Branch of the Attorney General's Office. C242 CB1869 Roll 428.

Cohen, David. "New Orleans." *The Atlantic Monthly* 165, no. 4 (April 1940): 84–491.

Dimick, Howard. "The Bonfoey Case at Marshall." *Southwestern Historical Society* 48, no. 4 (1945).

Dippie, Brian. "Sole Survivors." *True West* (June, 2001): 55–58.

East Texas Baptist University, Jarrett Library. Bonfoey Tree, Folder 30, Item 14. Marshall, Texas.

Frei, Winifred. "*Memoirs of Edson Dean Washburn,*" Maryville, TN: October, 1907.

Galveston, Texas, City Directories, 1886–1906. Rosenberg Library, Galveston, Texas.

Harrison County Genealogical Society. Bonfoey Family Folders. Marshall, Texas.

Hillhouse, Don. "The Colors Twice Lost." *Confederate Veteran* (September–October 1988).

House of Representatives, 46th Congress, Washington, D.C. 2nd Session. April 13, 1880. H.R. 1039, regarding William McGee.

House of Representatives, 48th Congress. Washington, D.C. 1st Session. December 10, 1883. H.R. 758, regarding William Magee.

Jaeger, Katherine. *The Molly Maguires of Northumberland County, Pa*. Electronic Copyright. April, 2001.

Jones, General John S. "History of the 174th Ohio Volunteer Infantry." *Dyers Compendium*. Marysville, OH: 1894.

Lewis, Jim. *The Legacy of Stone River: Occupation and the Home Front in Tennessee*. A Symposium in Murfreesboro, Tennessee. October 22, 2005. A summary.

Library of Congress. Printers No. 778, 48th Congress, 1st Session. December 10, 1883. H.R. 758.

Louisiana State University Library, Baton Rouge, LA. Case No. 1028, 5th Judicial District Court Civil Trial Transcript, *State vs. McGee.*

Marcus Ward Collection. New Jersey Historical Society and Alexander Library, Rutgers University Library, New Brunswick, New Jersey.

Minnesota Historical Society. Convict Registers, 1854–1902. 4 volumes. Box 112.d.4.7B-2, arranged by inmate register number.

National Archives Records Administration, Pennsylvania Avenue, Washington D.C. Civil War Pension Files, Regular Army Records, Medal of Honor Files, Registry of Trials by General Court-martial, 1868. Special Order No. 98, Transcript, Attorney General's Office, 1869.

New York vs. William McGee. Indictment Number 49148, December 15, 1904. A True Bill. Court of General Sessions of the Peace, in the County of New York.

Nez Perce National Historic Park. Appendix A: U.S. Army Casualties, Nez Perce War, 1877. XII. Bear's Paw, September 30-October 5, 1877.

Norris, Herbert, and James Long. "The Road to Redemption." *Civil War Times* (August 1997).

Noylas, Jonathan. "My Will Is Law — General Robert Milroy and Winchester, Virginia." Master of arts thesis, Virginia Polytechnic Institute, April, 2003.

Old Military and Service Records, NARA. Textual Archives Services Division, Washington, D.C. Microfilm T264, roll 1138, and microfilm T1270, roll 88–89.

Records of East Baton Rouge Parish, Louisiana Commission, 1874–1900. Reel 6, case 03, number1028.

Secretary's Report. Harvard University Class of 1864. Report Number 6, 1864–1889. Boston, 1889.

Sing Sing Correctional Facility. BO143. Inmate Registers, 1865–1971. William McGee, No. 55477.

Smoot, Frederick. "*A Yankee Writes to God's Land, 1864.*" Rutherford County Tennessee Letters from Forgotten Ancestors. www.tngenweb.org/tnletters.

Index

Page numbers in **_bold italics_** indicate pages with photographs.